C# COM+ Programming

C# COM+ Programming

Derek Beyer

M&T Books
An imprint of Hungry Minds, Inc.

Best-Selling Books • Digital Downloads • e-Books • Answer Networks •
e-Newsletters • Branded Web Sites • e-Learning

New York, NY • Cleveland, OH • Indianapolis, IN

C# COM+ Programming

Published by
M&T Books
an imprint of Hungry Minds, Inc.
909 Third Avenue
New York, NY 10022
www.hungryminds.com

Library of Congress Control Number: 2001089342

ISBN: 0-7645-4835-2

Printed in the United States of America

10 9 8 7 6 5 4 3 2 1

1B/SR/QZ/QR/IN

Distributed in the United States by Hungry Minds, Inc.

Distributed by CDG Books Canada Inc. for Canada; by Transworld Publishers Limited in the United Kingdom; by IDG Norge Books for Norway; by IDG Sweden Books for Sweden; by IDG Books Australia Publishing Corporation Pty. Ltd. for Australia and New Zealand; by TransQuest Publishers Pte Ltd. for Singapore, Malaysia, Thailand, Indonesia, and Hong Kong; by Gotop Information Inc. for Taiwan; by ICG Muse, Inc. for Japan; by Intersoft for South Africa; by Eyrolles for France; by International Thomson Publishing for Germany, Austria, and Switzerland; by Distribuidora Cuspide for Argentina; by LR International for Brazil; by Galileo Libros for Chile; by Ediciones ZETA S.C.R. Ltda. for Peru; by WS Computer Publishing Corporation, Inc., for the Philippines; by Contemporanea de Ediciones for Venezuela; by Express Computer Distributors for the Caribbean and West Indies; by Micronesia Media Distributor, Inc. for Micronesia; by Chips Computadoras S.A. de C.V. for Mexico; by Editorial Norma de Panama S.A. for Panama; by American Bookshops for Finland.

For general information on Hungry Minds' products and services please contact our Customer Care department within the U.S. at 800-762-2974, outside the U.S. at 317-572-3993 or fax 317-572-4002.

For sales inquiries and reseller information, including discounts, premium and bulk quantity sales, and foreign-language translations, please contact our Customer Care department at 800-434-3422, fax 317-572-4002 or write to Hungry Minds, Inc., Attn: Customer Care Department, 10475 Crosspoint Boulevard, Indianapolis, IN 46256.

For information on licensing foreign or domestic rights, please contact our Sub-Rights Customer Care department at 212-884-5000.

For information on using Hungry Minds' products and services in the classroom or for ordering examination copies, please contact our Educational Sales department at 800-434-2086 or fax 317-572-4005.

For press review copies, author interviews, or other publicity information, please contact our Public Relations department at 317-572-3168 or fax 317-572-4168.

For authorization to photocopy items for corporate, personal, or educational use, please contact Copyright Clearance Center, 222 Rosewood Drive, Danvers, MA 01923, or fax 978-750-4470.

About the Author

Derek Beyer is currently working as a Web development specialist at Meijer Stores in Grand Rapids, Michigan. Derek mentors other developers on application design issues and development techniques. He is also responsible for implementing and maintaining core infrastructure components such as Web and application servers. Derek has developed and evangelized development guidelines for corporate developers in the areas of MTS, COM+, Visual Basic, and Active Server Pages.

Derek has also worked as a consultant for the Chicago-based consulting company March First. He has been involved with projects ranging from developing applications for a major Internet-based consumer Web site to Web integration of SAP R/3 applications. Derek also speaks at user group meetings on the topic of COM+ and .NET.

In his free time, Derek can usually be found getting some much-needed exercise at the gym or enjoying outdoor activities such as hunting and fishing.

About the Series Editor

Michael Lane Thomas is an active development community and computer industry analyst who presently spends a great deal of time spreading the gospel of Microsoft .NET in his current role as a .NET technology evangelist for Microsoft. In working with over a half-dozen publishing companies, Michael has written numerous technical articles and written or contributed to almost 20 books on numerous technical topics, including Visual Basic, Visual C++, and .NET technologies. He is a prolific supporter of the Microsoft certification programs, having earned his MCSD, MCSE+I, MCT, MCP+SB, and MCDBA.

In addition to technical writing, Michael can also be heard over the airwaves from time to time, including two weekly radio programs on Entercom (`http://www.entercom.com/`) stations, including most often in Kansas City on News Radio 980KMBZ (`http://www.kmbz.com/`). He can also occasionally be caught on the Internet doing an MSDN Webcast (`http://www.microsoft.com/usa/webcasts/`) discussing .NET, the next generation of Web application technologies.

Michael started his journey through the technical ranks back in college at the University of Kansas, where he earned his stripes and a couple of degrees. After a brief stint as a technical and business consultant to Tokyo-based Global Online Japan, he returned to the States to climb the corporate ladder. He has held assorted roles, including those of IT manager, field engineer, trainer, independent consultant, and even a brief stint as Interim CTO of a successful dot-com, although he believes his current role as .NET evangelist for Microsoft is the best of the lot. He can be reached via email at mlthomas@microsoft.com.

Credits

ACQUISITIONS EDITOR
Sharon Cox

PROJECT EDITOR
Matthew E. Lusher

TECHNICAL EDITOR
Nick McCollum

COPY EDITOR
C. M. Jones

EDITORIAL MANAGER
Colleen Totz

PROJECT COORDINATOR
Dale White

GRAPHICS AND PRODUCTION SPECIALISTS
Laurie Stevens
Brian Torwelle
Erin Zeltner

QUALITY CONTROL TECHNICIANS
Carl Pierce
Charles Spencer

PERMISSIONS EDITOR
Carmen Krikorian

MEDIA DEVELOPMENT SPECIALIST
Gregory W. Stephens

MEDIA DEVELOPMENT COORDINATOR
Marisa Pearman

BOOK DESIGNER
Jim Donohue

PROOFREADING AND INDEXING
TECHBOOKS Production Services

COVER IMAGE
© Noma/Images.com

For

Mom and Dad,

without whom none of this would have been possible for so many reasons

Preface

Welcome to *C# COM+ Programming.* If you have purchased this book or are currently contemplating this purchase, you may have a number of questions you are hoping this book will answer. The most common questions I get are "Is COM+ dead?" and "What is COM+'s role in .NET applications?" The answer to the first question is a definite "no"! The COM+ technology that Microsoft has included with Windows 2000 is still available to .NET programmers. In fact, some COM+ technologies that were previously available only to C++ programmers can now be used by Visual Basic .NET and C# programmers. The second question is always a little harder to answer. The typical response you would get from me is "it depends." The technologies found in COM+ such as distributed transactions and queued components can be found only in COM+. The question to ask yourself when trying to decide if you should use a particular COM+ service is "Do I need this service in my application?" If the answer is yes, then feel free to use COM+. If the answer is no, then COM+ is not a good fit for your application.

All of the code examples used in the book use the new programming language C#. C# is an object-oriented programming language developed specifically for .NET. In fact, .NET applications are the only applications you can write with C#. Throughout the book I point out the language features of C# that can help you write better COM+ components. Although all of the code is in C#, the examples can also be rewritten in C++ if you like.

Whom This Book Is For

COM+ is not a topic for novice programmers. If you have never developed an application before, then this book probably is not for you. When talking about COM+, the conversation invariably goes toward distributed computing. If you have developed applications, particularly distributed Web applications, then the topics covered in this book will make much more sense to you.

If you are new to .NET programming or COM+ programming, do not fear. Part I of this book covers the basics of .NET and interacting with COM components. Part I provides you with the grounding you will need to understand how .NET applications work and how they interact with legacy COM components. If you are new to .NET programming, I strongly suggest you read Chapter 1 before reading any of the other chapters. Chapter 1 introduces you to the .NET environment. If you don't understand how the environment works, the rest of the book will not make much sense to you.

For those of you new to C#, Appendix C provides you with an introduction to the language. Appendix C covers the basic features of the language such as data types, loops, and flow control statements as well as the specific language features used in the rest of the book.

This book assumes that you are not familiar with COM+ programming. Each chapter covers the basics features and issues about each COM+ service. You do not have to be an experienced COM+ developer to learn how to develop COM+ components with this book.

How This Book Is Organized

This book is divided into three parts. Each part provides information that you will need to understand the following part. The parts of this book provide a logical progression that you will need in order to build your skills and understanding of COM+ programming in .NET.

Part I: Interoperating with COM

Part I covers the basics of the .NET runtime environment called the Common Language Runtime. Because every .NET application runs in the Common Language Runtime, it is crucial that you understand this environment if you are to develop COM+ components with C#. The bulk of Part I covers interoperating with the COM world. I show you how to consume legacy COM components from C# applications. I also show you how to write C# components that COM clients can consume. An understanding of COM interoperation with .NET is important if you develop distributed applications that use COM components or are used from COM components.

Part II: COM+ Core Services

Part II covers the core services of COM+. All of the typical services such as distributed transactions, role-based security, loosely coupled events, and queued components, among others, are covered in Part II. The chapters in this part are organized (as best as possible) from the more easy services to more advance services.

Part III: Advanced COM+ Computing

The final part of this book, Part III, covers some of the more advanced topics of COM+. Part III covers the .NET remoting framework. The .NET remoting framework provides a developer with a way to call methods of a component from across the network. As you will see, COM+ components written with C# can plug into the remoting framework by virtue of their class hierarchy. Part III also discusses the new features of COM+, Internet Information Server and Microsoft Message Queue (all of these technologies are used in the book) currently slated for Windows XP. Many of the new features of COM+ center on providing a more stable environment for COM+ components.

Conventions Used in This Book

Every book uses some several conventions to help the reader understand the material better. This book is no exception. In this book I used typographical and coding conventions to help make the material more clear.

Typographical Conventions

Because this is a programming book, I have included lots of code examples. I cover each code example (the larger ones have their own listing numbers) almost line for line. Paragraphs that explain a particular code example often refer to the code from the example. When I refer to code from the example, it is always in `monospaced` font. Here is an example from Chapter 5.

```
using System;
using Microsoft.ComServices;
[assembly: ApplicationAccessControl(
    AccessChecksLevel = AccessChecksLevelOption.ApplicationComponent
  )
]
public class SecuredComponent {
    // some method implementations
}
```

Notice that I use the `assembly` keyword inside the attribute tags. This tells the C# compiler that the attribute is an assembly-level attribute. Inside the attribute declaration, I have set the `AccessChecksLevel` property to application and component by using the `AccessChecksLevelOption` enumeration.

The code example above (the line starting with `using System;`) is set entirely in monospaced font. The paragraph above explains the code example. In this paragraph I refer to keywords from the code example such as `assembly`, `AccessChecksLevel`, and `AccessChecksLevelOption`. Wherever you see something in monospaced font inside a paragraph, there is a good chance that it is a keyword that was used in a previous or forthcoming code example.

Coding Conventions

The .NET framework uses Pascal casing to name most of its classes, method parameters, enumerations, and so on. The code examples used in this book follow this practice. Pascal casing capitalizes the first letter of each word in a name. For example, if I wrote a class that accessed customer order information, I might name it `CustomerOrders`. Because I use Pascal casing, I must capitalize the `C` of `Customer` and the `O` of `Orders`. I use this convention to help make the code examples more readable.

Icons Used in This Book

Many of the topics covered in this book have related topics. Quite often it is important for you to understand these related topics if you are to understand the central topic being discussed. It is can be rather easy however, to lose a reader if you go too far off on a tangent. In order to both cover the important information and not lose you, the reader, I've put these topics into a Note. For example:

Notes explain a related topic. They are also used to remind you of particular features of C# that can help you write good COM+ components.

Acknowledgments

I am truly grateful to the team of reviewers and editors who worked so hard and diligently on this book. Although my name appears on the cover, this book is truly a team effort. Matt Lusher and Eric Newman filled the project editor role on this project and provided great feedback. Matt made stressful times much more bearable through his professionalism and good humor. Chris Jones caught the grammar mistakes I made late at night while I was sleepy and bleary-eyed. A good acquisitions editor glues the whole book together and tries to keep everyone happy, and Sharon Cox was terrific in this capacity. Sharon no doubt buffered me from lots of issues that I would normally have had to deal with. Thank you, Sharon! I owe a huge debt of gratitude to the Production Department at Hungry Minds; these folks are the ones who suffered my artwork and screenshot mistakes. You guys really came through in a pinch. I should also thank Rolf Crozier, who was the acquisitions editor early on in this book. Rolf pitched the book idea to Hungry Minds and got the whole ball rolling.

The best part about being in a field that you love is the people you get to share your ideas with and learn from. Steve Schofield is the most enthusiastic guy I have ever met when it comes to learning new technology. His excitement for .NET is infectious. Steve also provided me with the contacts inside Hungry Minds I needed to make this book a reality. Nick McCollum was an awesome technical editor for the book. He kept me honest throughout and helped me relate many topics better to the reader. I would also like to thank a couple of key Microsoft employees, Mike Swanson and Shannon Paul. Mike was always there to offer assistance and get things I needed. He also absorbed many of my complaints about the technology with a smile and a nod. Shannon provided me with key information about COM+ events. He also kept me on track when it came to that subject. Thank you, Shannon.

I now realize that writing a book is a monumental undertaking. No one can undertake such an endeavor without the proper support system of friends and family. I am fortunate enough to have a wonderful support system. The cornerstone of that system are my parents. My dad showed me by example what a work ethic *really* is. This is the hardest-working man I have ever seen. I am grateful that some of his work ethic rubbed off on me. My mother provides me with unconditional support and encouragement. I must thank her for understanding why she hardly saw me for months while I was cooped up writing this book. Last but certainly not least I must thank Jacque. Jacque is a very special friend who bore the brunt of my crankiness during the course of this book. She was able to pick me up at my lowest times with her compassion and positive energy. Thank you, sweetie!

Contents at a Glance

Contents

Part III Advanced COM+ Computing

Part I

Interoperating with COM

Chapter 1

Understanding .NET Architecture

IN THIS CHAPTER

- Loading and executing code inside the Common Language Runtime
- Automatic memory management
- Assemblies
- Application domains
- The Common Type System

THE .NET FRAMEWORK attempts to solve many of the problems historically associated with application development and deployment in the Microsoft Windows environment. For example, using Visual Studio 6 and earlier versions it was impossible to write a class in C++ and consume it directly inside Visual Basic. COM has attempted to ease this pain by allowing compiled components to talk to one another via a binary contract. However, COM has had its flaws. COM has provided no clean way of discovering the services a component provides at runtime. The .NET Framework provides mechanisms that solve this problem through a concept known as *reflection*. Error handling is another issue the Framework solves. Depending on what API call you are making, the API call might raise an error, or it might return an error code. If the call returns an error code, you must have knowledge of the common errors that might be returned. The Framework simplifies error handling by raising an exception for all errors. The Framework library provides access to lower-level features that were traditionally the domain of C++ programmers. Windows services, COM+ Object Pooling, and access to Internet protocols such as HTTP, SMTP, and FTP are now firmly within the grasp of the Visual Basic .NET or C# developer.

As you can see, the .NET Framework provides a number of services that level the playing field for applications that run in its environment. All applications written for .NET (including COM+ components written in C#) run inside an environment called the Common Language Runtime (CLR). An application written to run inside the CLR is considered *managed code*. Managed code can take advantage of the services the CLR provides. Some of these services, such as Garbage Collection, are provided for you automatically. Other services, such as software versioning, require your involvement.

This chapter covers the services provided by the CLR. An understanding of the CLR will provide you with the proper grounding you need to develop COM+ components in C#.

Loading and Executing Code Inside the Common Language Runtime

As mentioned previously, the CLR provides many services that simplify development and deployment of applications. Part of the reason the CLR is able to provide these services is that all applications run on top of the same execution engine, called the Virtual Execution System (VES). In fact, it is a combination of compiler support and runtime enforcement of certain rules that allows the CLR to provide its services. This section describes the runtime support available to your application as well as the compiler and VES support needed to provide those services. Throughout this chapter, the terms *class* and *dll* are used to illustrate the concepts because they apply directly to the COM+ programming model. These concepts apply to all types and file formats (exes and dlls).

Microsoft Intermediate Language and Metadata

When you compile a C# application, you do not get the typical file you expect. Instead, you get a Portable Executable (PE) file that contains Microsoft Intermediate Language (MSIL) code and metadata that describes your components. MSIL is an instruction set that the CLR interprets. MSIL tells the CLR how to load and initialize classes, how to call methods on objects, and how to handle logical and arithmetic operations. At runtime, a component of the CLR, the Just In Time Compiler (JIT), converts the MSIL instruction set into code that the operating system can run.

The MSIL instruction set is not specific to any hardware or operating system. Microsoft has set the groundwork to allow MSIL code to be ported to other platforms that support the CLR. Visual Studio .NET and Windows 2000 provide the only tool and platform combination the CLR runs on, but it is conceivable that the CLR can be ported to other platforms. If this becomes the case, your MSIL code can be ported directly to these other platforms. Of course, making use of platform-specific services such as those COM+ provides makes it more difficult to port your application to other platforms.

As I mentioned previously, metadata is also present in your dll (Dynamic Link Library) along with the MSIL. Metadata is used extensively throughout the CLR, and it is an important concept to grasp if you want to understand how the .NET Framework operates. Metadata provides information about your application that

C# Code: Truly Portable?

If your application uses COM+ services or other services specific to Microsoft or another vendor, then you run the chance of those services being unavailable on other platforms. If, on the other hand, your application uses services such as the TCP/IP support provided in the `System.Net.Sockets` namespace, your application might be relatively portable. TCP/IP is a well supported and common service that most platforms are likely to support. As long as the support does not differ greatly from platform to platform, chances are that this type of code will be highly portable. The point to understand here is that MSIL and the CLR provide a consistent set of standards for various vendors to shoot for. Although true portability with code written for the CLR is not a reality yet, it soon may be.

the CLR needs for registration (into the COM+ catalog), debugging, memory management, and security. For COM+ components, metadata tells the CLR and the COM+ runtime such things as the transaction level your class should use and the minimum and maximum pool size for pooled components, to name just a few. This metadata is queried at registration time to set the appropriate attributes for your class in the COM+ Catalog. When you write the code for your class, you use coding constructs called attributes to manipulate the metadata. Attributes are the primary method for manipulating metadata in the .NET Framework.

Metadata provides a means for all of an application's information to be stored in a central location. Developers who write COM+ applications with an earlier version of Visual Studio store an application's information in a variety of locations. A component's type library stores information about the components, their methods, and interfaces. The Windows registry and the COM+ Catalog store information about where the dll is located and how the COM+ runtime must load and activate the component. In addition, other files may be used to store information that the component needs at runtime. This dislocation of information results in confusion for developers and administrators. Visual Studio .NET attempts to resolve this problem by using metadata to describe all of an application's dependencies.

Metadata goes beyond describing the attributes you have placed in your code. Compilers use metadata to build tables inside your dll that tell where your class is located inside the dll and which methods, events, fields, and properties your class supports. At runtime, the Class Loader and JIT query these tables to load and execute your class.

Class Loader

Once you have written and compiled your code, you want to run it, right? Of course. However, before the CLR can run your class, your class must be loaded and initialized. This is the Class Loader's job. When application *A* attempts to create a new instance of class *C*, the Class Loader combines information it already knows about *A* with information from administratively defined XML configuration files and determines where *C* is physically located. (The process of locating a particular type is covered in more detail in the "Assemblies" section, later in this chapter.) Once the Class Loader finds the class, it loads the dll into memory and queries the dll's metadata tables for the offset of the class. The offset is a location where the Class Loader can find the class inside the dll. The Class Loader also queries the metadata to determine how it should lay out the class in memory. Generally, the Class Loader is allowed to construct the class in memory any way it sees fit, but there are times when the compiler needs to tell the Class Loader how the class must be constructed in memory. Three options are available to tell the Class Loader how to lay out the class:

- `autolayout` is the default and allows the Class Loader to load the class into memory in any manner acceptable to the Class Loader.
- `layoutsequential` forces the loader to lay out the class with its fields in the same order the compiler emits.
- `explicitlayout` gives the compiler direct control over how the class is constructed in memory.

I should emphasize that the compiler has the responsibility for generating the correct MSIL code to instruct the Class Loader on how it should lay out classes in memory. Microsoft provides documentation on how to instruct the Class Loader on a class's layout in the Tool Developer Guide. The Tool Developers Guide comes as part of the Visual Studio .NET product documentation. As a COM+ developer you do not need to worry about specifying the layout scheme of your classes.

The Class Loader performs a cursory verification of the loaded class and its caller. The Class Loader examines the class to see if it has references to other classes that have not been loaded. If it does have such references, the Class Loader either loads the next class or, if it cannot, records this fact for later use. The Class Loader also enforces accessibility rules. For example, if a class being loaded inherits from another class, the Class Loader ensures that the child has not attempted to inherit from a sealed class or to extend a method the base class has deemed final. Any references made by classes already loaded to the newly created class are verified. Conversely, any references made by the new class to classes already loaded are verified.

Once the class has been located and verified as safe to execute, the Class Loader creates a *stub* for each of the methods that have been loaded for the class. The stub acts as an intermediary between the consumer of the class and the method being called. The stub's responsibility is to invoke the JIT.

Just In Time Compiler

The Just In Time Compiler is responsible for converting MSIL instructions into native machine code. It performs this task only when methods are first called on a object. Once invoked, the JIT preserves the converted MSIL in memory. Subsequent calls to the method go directly to the native machine code.

The JIT compiler is responsible for performing a much more thorough verification process than the Class Loader performs. The JIT verification process ensures that only legal operations are performed against a class. It also ensures that the type being referenced is compatible with the type being accessed. For example, if a class `A` references an instance of class `CFoo` and calls one of `CFoo`'s methods, `ToString()`, the JITer ensures that the call to `Cfoo.ToString()` is being called for an instance of `CFoo`. The JIT compiler also checks memory access at this point. The JIT does not allow a class to reference memory that the class is not supposed to access. Security access permissions are also checked at this point on various levels.

The JIT operates on the concept that not all of an application's code is always executed. Rather than waste CPU time and memory by converting an entire MSIL file to native code, the JIT converts only the code the application needs at any given time. This is one of the key strategies behind improving the performance and scalability of applications written for the .NET Framework.

Automatic Memory Management

The task of allocating and deallocating memory has often been a source of bugs in many applications, particularly those written in C++ where this is more of a manual process than in languages such as Visual Basic. The CLR addresses this issue by allocating and deallocating memory from a managed heap.

The CLR creates and initializes the managed heap when it starts an application. In addition, the CLR initializes the heap's pointer to the base address of the heap. The heap's pointer contains the address of the next available block of memory. Figure 1-1 shows the managed heap after it has been initialized and before any objects have been created.

When you create an object by using the `new` keyword in C#, the CLR allocates memory from the heap and increments the heap's pointer to the next available block of memory. Figure 1-2 shows the heap after the first call to `new` in an application.

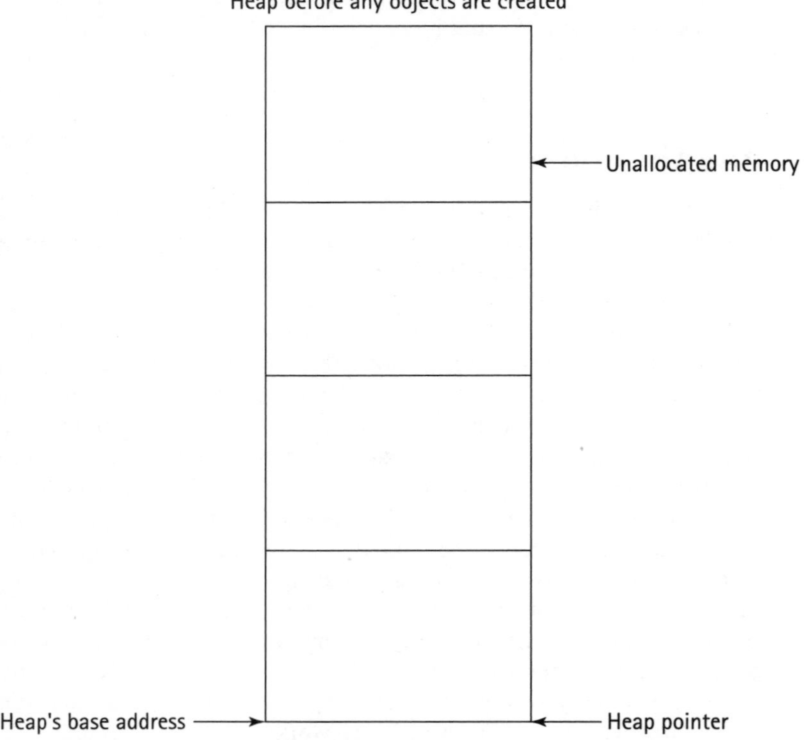

Figure 1-1: Managed heap before Garbage Collection

The CLR can allocate memory from the managed heap much faster than it can allocate memory from a traditional unmanaged Win32 heap. In a typical unmanaged Win32 heap, allocation is not sequential. When memory is allocated from a Win32 heap, the heap must be examined to find a block of memory that can satisfy the request. Once a block of memory is found, data structures that the heap maintains must be updated. The managed heap, on the other hand, only needs to increment the heap pointer.

At some point, the heap pointer is incremented to the top of the heap, and no more memory is available for allocation. When this occurs, a process known as *Garbage Collection* is started to free resources that are no longer in use. The Garbage Collector starts by building a list of all objects the application is using. The first place the Garbage Collector looks is the application's roots, which include the following:

- Global object references
- Static object references
- Local variables (for the currently executing method)
- Parameters (for the currently executing method)
- CPU Registers that contain object references

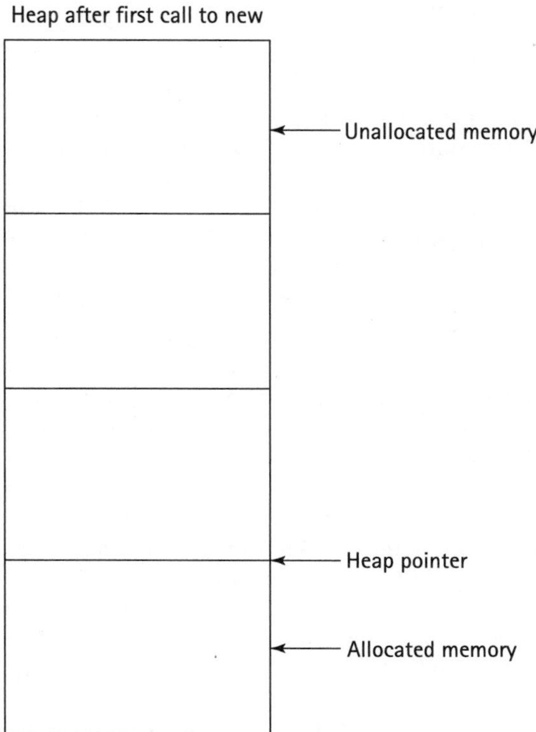

Figure 1-2: Managed heap after memory allocation

A full list of application roots is maintained by the JIT compiler, which the Garbage Collector is allowed to query at runtime. Once the full list of roots has been identified, the Garbage Collector walks through each object reference in each of the roots. If a root contains references to other objects, these references are also added to the list. Once the Garbage Collector has walked through the entire chain of object references, it examines the heap to find any references that are not in its list. References not in the list are considered unreachable and can be freed. After the memory has been released for the unreachable objects, the Garbage Collector compacts the heap and sets the heap pointer to the next available block in the heap.

It may seem that any time saved by memory allocation is now consumed by the Garbage Collection process. This is not entirely the case. The Garbage Collector uses a technique called *Generational Garbage Collection* to optimize the Garbage Collection process. Generational Garbage Collection assumes the following is true about an application:

- New objects have shorter lifetimes than old objects.
- A new object's memory can be released sooner than an old object's memory.
- New objects have strong relationships with one another.

- New objects are accessed at about the same time.
- Compacting a portion of the heap is faster than compacting the entire heap.

Based on these assumptions, the Garbage Collector logically breaks the heap into three generations: Generation 0, Generation 1, and Generation 2. Generation 0 objects are newly created objects that have not undergone a Garbage Collection cycle. Generation 1 objects have survived one Garbage Collection cycle. Objects in Generation 2 have gone through at least two Garbage Collection cycles and are considered the oldest objects. When a Garbage Collection occurs, the Garbage Collector looks at Generation 0 objects first for any garbage that can be cleaned up. If the Garbage Collector is able to reclaim enough space from a Generation 0 collection, it does not attempt to collect objects from older generations. The Garbage Collector works through Generations 0, 1, and 2 as needed to reclaim enough memory to satisfy a request. The Garbage Collector has to walk through only a subsection of the heap to perform a Garbage Collection. This greatly enhances the Garbage Collector's performance.

The Garbage Collection feature in .NET has sparked much controversy. The controversy stems from the fact that a programmer does not know when his or her object will be destroyed. This is referred to as *nondeterministic finalization.* Nondeterministic finalization can be a particular problem for objects that hold on to expensive resources such as handles to files or database connections. The problem arises when the object waits to release its resources until it is destroyed by the Garbage Collector.

In traditional applications, this is not a problem because the object's destructor (or `Class_Terminate` in the case of Visual Basic) is called when the client frees its reference to the object. In this scenario, the object has a chance to release its resources immediately after the client is done with it. In .NET, objects do not have destructors or `Class_Terminate` events. The closest you can come to the Visual Basic `Class_Terminate` event if you are writing your application in C# is a method called `Finalize`. The problem is that the Garbage Collector calls the `Finalize` method – you do not. `Finalize` is not necessarily called when the client releases its reference to the object. Resources such as database connections and file locks remain open in your object until a Garbage Collection is run if they are closed in the `Finalize` method. Microsoft's workaround for these types of objects is a recommendation that you implement a `Dispose` or a `Close` method. The client can call these methods explicitly just before it is done with your object in order to allow you to free any resources.

Before we continue, let's discuss what the `Finalize` method is intended for and what the costs are of using it. First of all, as mentioned previously, the `Finalize` method is called by the Garbage Collector, *not* by the client using the object. The `Finalize` method should not be called by a program consuming your object. In fact, the C# compiler does not compile a class if it has implemented a public finalizer. The finalizer should be declared protected so that only classes that inherit from the object can call the `Finalize` method. The key points to remember about implementing a `Finalize` method are as follows:

- Implement this method only if you must. A performance hit is associated with implementing this method (see the next paragraph for details).
- Release only references held by the object. Do not create new references.
- If you are inheriting from another class, call your base class's `Finalize` method via `base.Finalize()` – assuming it has a `Finalize` method.
- Declare the `Finalize` method as protected only. Currently, this is the only access attribute the C# compiler allows.

The first bullet brings up an important point. When an object is created with the `new` keyword, the CLR notices that the object has implemented a `Finalize` method. These types of objects are recorded onto an internal Garbage Collector queue called the Finalization Queue. Remember that when a Garbage Collection cycle occurs, the Garbage Collector walks the managed heap, looking for objects that are not reachable. If the Garbage Collector sees an unreachable object on the heap that has implemented a `Finalize` method, it removes the reference to the object from the Finalization Queue and places it on another queue called the Freachable Queue. Objects on this queue are considered reachable and are not freed by the Garbage Collector. As objects are placed on the Freachable Queue, another thread awakes to call the `Finalize` method on each of the objects. The next time the Garbage Collector runs, it sees that these objects are no longer reachable and frees them from the heap. The result of all this is that an object with a `Finalize` method requires two Garbage Collection cycles in order to be released from the heap.

As you can see, the CLR does a lot of work on your behalf behind the scenes. This can be good and bad at times. It can improve your productivity because the task of tracking down memory leaks and bugs is greatly simplified. On the other hand, this type of *black-box* functionality can make it difficult to see what your application is really doing. Fortunately, the SDK comes with several performance counters that can help you monitor the performance of your application. Some of the counters relevant to our discussion are JIT Compilation Counters, Loading Counters, and Memory Counters. These counters are highlighted as follows.

- **JIT Compilation Counters:**
  - **IL Bytes Jitted / sec:** the number of bytes of IL code being converted to native code per second
  - **# of IL Bytes Jitted:** the number of IL bytes that have been JITed since application startup
  - **# of Methods Jitted:** the number of methods that have been JITed since application startup
- **Loading Counters:**
  - **Current Classes Loaded:** the current number of classes loaded into the CLR

- **Total # of Failures:** the total number of classes that have failed to load since the application started up
- **Total Classes Loaded:** the total number of classes that have been loaded since application startup

- Memory Counters:
  - **# Bytes in Heap:** The total number of bytes in the managed heap. This includes all generations.
  - **Gen 0 Heap Size:** The size of the Generation 0 heap. Similar counters for Generations 1 and 2 are also provided.
  - **# Gen 0 Collections:** The number of collections on Generation 0. Similar counters for Generations 1 and 2 are also provided.

Assemblies

Assemblies are the point at which the CLR implements versioning. Assemblies are also the point at which name resolution occurs. Assemblies can be thought of as logical dlls that contain the implementation of types (such as classes and interfaces), references to other assemblies, and resource files such as JPEGs. Assemblies in and of themselves are not applications. Applications reference assemblies to access types and resources of the assembly. Think of .NET applications as made up of one or more assemblies. A reference to an assembly can be made at compile time or at runtime. Usually, references are made at compile time. This is similar to setting a reference to a COM library in a Visual Basic project. These references are contained in a section of the assembly called the manifest.

The Manifest

The *manifest* contains the information the CLR needs to load the assembly and to access its types. Specifically, the manifest contains the following information:

- The name of the assembly
- The version of the assembly (includes major and minor numbers as well as build and revision numbers)
- The shared name for the assembly
- Information about the type of environment the assembly supports, such as operating system and languages
- A list of all files in the assembly
- Information that allows the CLR to match an application's reference of a type to a file that contains the type's implementation
- A list of all other assemblies this assembly references. This contains the version number of the assembly being referenced.

Usually, the manifest is stored in the file that contains the assembly's most commonly accessed types. Less commonly accessed types are stored in files called *modules*. This scenario works particularly well for browser-based applications because the entire assembly does not need to be downloaded at once. The manifest identifies modules that can be downloaded as needed.

Figure 1-3 shows a logical representation of a file that contains both the assembly's manifest and types implemented in the file.

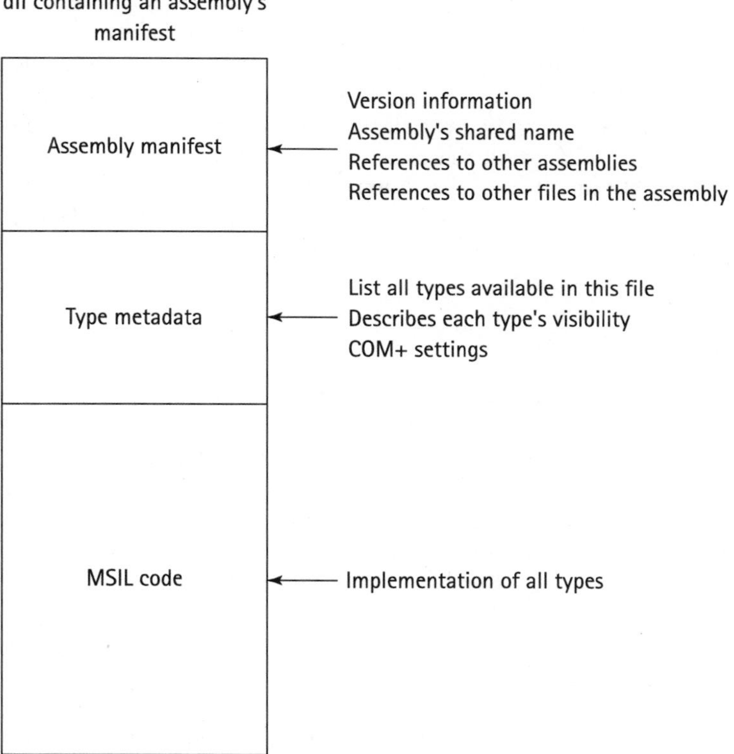

Figure 1-3: Assembly's logical dll structure

Versioning

As stated previously, the assembly's manifest contains the version of the assembly. The version is made up of four parts: the major version, the minor version, the build number, and the revision number. For example, the version of the System.Windows.Forms assembly in the .NET SDK Beta 2 is 1.0.2411.0, where 1 is the major version, 0 is the minor version, 2411 is the build number, and 0 is the revision number. The CLR compares the major and minor version numbers with those the application asks for. The CLR considers the assembly to be incompatible if the major and minor version numbers do not match what the application is asking for. By default, the CLR loads the assembly with the highest build and revision numbers. This behavior is known as Quick Fix Engineering (QFE). QFE is intended to allow developers to deploy fixes or patches to applications such as fixing a security hole. These changes should not break compatibility for applications using the assembly.

Shared Names

In addition to the version number, the assembly's manifest contains the name of the assembly, which is simply a string describing the assembly and optionally a *shared name* (also referred to as a "strong" name). Shared names are used for assemblies that need to be shared among multiple applications. Shared names are generated using standard public key cryptography. Specifically, a shared name is a combination of the developer's private key and the assembly's name. The shared name is embedded into the assembly manifest at development time using either tools provided in the .NET SDK or the Visual Studio .NET development environment. The CLR uses shared names to ensure that the assembly the application references is indeed the assembly being accessed.

Global Assembly Cache

Now that we have a mechanism for uniquely identifying an assembly that multiple applications can use, we need a place to store these assemblies. This is the Global Assembly Cache's job. The *Global Assembly Cache* is a logical folder that stores all assemblies that can be shared among applications. I say it is a logical folder because the assemblies themselves can be stored anywhere in the file system. An assembly is placed in the Global Assembly Cache at deployment time using either an installer that knows about the assembly cache, the Global Assembly Cache Utility (`gacutil.exe`) found in the .NET Framework SDK, or by dragging and dropping the file with the assembly manifest into the `\winnt\assembly` folder. The `\winnt\assembly` folder is implemented with a Windows Shell extension, so it can be viewed from Windows Explorer or from My Computer. Figure 1-4 shows what the Global Assembly Cache looks like when viewed from My Computer.

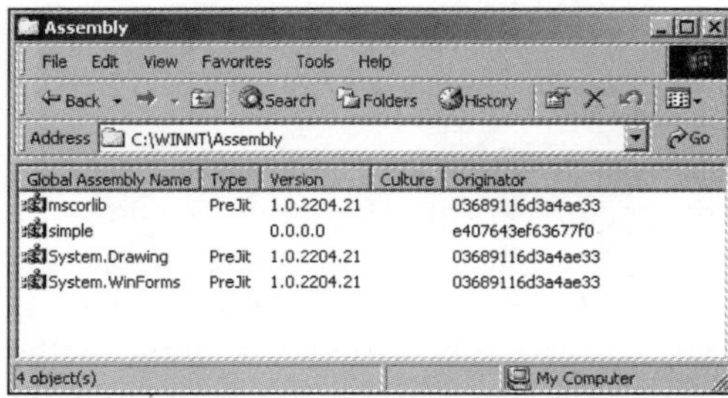

Figure 1-4: Global Assembly Cache

The Global Assembly Cache stores basic information about the assembly, including the assembly name, the version, the last modified date, the public key used to sign the assembly, and the location in the file system of the file that contains the manifest. There are several benefits to adding an assembly to the Global Assembly Cache:

- The Global Assembly Cache allows you to share assemblies among applications.
- An application can gain several performance improvements.
- Integrity checks are made on all files the assembly references.
- Multiple versions of an assembly can be stored in the Global Assembly Cache; QFE is applied automatically if multiple versions exist.

The Global Assembly Cache improves performance for assemblies in two ways. First, assemblies in the Global Assembly Cache do not need to be verified each time they are accessed. If you remember our previous discussion, when an assembly is referenced the CLR ensures that the assembly an application is referencing is the one being accessed. If an assembly is in the Global Assembly Cache, this verification process is skipped. Second, assemblies in the Global Assembly Cache need to be loaded into the CLR only once. Multiple applications access a single instance of the assembly. This decreases the load time for assemblies in the Global Assembly Cache. In addition, because all applications are accessing the same instance, a greater chance exists that methods being called are already JIT compiled. Of course, there is a down side to using the Global Assembly Cache. If most of your assemblies are application specific (that is, only one application uses them), you are introducing an extra administrative step by installing these types of assemblies into the Global Assembly Cache.

Locating Assemblies

Before the CLR can access any types in an assembly, it must locate the assembly. This is a multistep process that begins with the application's configuration file. The application's configuration file is XML formatted. It is named the same as the application except it uses a `.cfg` extension. The configuration file, if it exists, is in the same folder as the application. For instance, if the application is `c:\program files\Microsoft office\Word.exe`, the application's configuration file is `c:\program files\Microsoft office\Word.exe.cfg`. The configuration file tells the CLR several things when it tries to locate an assembly:

- The version of the assembly to use instead of the one being asked for
- Whether to enforce QFE
- Whether the application should use the exact version it is compiled against (known as safe mode)
- The exact location to find the assembly being referenced (known as a codebase)

The example that follows shows a section of the configuration file called the BindingPolicy.

```
<BindingPolicy>
      <BindingRedir Name="myAssembly"
                    Originator="e407643ef63677f0"
                    Version="1.0.0.0" VersionNew="2.1.0.0"
                    UseLatestBuildRevision="no"/>
</BindingPolicy>
```

The BindingPolicy section tells the runtime which version of an assembly to replace with another version. In this example, we are telling the CLR to use version 2.1.0.0 instead of version 1.0.0.0 for the assembly named myAssembly. Notice that the major and minor versions are different. This overrides the default behavior of the CLR, which normally does not allow us to load an assembly with a different major or minor version number. The other tag of interest to us is UseLatestBuildRevision. This tag allows us to turn off or turn on the CLR's QFE policy. In our example, we have set this tag to "no," which tells the CLR not to use assemblies that have greater build or revision numbers. If we omit this tag or set it to "yes," the CLR loads the assembly that has the greatest build and/or revision number. Finally, the Originator tag represents the assembly creator's public key that has been used to sign the assembly.

The safe mode section of the configuration file tells the CLR whether or not it should use only assemblies the application is compiled against. If safe mode is turned on, the CLR loads only assemblies the application has referenced directly. Safe mode is intended to be used to revert the application to a state where it can reference only assemblies it was originally compiled against. The example that follows shows how safe mode can be turned on for an application.

```
<BindingMode>
<AppBindingMode Mode="safe"/>
</BindingMode>
```

It is important to note that safe mode is turned on for an entire application. Once safe mode is set to "safe," it is applied for all assemblies. Safe mode is turned off by default; however, it can be explicitly turned off by setting the Mode attribute to "normal."

In addition to overriding the versioning rules, the configuration file can specify exactly where an assembly can be found. The Assemblies collection specifies locations for each of the application's assemblies through a CodeBase attribute.

```
<Assemblies>
      <CodeBaseHint Name="myAssembly"
                    Originator="e407643ef63677f0"
```

```
                        Version="2.1.0.0"
                        CodeBase="c:\winnt\myNewDll.dll"/>
</Assemblies>
```

In this example, we are telling the CLR that version 2.1.0.0 of `myAssembly` can be found at `c:\winnt\myNewDll.dll`. If a code base is specified and the assembly is not found, the CLR raises an exception.

But what happens if the code base is not specified? At this point, the CLR starts a process known as probing. When the CLR probes for an assembly, it searches for the assembly in a specific set of paths, in the following order:

1. The application's current directory. The CLR appends `.mcl`, `.dll`, and `.exe` file extensions when referencing the assembly.
2. Any `PrivatePaths` specified in the application's configuration file. The name of the assembly is also added to this path.
3. Any language-specific subdirectories
4. The Global Assembly Cache

Step four is where things get interesting. If the configuration file does not contain an `Originator` attribute, probing stops, and an exception is raised. However, if an `Originator` ***has been*** specified ***and*** QFE is enabled, the CLR searches the Global Assembly Cache for the assembly that has the highest build and revision numbers.

Let's go though an example of probing. Assume the following conditions are true about our application:

- The application's name is `myapp.exe`.
- The application directory is `c:\program files\myapp\`.
- Our configuration files specify `PrivatePaths` as `<AppDomain PrivatePath="complus">`.
- `myassembly` is located in the Global Assembly Cache with the same major and minor version number the application references, and an `Originator` entry is included in our configuration file.
- QFE is enabled.

With our conditions defined previously, our probing paths look like the following:

1. `C:\program files\myapp\myassembly.mcl`
2. `C:\program files\myapp\myassembly.dll`
3. `C:\program files\myapp\myassembly.exe`
4. `C:\program files\myapp\myassembly\myassembly.mcl`

5. `C:\program files\myapp\myassembly\myassembly.dll`
6. `C:\program files\myapp\myassembly\myassembly.exe`
7. `C:\program files\myapp\complus\myassembly.mcl`
8. `C:\program files\myapp\complus\myassembly.dll`
9. `C:\program files\myapp\complus\myassembly.exe`
10. Global Assembly Cache

Application Domains

Just as assemblies can be thought of as "logical dlls," application domains can be thought of as "logical exes." On a Windows platform, a Win32 process provides isolation for applications running on the system. This isolation provides a number of services to applications:

- Faults in one application cannot harm the other application.
- Code running in one application cannot directly access another application's memory space.
- Win32 processes can be stopped, started, and debugged.

The CLR is able to provide these services to application domains through its type safety and its rigorous code verification process. The CLR is able to provide these features at a much lower cost than traditional Win32 applications because it can host multiple application domains in a single Win32 process, thus reducing the number of Win32 processes needed to run applications. The CLR improves performance by reducing the number of context switches the operating system must perform on physical processes. In addition, when code in an application domain accesses types in another application domain, only a thread switch may need to occur as opposed to a process context switch, which is much more costly.

Common Type System

The Common Type System defines the rules of how types interact with one another and how they are represented with metadata. These rules help solve some of the conventional problems associated with reuse among programming languages. In the .NET Framework, almost every entity is considered a type. Types can be classes, interfaces, structures, enumerations, and even basic data types such as integers and characters. All types can be classified into two categories: reference types and value types.

In .NET, reference types include classes, interfaces, pointers, and delegates (similar to C++ function pointers). Essentially, any reference type consists of three parts: the sequence of bits that represent the current value of the type, the memory address at which the bits start, and the information that describes the operations allowed on the type. I realize this description is pretty vague, so let's make these concepts more concrete. As you know from our discussion about Garbage Collection, when you use the `new` keyword, the CLR allocates a block of memory for the class and returns that memory location to your application. This is the memory location where the class's (read *type*'s) bits start. The "sequence of bits" is the value of any fields, properties, method parameters, method return values, and so on at any point in time. The final part of a reference type, the "description," is the metadata that describes the public and private fields, properties, and methods. Reference types come in three forms: object types, interface types, and pointer types. For the purposes of this book, you can think of classes as object types, interfaces as interface types, and pointer types as pointers in C++ (yes, C# supports pointers). Reference types are always passed by reference, whereas value types are always passed by value. For example, when a reference type is passed into a method as a parameter, the memory address is passed to the method. When a value type is passed to a method, a copy of the value's bits is passed instead.

Value types can be built-in data types such as integers, or they can be user defined such as enumerations and structures. Value types are a sequence of bits that represents the value of the type at any point in time. Unlike reference types, which are created from the managed heap, value types are created from a thread's stack. Value types are always initialized to 0 by the CLR.

Every value type has a corresponding reference type called a *boxed type*. To access the boxed type of a value, the value must be cast to an object type. Consider the following code example:

```
int iNum = 1;
Object oObj = iNum;
oObj = 2;
WriteLine(iNum);
WriteLine(oObj);
/* OUTPUT */
1
2
```

In this example, an integer value type, `iNum`, is declared and set equal to 1. Then an `Object` reference type, `oObj`, is declared and set equal to `iNum`. An implicit cast from `iNum` to `oObj` is performed at this point. Reference types can be converted to value types. This is possible only if the reference type in question has a corresponding value type.

Summary

As you can see, the CLR provides a lot of features and services. Many of these, if not all, are completely new to someone with a Visual Basic or Visual C++ background. The better you understand how the CLR works, the better you are able to diagnose problems as they arise, and the better you are able to plan the implementation of your components. As you work your way through the rest of this book, remember a few key points about the CLR:

- Metadata is used to describe the attributes – such as transaction level – of your COM+ components to the CLR and the COM+ runtime.
- The Global Assembly Cache can be used to store assemblies used by multiple applications. It is likely that most C# components that use COM+ services are used by multiple applications.
- Shared names are required for assemblies that reside in the Global Assembly Cache.
- The Garbage Collector can greatly simplify the development of components, but it can also introduce complexity to components that access expensive resources such as database connections.
- Assembly-versioning rules can be overridden with an application's configuration file.

In the next chapter, we discuss how COM interacts with the .NET CLR and how the CLR interacts with COM.

Chapter 2

Consuming COM Components from .NET

IN THIS CHAPTER

- Converting type libraries to .NET namespaces
- The Runtime Callable Wrapper
- Threading and performance issues between .NET and COM

AS YOU CAN SEE from Chapter 1, the .NET Framework provides many new features for developers to consider when developing applications. The combination of all these features requires us to adjust our mindset from the *old* ways of developing applications with COM.

We cannot, however, throw out everything we know about COM just yet. It is illogical to think that when a company starts developing applications with the .NET Framework, the COM legacy will just disappear. In reality, there will be a long period where .NET applications need to interact with COM and vice versa.

Today, many large e-commerce, Intranet, and other types of applications are built with the Microsoft toolset that heavily leverage COM. Because time always comes at a premium, it may not be possible to convert an application entirely to .NET overnight. In addition, you may have to continue to use COM APIs exposed by third party applications.

So what do you do if you want to use .NET to upgrade components of your legacy COM application or to add new features? The answer lies in the COM Interoperation (COM Interop) features of .NET. The COM Interop specification allows .NET components to use COM objects, and vice versa.

Converting Type Libraries to .NET Namespaces

If you remember from Chapter 1, .NET components talk to other .NET components through assemblies. For a .NET component to talk to a COM component, an assembly *wrapper* must be generated from the COM type library (`TypeLib`). The framework provides a tool called the *Type Library Importer* (`tlbimp.exe`) to do just that. The

Type Library Importer utility takes a COM type library as input and produces a .NET assembly as output. The assembly this tool produces contains stub code that calls the COM component's methods and properties on your behalf. This stub code is the actual implementation of the Runtime Callable Wrapper discussed in the next section.

Let's see how the tlbimp.exe utility works by creating a simple HelloWorld COM component using Visual Basic 6. The HelloWorld component contains one function, Hello, which returns a string to the caller. The implementation of this function is illustrated as follows:

```
' VB project name: prjHelloWorld
' class name: CHelloWorld
Public Function Hello() as string
     Hello = "Hello World"
End Function
```

Let's assume our project name is prjHelloWorld and our class name is CHelloWorld, making the COM ProgID for this component prjHelloWorld.CHelloWorld. The COM server is compiled to prjHelloWorld.dll.

The relevant information from the type library is depicted as follows.

```
Library prjHelloWorld {
     Interface _CHelloWorld {
          HRESULT Hello([out, retval] BSTR* );
     }
     coclass CHelloWorld {
          [default] interface _CHelloWorld;
}
```

Notice that the Visual Basic project name has been converted to the name of the type library. Also, Visual Basic has created a default interface for us by adding an underscore to the class name.

Once we have our type library, we are ready to use the Type Library Importer. The Type Library Importer is a command-line utility that requires a number of parameters to build the assembly. For the moment, all we want to do is generate a simple, private assembly. To do this, go to the command prompt, and change to the directory containing the dll we have created. The following command generates an assembly called AsmHelloWorld.dll:

```
tlbimp.exe /out:AsmHelloWorld.dll prjHelloWorld.dll
```

The /out: switch provides the name of the assembly file, and the HelloWorld.dll provides the name of the file containing the type library. So now we have an assembly that contains the stub code mentioned previously. But what does this stub code look like? Let's use the Framework's MSIL Disassembler (ildasm.exe) to peek inside the assembly. MSIL Disassembler is another utility that

reads the metadata of an assembly to give you a vie
assembly. To view the assembly with the MSIL Disass
command at the prompt:

```
Ildasm.exe AsmHelloWorld.dll
```

After running this command, you should see the MSIL Disassemb
shown in Figure 2-1.

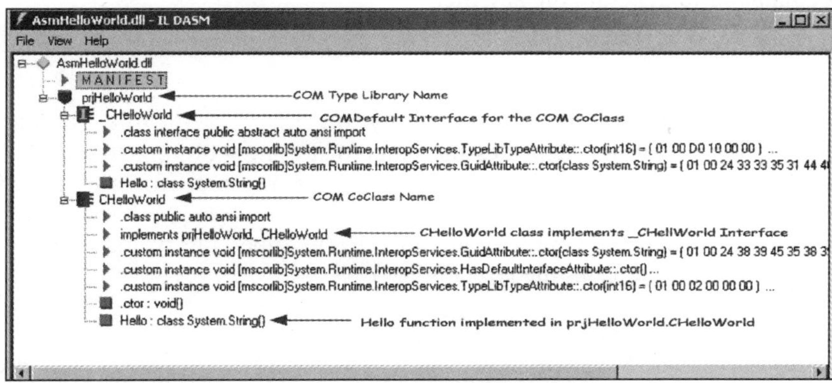

Figure 2-1: MSIL Disassembler View of AsmHelloWorld.dll

The MSIL Disassembler provides quite a bit of information. For now, we are concerned with only three items:

- The .NET Namespace
- The default interface from COM
- The COM CoClass - `CHelloWorld`

At the top of the window, just under the key labeled "MANIFEST," you see the namespace `prjHelloWorld`. The Type Library Importer maps the COM type library name to the name of the namespace for the assembly. Below the `prjHelloWorld` namespace, you see the COM default interface of `CHelloWorld` implemented as a .NET interface. Again, the type name from COM is carried directly to .NET. Below the definition of the interface, you see the definition of the .NET class. Inside the class definition, you find the line "implements `prjHelloWorld._CHelloWorld`," which tells the .NET runtime that this class implements the `_CHelloWorld` interface defined previously. Finally, you have the definition of the `Hello` method. As you can see, this function takes no parameters and returns a string. The method's signature has changed slightly from the definition in the type library. Notice the `HRESULT` is not present. I discuss the reason for this later in this chapter. Also, the `[out, retval]` parameter from the type library has been removed.

plication is in the same directory as you want to use the new assembly er from Chapter 1, assemblies must ıred among multiple .NET applica- mbly Cache, the assembly must be ype Library Importer provides a ıssembly with your public/private that contains the public/private d Name Utility (sn.exe). Use the

to generate the keyfile. The file of the new file that the utility rivate key pair in a file called

the Type Library Importer by

```
Tlbimp /out:AsmHelloWorld.dll
       /keyfile:AsmHelloWorld.snk prjHelloWorld.dll
```

At this point, you can add the assembly to the Global Assembly Cache and use it from any .NET application.

Properties of a COM object can be imported from its type library into an assembly. If our CDog CoClass implements a property called Breed, the type library contains property fields that let our users set and get the value of Breed.

```
Library Animals {
     interface IDog {
          [propput] HRESULT Breed ([in] BSTR);
          [propget] HRESULT Breed ([out, retval] BSTR*);
     }
     coclass CDog {
          [default] interface IDog;
     }
}
```

When the Type Library Importer converts a type library such as the one shown previously, it creates accessor methods for each property. Logically speaking, the class is implemented in the following manner.

```
Namespace Animals {
     Class CDog {
          // private get accessor method called by runtime
          private string get_Breed() { ... };

          // private set accessor method called by runtime
          private void set_Breed(string) { ... };

          // public class field that you will Interop with
          public string Breed; // public class property
     }
}
```

If you are using Visual Studio .NET and you reference the `Animals` namespace in your code, you will only be able to call the public property `Breed` and not the private methods, `get_Breed()` and `set_Breed()`. Depending on where `Breed` is used in a line of code (that is, the right side of an equation or the left side), the runtime calls the proper accessor method for you.

Accessors are glorified fields that allow you to intercept the assignment and retrieval of a field. Accessors are similar to the Let/Set/Get property procedures you may have used when developing COM components in Visual Basic 5 and 6. Appendix C, "Introduction to C#," at the end of this book, explains accessors in greater depth.

Converting Typedefs, Enums, and Modules

The preceding examples are intended to demonstrate how the common elements of a type library map to a .NET namespace. However, type libraries do not contain only classes and interfaces. They may contain enumerations (`enums`), type definitions (`typedefs`), module-level constants, and methods (among other things).

Typedefs are used in COM just as they are used in programming languages such as Visual Basic and C++. The Type Library Importer does not import COM `typedefs` directly into an assembly. Consider the following `typedef`:

```
Library Animals {
     Typedef [public] int AGE;
     Interface _CDog {
          HRESULT GetAgeInDogYears(
               [in] AGE humanyears,
```

```
                [out, retval] AGE dogyears
                );
        }
}
```

Because the Type Library Importer cannot import the typedef directly, it produces the interface as follows:

```
Namespace Animals {
        Interface _CDog {
                Int GetAgeInDogYears([ComAliasName(AGE)] int humanyears);
        }
}
```

Notice that the type definition has been converted to its underlying type: int. The importer also added the attribute, ComAliasName, to the method signature. The ComAliasName attribute can be accessed through a technique known as reflection. Reflection allows you to examine a type's metadata for the purpose of determining a type's interfaces, methods, constructors and other similar details. The Visual Studio .NET documentation contains more information on the topic of reflection if you are interested.

Converting an enum from a type library to an assembly is pretty straightforward. Consider the following enum defined in a COM type library.

```
Enum {
        GoldenRetriever = 0,
        Labrador = 1,
        ChowChow = 2
} Breeds;
```

The Type Library Importer converts this enum into a managed enum with the same name and fields. The managed enum is accessible directly from the managed namespace.

In addition to typedefs and enums, a type library can define module-level methods and constants. When modules are converted from a type library to an assembly, the name of the module is carried over and used to create a class with the same name. The new .NET class contains the members of the original module. For example, let's look at a simple COM module called Security.

```
Module Security {
        Const long SIDToken = 0x009312;
        [entry("ApplySidToThread")]
        pascal void ApplySidToThread([in] long SID);
}
```

When the Type Library Importer sees this module, it creates a new class called Security, as follows.

```
Public class Security {
     Public static const SIDToken = 0x009312;
     Public static void ApplySidToThread(long SID);
}
```

In this example, I have deliberately left out some of the attributes, such as the calling convention, extraneous to the discussion. The important thing to note here is that members of the original module are converted to public, static members of the new class.

Runtime Callable Wrapper

Now that you know how to convert a COM type library to a .NET assembly, you need to learn how the .NET runtime interacts with COM. As I mention previously, the assembly the Type Library Importer generates acts as a wrapper for the actual COM class. This wrapper is referred to as the *Runtime Callable Wrapper* (RCW). The RCW has several responsibilities:

- preserves object identity
- maintains COM object lifetime
- proxies COM interfaces
- marshals method calls
- consumes default interfaces such as `IUnknown` and `IDispatch`

Preserving Object Identity

To understand how the RCW maintains a COM object's identity, let's examine what happens when you create a new instance of a managed class that wraps a COM object. Calling `new` on a managed class has the effect of creating a new instance of the RCW and a new instance of the underlying COM object. As methods are called against the RCW, the RCW ensures that those methods are implemented by one of the COM object's supported interfaces. The RCW accomplishes this by calling `IUnknown->QueryInterface()` for you behind the scenes. When you cast an instance of the RCW class from one interface to another, the RCW looks in its internal cache to see if it already has a reference to the requested interface. If the interface is not cached, the RCW calls `IUnknown->QueryInterface` to see if the COM object supports the interface. If the requested interface does not exist, the runtime raises an exception. COM object identity is maintained by the RCW by not allowing .NET clients to gain references to interfaces the underlying COM object does not support.

Maintaining COM Object Lifetime

In Chapter 1, we discuss the non-deterministic finalization problem. Non-deterministic finalization deals with the fact that a type in .NET is not necessarily destroyed when it is set to null or goes out of scope. Types in .NET are destroyed only when a Garbage Collection occurs. This can be a particular problem for managed classes such as RCWs that reference unmanaged COM objects.

COM implements a completely alternate system for maintaining object lifetime. In COM, objects are reference-counted. Each time a COM client references an object, it calls `IUnknown->AddRef()`, and each time it releases an object, it calls `IUnknown->Release()`, allowing the COM object to decrement its internal-reference count. Once the reference count reaches zero, the instance is released. The RCW behaves the same as a traditional COM client by calling `AddRef` and `Release` at the appropriate times. The difference is that `Release` is called by the RCW's `Finalize` method. Usually, this does not present much of a problem, but there are two special circumstances when this can be problematic.

Take the case of a RCW wrapping a COM object that holds expensive resources such as a database connection. If a COM object such as this releases its resources only when its reference count goes to zero, the resources might be tied up until a Garbage Collection occurs. Obviously, this is a wasteful use of resources.

The second problem may occur when the managed application shuts down. The .NET runtime does not guarantee that finalizers are called during an application shutdown. If an RCW's finalizer is not called before the application shuts down, `Release` cannot be called on any of the interfaces the RCW holds. The `GC` class located in the `System` namespace has two methods — `RequestFinalizeOnShutdown` and `WaitForPendingFinalizers` — that can be used to alleviate this problem. `RequestFinalizeOnShutown` forces the runtime to call finalizers on classes during shutdown. If you remember, a separate thread calls the `Finalize` method for classes. `WaitForPendingFinalizers` tells the runtime to wait for the finalizer thread to finish before shutting down. These methods must be used with caution because they can significantly slow down an application's shutdown time.

There is another way around the non-deterministic finalization problem. The .NET framework allows you to take the responsibility of calling `Release()` yourself. The `System.Runtime.InteropServices` namespace provides a class called `Marshal`. `Marshal.RelaseComObject` takes an instance of an RCW class and decrements its reference count by 1.

```
Using System.Runtime.InteropServices;
Class CMain {
     Public void MakeDogBark() {
          // RCW that maps to the CDog COM Class
          CDog dog = new CDog();
          dog.Bark();
          Marshal.ReleaseComObject ((object)dog);
     }
}
```

In the preceding code example, once we are finished with our RCW instance, we decrement the reference to the underlying COM object by calling `Marshal.ReleaseComObject()`. If the RCW is the only client using the underlying `CDog` COM object, its reference count goes to zero, and its memory is freed. When the next Garbage Collection occurs, the RCW instance of `dog` is freed. Any further use of an RCW after its reference count reaches zero raises an exception.

Proxying Interfaces

The RCW is responsible for proxying interfaces exposed to managed clients and consuming some "standard" COM interfaces not directly exposed to managed clients. You can call any method on any interface exposed to a managed client. The RCW is responsible for directing these method calls to the appropriate COM interface. By doing this, the RCW prevents you from having to cast instances of the RCW to the appropriate interface before calling the methods.

As you may have guessed already, the purpose of the RCW is to make a .NET client think it is accessing another .NET object and to make the COM object think it is being accessed by a COM client. One of the ways the RCW is able to do this is by hiding certain interfaces from the .NET client. Table 2-1 lists some of the more common interfaces the RCW consumes directly.

TABLE 2-1 INTERFACES THE RCW CONSUMES

COM Interface	Description
`Iunknown`	RCW consumes this interface when the .NET client uses early binding to access COM objects. Early binding to COM is accomplished by exporting the COM type library into a .NET assembly and then accessing the assembly types as if they were ordinary .NET types. When a member is called on a type from one of these assemblies, the RCW determines the interface the member belongs to. If the interface is not currently cached in the RCW's internal table of interfaces, the RCW calls `IUnknown-QueryInterface`, passing the name of the COM interface. If the interface exists, `IUnknown->AddRef` is called. If the interface does not exist, an exception is raised to the client.

Continued

TABLE 2-1 INTERFACES THE RCW CONSUMES *(Continued)*

COM Interface	Description
`Idispatch`	The RCW consumes this interface when the .NET client is using late binding to access members of the COM object. Late binding to COM objects is accomplished in .NET through a technique known as reflection.
`ISupportErrorInfo` and `IErrorInfo`	If the COM object implements these interfaces, the RCW uses them to get extended information about an error when a COM method returns a failure `HRESULT`. The RCW maps the information provided by these interfaces to the exception thrown to the .NET client.
`IConnectionPoint` and `IConnectionPointContainer`	These interfaces are used in COM to support the COM event architecture. The RCW uses these interfaces to map COM events to .NET events.

Marshalling Method Calls

In addition to all of its other responsibilities, the RCW is responsible for marshalling method calls from the .NET client to the COM object. The RCW performs several functions on behalf of the .NET client:

- Converts failure `HRESULT`s from COM to .NET exceptions. Failure `HRESULT`s force an exception to be raised; success `HRESULT`s do not.
- Converts COM `retval` parameters to .NET function return values
- Marshals COM data types to .NET data types
- Handles the transitions from managed code to unmanaged code and vice versa

Threading Issues

To write efficient .NET applications that use COM objects, it is important to understand the threading differences between COM and .NET. The COM threading model uses the concept of *apartments*. In the COM world, processes are logically broken down into one or more apartments. Apartments can have a single thread running inside them or they can have multiple threads. An apartment with a single thread is called a Single Threaded Apartment (STA); an apartment running multiple threads is called a Multi-Threaded Apartment (MTA). When a COM client calls into the COM runtime to create a new instance of a component, the COM runtime reads the component's thread value from the Windows registry. The registry value tells the COM runtime which apartment model the component supports. Most components, including those Visual Basic 6 creates, are STA. Clients that run in different apartment models from their components must go through a proxy-stub pair to make method calls. The proxy-stub architecture allows seamless integration between clients and components running in different apartments. This seamless integration comes at a price, however. Your applications take an additional performance hit when calls must be made across apartments. This is due to the fact that extra marshalling must occur in order for the method calls to work properly.

In COM+, apartments are further divided into "contexts." Contexts are objects that contain COM+ properties such as the current state of a transaction. Each apartment can have one or more contexts associated with it. Contexts are the smallest unit of execution in COM+ in that an object can only run in one context at any point in time.

The .NET runtime does not exactly follow the COM threading model. By default, objects inside the .NET runtime run in an MTA. If the COM object and the .NET thread do not support the same threading model, calls have to be made through the proxy-stub pair.

To reduce the cost of crossing the runtime boundaries, you should understand the threading of the COM component you are using. If you are using a STA COM component, it is wise to set the state of the current .NET thread to STA. This can be accomplished through the `Thread` class in the framework's `System.Threading` namespace. You can set the state of the current .NET thread to STA by calling the following:

```
System.Thread.CurrentThread.ApartmentState = ApartmentState.STA.
```

The thread state must be set *before* any COM objects are created. By doing this, the RCW can call directly into the underlying COM component without going through a proxy-stub pair.

Summary

In this chapter, we have covered the aspects of converting a COM type library to a .NET assembly by using the Type Library Importer. As you have seen, this utility is responsible for the following:

- converting type libraries to namespaces
- converting `typedef`s to their native types
- converting `enum`s to .NET `enum`s
- converting module-level methods and constants to static classes and members

We have explored how the RCW is responsible for marshalling method calls from .NET applications to COM components. In short, the RCW is responsible for the following:

- preserving object identity
- maintaining COM object lifetime
- proxying COM interfaces
- marshalling method calls
- consuming default interfaces such as `IUnknown` and `IDispatch`

In the next chapter, we learn to make .NET classes available to COM-based clients.

Chapter 3

Consuming .NET Components from COM

IN THIS CHAPTER

- Converting assemblies to COM type libraries
- Registering assemblies with COM
- COM Callable Wrapper
- Design guidelines for .NET components

JUST AS COM COMPONENTS can be consumed from .NET applications, .NET components can be used from COM clients. In fact, the development model for doing this is very similar to the model used for making COM components available to .NET clients. In this chapter, we cover the steps necessary to make a .NET assembly accessible from COM.

Converting Assemblies to COM Type Libraries

The .NET SDK comes with two tools that can be used to generate type libraries from assemblies: the Type Library Exporter (`tlbexp.exe`) and the Assembly Registration Tool (`regasm.exe`). The Type Library Exporter takes an assembly as input and produces the corresponding type library as output. The Assembly Registration Tool also produces a type library from a .NET assembly and registers the type library and its COM classes in the Windows Registry. Because we are concerned with more than just creating type libraries, let's focus on the Assembly Registration Tool.

The Assembly Registration Tool is yet another command-line utility. Let's take a look at some of its more common parameters. Table 3-1 identifies the parameters we are using in this section.

TABLE 3-1 ASSEMBLY REGISTRATION TOOL OPTIONS

Options	Description
`/regfile:RegFileName.reg`	Prevents the normal COM registry entries from being entered into the registry. The `RegFileName.reg` contains the entries that would have gone into the Windows Registry.
`/tlb:TypeLibFileName.tlb`	Specifies the destination file for the newly generated COM type library. This switch cannot be used in conjunction with `/regfile`.
`/u` and `/unregister`	Unregisters any classes that have been registered from this assembly.

Let's go through a simple example to see how this tool is used. Consider the following .NET class.

```
// Assembly file name: Animal.dll
using System;
namespace Animals {
     public class CDog {
          public void Bark() {
               Console.WriteLine("Woof Woof");
          }
     }
}
```

We compile this class to `Animal.dll` and run it through the Assembly Registration Tool with the following syntax: `regasm /tlb:animal.tlb animal.dll`. Next, if we look at the resulting type library, we find something similar to the following:

```
Library Animals {
     CoClass CDog {
          [default] interface _CDog;
          interface _Object;
     };

     interface _CDog : IDispatch {
          HRESULT ToString([out, retval] BSTR* pRetVal);
          HRESULT Equals([in] VARIANT obj,
               [out, retval] VARIANT_BOOL* pRetVal);
          HRESULT GetHashCode([out, retval] long* pRetVal);
```

```
          HRESULT GetType([out, retval] _Type** pRetVal);
          HRESULT Bark();
     }
}
```

Let's start off by examining the CoClass definition of CDog. Notice there are two interfaces: _CDog, and _Object. .NET supports single inheritance by allowing one object to inherit members of another class. In .NET, each class inherits from System.Object either directly or indirectly. When the Assembly Registration Tool reads an assembly, it is able to extract the inheritance hierarchy for each public class. Members of each class in the inheritance tree are added as members of the class being evaluated. So when the Assembly Registration Tool sees that CDog inherits from System.Object, it adds System.Object's members to CDog.

As you can see, many of the names in the .NET namespace map directly into the type library. For instance, the namespace Animals maps directly to the library name. In addition, the class name CDog maps directly to the CDog CoClass. There are circumstances where a type name in an assembly cannot map directly into the type library. In .NET, a type name can be reused throughout multiple namespaces. The class CDog can exist in the Animals namespace and in the Mammals namespace. To understand how the Assembly Registration Tool handles this naming conflict, let's modify our assembly to contain the Mammals namespace.

```
// Assembly file name: Animal.dll
using System;
namespace Animals {
     public class CDog {
     public void Bark() {
          Console.WriteLine("Woof Woof");
     }
}
namespace Mammals {
     public class CDog {
          public void RollOver(){
               Console.WriteLine("Rolling Over");
          }
     }
}
```

If we repeat our previous step, we get something similar to the following type library:

```
Library Animals {
     CoClass CDog {
          [default] interface _CDog;
          interface _Object;
```

```
    };
    interface CDog : IDispatch {
        // .. Declaration of System.Object's members
        HRESULT Bark();
    };
    CoClass CDog_2 {
        [default] interface _CDog_2;
        interface _Object;
    };
    interface _CDog_2 : IDispatch {
        // .. Declaration of System.Object's members
        HRESULT RollOver();
    }
}
```

Notice that the Assembly Registration tool has added an underscore and 2 to the second instance of `CDog` in the assembly. Because `Animal.CDog` is defined first in the source code, it gets to keep its original name in the type library. Subsequent uses of the `CDog` name are suffixed with an underscore and a running index number. If `CDog` were an interface instead of a class, the same rules would apply. Be forewarned, however, that this naming convention could change in future releases of the framework.

There are a few limitations when converting assemblies to type libraries. For instance, only public classes and interfaces can be exported. In addition, any public class you wish to export must implement a constructor with no parameters. Any static members such as fields and methods cannot be exported. If you wish to provide access to a static member, you must wrap it in an instance-level method call.

If you have classes that meet these criteria and you still do not want to make them available to COM, you can use the `System.Runtime.InteropServices.ComVisible` attribute. The `ComVisible` attribute can be used to hide assemblies, classes, and interfaces from COM. Although this attribute takes a true or false value, it cannot be used to make an otherwise invisible type available to COM. Types that are marked private, internal, or those that do not have a default constructor (no parameters) cannot be made visible to COM, regardless of the value of the `ComVisible` attribute.

Assemblies contain more than just the definition of their types. As you have learned from Chapter 1, assemblies contain a four-part version number, a simple string name, the originator's public key, and, optionally, a strong name if the assembly is shared among multiple applications. When an assembly is converted to a type library, a unique TypeLib ID must be created for COM clients to find the type library in the registry. During the conversion process, an assembly's simple name and originator key are used to generate the new TypeLib ID. A given simple name originator key always generates the same TypeLib ID.

Type libraries also contain version numbers. An assembly's major and minor version numbers are converted to the type library's major and minor version numbers. Build and revision numbers from an assembly are discarded. If an assembly does not contain a version number, the Assembly Registration Tool and the TlbExp utility use 0.1 for the type library version number.

Registering Assemblies with COM

When the Assembly Registration Tool registers an assembly with COM, it makes all the necessary entries for classes and the type library into the Windows registry. The /regfile switch of the Assembly Registration Tool is used to save the resulting registry entries to a file. This file can be copied to other machines that need the assembly registered with COM.

Let's run our CDog class through the Assembly Registration Tool with the /regfile switch turned on.

```
// Assembly file name: Animal.dll
using System;
     namespace Animals {
          public class CDog {
          public void Bark() {
               Console.WriteLine("Woof Woof");
          }
     }
}
```

Using the CDog class defined in the preceding code, the Assembly Registration Tool yields the following registry file. Note that when this switch is used the registry entries are not made to the Windows registry.

```
REGEDIT4

[HKEY_CLASSES_ROOT\Animals.CDog]
@="Animals.CDog"

[HKEY_CLASSES_ROOT\Animals.CDog\CLSID]
@="{AC480224-1FA7-3047-AE40-CCDD09CDC84E}"

[HKEY_CLASSES_ROOT\CLSID\{AC480224-1FA7-3047-AE40-CCDD09CDC84E}]
@="Animals.CDog"
```

```
[HKEY_CLASSES_ROOT\CLSID\{AC480224-1FA7-3047-AE40-CCDD09CDC84E}\InprocServer32]
@="C:\WINNT\System32\MSCorEE.dll"
"ThreadingModel"="Both"
"Class"="Animals.CDog"
"Assembly"="animal, Ver=0.0.0.0, Loc="""

[HKEY_CLASSES_ROOT\CLSID\{AC480224-1FA7-3047-AE40-CCDD09CDC84E}\ProgID]
@="Animals.CDog"

[HKEY_CLASSES_ROOT\CLSID\{AC480224-1FA7-3047-AE40-CCDD09CDC84E}\Implemented
Categories\{62C8FE65-4EBB-45e7-B440-6E39B2CDBF29}]
```

The `ProgID` for the class follows the format of `namespace.class_name`. The Assembly Registration Tool registers the `CDog` class as `Animals.CDog`.

In the registry file shown previously, I have highlighted the most interesting key of all. We can learn a lot from this particular registry entry. First, the COM `InprocServer32` is not `animal.dll` as you may expect, but it is `MSCorEE.dll`. This dll provides a level of indirection that allows COM clients to talk to .NET. This dll implements the COM Callable Wrapper discussed in the next section.

The threading model is defined as "Both." This allows our .NET class to run in either a single threaded apartment or a multi-threaded apartment – depending on the apartment model the unmanaged client is running in.

Finally, notice a brand new registry entry for the assembly. The Assembly registry key tells `MSCorEE.dll` which assembly is implementing the class the ProgID identifies. The assembly's version and locale is also present in the registry. This information is passed to the .NET assembly resolver at runtime to ensure that the proper assembly is located.

COM Callable Wrapper

The counterpart to the Runtime Callable Wrapper is the COM Callable Wrapper (CCW). As you see in the previous section, when a .NET assembly is made available to COM via the Assembly Registration Tool, `MSCorEE.dll` is registered as the COM server. This dll implements the CCW that COM clients call when they use .NET classes. Unlike the RCW, the CCW is unmanaged code running outside the .NET runtime. The CCW has the following responsibilities:

- preserving .NET object identity
- maintaining .NET object lifetime
- proxying explicit interfaces
- providing *standard* COM interfaces on demand
- marshalling method calls between runtimes

Preserving Object Identity

The CCW ensures that there is always a one- to-one relationship between a .NET class and the CCW acting as its wrapper. For instance, when a managed method call returns another class instance (either from a return value or an out parameter), the runtime ensures that a new CCW instance is created. Conversely, when a COM client casts its reference to an interface the underlying managed class supports, the CCW ensures that the interface is supported by the managed class and that a new instance of the managed class is not created just to serve the requested interface.

Maintaining Object Lifetime

When a COM client receives a reference to a COM object, it calls `IUnknown->AddRef` in order to increment the count on the object. Conversely, when it releases a reference to an object, it calls `IUnknown->Release`. The CCW provides an `IUnknown` interface for COM clients to call these methods. Because .NET classes do not implement a reference count, the CCW maintains this count and releases the .NET class when its internal reference count reaches zero. Once the CCW releases its reference to the .NET class, the class becomes eligible for garbage collection, assuming there are no other managed references to the class.

It is possible to leak memory from a .NET class a CCW is wrapping. If the unmanaged process using the .NET class via the CCW shuts down before a Garbage Collection occurs, the managed class is not freed from memory. To keep this problem from happening, the unmanaged process must call the function `CoEEShutDown`. This function is part of the unmanaged API the .NET runtime exposes. The .NET runtime performs one last Garbage Collection once this function is called. More information about this API can be found in the Tool Developers Guide section of the Visual Studio .NET documentation. The methods in this API can be consumed from any programming language that is capable of calling Windows API functions.

Standard COM Interfaces: IUnknown & IDispatch

`IUnknown` and `IDispatch` are two well-known interfaces in the COM world, but they have no meaning in the .NET world. The CCW is responsible for providing these interfaces to COM on demand. `IDispatch` is perhaps the most heavily used interface in COM. Automation clients such as Active Server Pages, Visual Basic (unmanaged versions), and Visual Basic for Applications use `IDispatch` exclusively. `IDispatch` exposes methods that allow clients to query type information from the type library at runtime. If your .NET application does not provide a pre-built type library, the .NET runtime may create one on the fly. This process can be rather time-consuming and can considerably slow down your application. It is wise to ship a type library with your application for this reason.

If you know ahead of time that an automation client will never call your .NET class, you can suppress support for the `IDispatch` interface. `System.Runtime.InteropServices` namespace provides `NoIDispatch`, an attribute that suppresses support for the `IDispatch` interface. If COM clients do query for this interface through `IUnknown->QueryInterface`, the `E_NOINTERFACE HRESULT` is returned.

Proxying Interfaces

Classes in .NET can implement any number of interfaces. When a COM client casts its CoClass instance of the .NET class to one of the explicitly implemented interfaces, the CCW creates a VTable containing the methods of that interface. Usually in COM, a VTable contains pointers to the functions the interface implements. Instead, the CCW places stub functions in the VTable rather than the function pointers. These stubs are responsible for marshalling method calls between COM and .NET. The stub functions are described in more detail in the "Activation Lifecycle" section that follows.

VTables (Virtual Function Tables) define a block of memory that contains pointers to functions the interface defines. When a client obtains a reference to an interface, be it a specific interface or the class's default interface, it receives a pointer to the VTable.

Marshalling Method Calls

Once a COM client has obtained a reference to one of the class's interfaces, it begins to call methods on that interface. The client makes its calls against stubs provided in the interface's VTable. These stubs have several responsibilities:

- managing the transition between managed and unmanaged code
- converting data types between the two runtimes
- changing .NET method return values to out, `retval` parameters
- converting .NET exceptions to `HRESULT`s

It is possible to prevent the CCW from marshalling method calls between the two runtimes. The `System.Runtime.InteropServices.PreserveSigAttribute` attribute is used to maintain the managed method signature when it is called from a COM client. For example, a managed method that has the following signature:

```
long SomeMethod(string sParameter);
```

is converted to the type library in the following format:

```
HRESULT SomeMethod([in] BSTR sParameter,
                   [out, retval] long* pRetVal);
```

When this attribute is applied, the method retains the original signature inside the type library:

```
long SomeMethod(string sParameter);
```

The second point above raises an interesting issue. Converting data types involves marshalling. The marshalling process acts similar to the marshalling process described in the previous chapter, except it works in reverse. The CCW converts .NET data types to their corresponding COM data types when parameters are passed to methods and returned from methods. Basic data types like strings and integers work well in this situation. However, other managed classes can also be returned from method calls. Managed classes returned from method calls do not necessarily have to be registered as COM components. The CCW will convert a managed class to a suitable COM component for the COM client.

Activation Lifecycle

Let's firm up these concepts by walking through each phase that must occur when a COM client loads a class and begins to call methods. Before a COM client can even get an instance of a managed class, it must find the COM dll, load it, and get access to its class factory. The process for doing this is as follows:

1. Query the Windows Registry for the CLSID, given a specific `ProgID`. (Remember for .NET classes the `ProgId` is the `namespace.classname`.)
2. Given the CLSID, the client queries the registry for the CLSID Key. The section "Registering Assemblies with COM" shows what this key looks like for a .NET class.
3. The client calls the COM API `DllGetClassObject`, passing in the CLSID, to get a reference to the class's `ClassFactory`.

Step 3 is where things start to get interesting. `MSCorEE.dll` is the COM server for all .NET classes – including COM+ classes. When a COM client requests a class factory, `MSCorEE.dll` queries the .NET Class Loader to see if that class has been loaded. If the class has been loaded, a class factory is returned to the client. The CCW is responsible for creating this class factory and returning it to the client. However, if the class is not loaded, the CCW looks at the assembly key in the registry to determine the name, version, and locale of the assembly. This information is passed off to the .NET assembly resolver. At this point, the assembly is located through the normal assembly location algorithm. All of the versioning rules, config-file overrides, and location rules we discussed in Chapter 1 are applied at this point. Remember, unless

Class Factories

Class factories are special kinds of COM classes responsible for creating instances of other COM classes. For the most part, each class or object in COM has a corresponding class factory responsible for creating instances of itself. A class factory is responsible for creating *only* one instance of the class it represents. Using class factories to control the creation process of classes has several advantages over simply making a call to the COM API, `CoCreateInstance`:

- The author of the COM class can use his or her knowledge of the class to improve efficiency of the class factory and thus improve the creation process.
- The class-factory model provides a level of indirection that can be used to catch errors during the creation process.
- The class factory simplifies the creation of classes for COM's clients.

Class factories also provide an efficient way to produce multiple instances of a class. In a multi-user environment, such as a Web server using COM+ components, class factories are used to create instances of COM+ objects as user requests are received. In fact, COM+ caches instances of class factories to improve the object-creation times of COM+ objects.

the assembly is in the same directory, in a subdirectory, or in the Global Assembly Cache, the assembly resolver is not able to find the assembly.

Once found, the assembly is passed back to the Class Loader. The Class Loader is responsible for loading the assembly and determining if the assembly implements the class (by reading its metadata). Assuming the class is found within the assembly, the CCW creates a class factory and returns it to the calling client.

The class factory returned to the client is a standard COM class factory on which the client can call `IClassFactory.CreateInstance()` to get an instance of the CCW that wraps the underlying .NET class. `IClassFactory.CreateInstance()` takes three parameters:

- a pointer to `IUnknown`
- an interface ID (GUID defined in the type library)
- a void pointer used to hold the reference to the object

When the client passes in the IUnknown pointer, the CCW compares the values of the pointer to the instance of the class for which the class factory has been returned. By doing this, the CCW preserves the identity of the .NET class.

When `CreateInstance()` is called, the CCW returns the interface to the client and sets up the VTable for the interface's methods. Figure 3-1 shows a VTable for an interface called `IList` that defines methods for `MoveFirst`, `MoveLast`, and `Goto`.

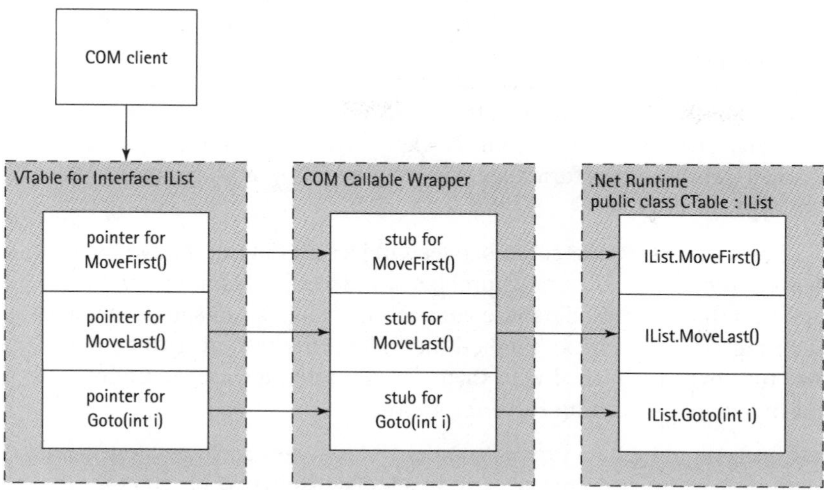

Figure 3-1: VTable for Interface IList

When the client calls `MoveFirst` and `MoveLast`, the CCW manages the transition between managed and unmanaged code and catches any exceptions the methods throw. For instance, the class `MoveLast` may throw an exception if it is called after the client has reached the last position in the list. When this exception is thrown, the CCW converts the exception to a `HRESULT`.

Design Guidelines for .NET Components

We have hit upon several concepts for designing efficient .NET classes to be used with COM. This may not have been entirely obvious, so let's hit upon a few of the key issues.

1. Minimize trips across the Interop boundary: as you can see, a lot of low-level COM and .NET interaction is done automatically for you. COM Interop in .NET provides you with a lot of flexibility. But this flexibility comes at the price of performance. When designing your component, try to minimize the trips your clients have to take across the Interop boundary.
2. Adopt a message-passing architecture: one way to minimize trips across the Interop boundary is to implement a message-passing format. Instead of following an object-oriented approach of setting properties, and calling methods, try passing multiple parameters into a single method call. As an option, you can pass in an XML string containing all of the method parameters as well. This type of approach sets you up well if you want to use a stateless programming model such as in COM+ or if you want to call your object from a remote machine using .NET Remoting.

3. Provide type libraries: the `IDispatch` interface consumes type libraries when `IDispatch->GetTypeInfo` and `IDispatch->GetTypeInfoCount` are called. As we mentioned previously, the .NET runtime can generate type libraries on the fly for these method calls by examining an assembly's metadata. This process is extremely expensive in terms of performance. You can gain a big performance win by generating and deploying your own type libraries.
4. Close and Dispose: differences between object lifetime in the two environments can cause some curious problems. Objects that hold onto expensive resources (file handles, database connections, and so on) should implement either a `Close` or `Dispose` method that allows the resources to be freed once the client is finished with them. Do not rely on Garbage Collection and finalizers to clean up these resources.
5. Stay with standard data types: "standard" data types such as integers and floating-point types do not need to be marshalled across the Interop boundary. Other, more complex types such as strings and dates are marshalled. Also, keep in mind that a CCW or RCW must be created for methods that return references (as a return value or out parameter) to other objects across the boundary.

Summary

In this chapter, we have discussed how .NET assemblies are converted to COM type libraries by using the Assembly Registration Tool. The Assembly Registration Tool is responsible not only for converting types in an assembly to types in a type library but also for registering the new type library in the Windows registry. Also remember that a new value, `Assembly`, is created in the `InprocServer32` key. The `Assembly` sub-key is passed onto the assembly resolver to locate the assembly the client is seeking. We have seen how the CCW plays an important role during method-marshalling between COM and .NET.

This chapter wraps up the first part of the book, Interoperating with COM. This part of the book is intended to provide you with the proper grounding you need as you go forward and learn to implement COM+ services in your .NET applications. The next part of the book teaches you to leverage COM+ services such as distributed transactions, object pooling, and queued components from your .NET applications.

Part II

COM+ Core Services

Chapter 4

Transactions

IN THIS CHAPTER

- ACID requirements
- Logical transaction lifecycle
- Physical transaction lifecycle
- Writing transactional components in C#

TRANSACTIONS are one of the cornerstone services of COM+. In fact, the benefits COM+ transactions provide applications are among the most driving factors in developers' decisions to use COM+. COM+ transactions are so compelling to developers because they provide the glue or plumbing necessary to tie together transactional services such as Oracle and SQL Server databases, CICS applications, and message queues in a single transaction. This type of plumbing code is difficult to design and develop correctly.

In this chapter, you learn some of the basic rules of transaction processing, such as ACID rules. From there, you learn how COM+ provides services such as the Two-Phase Commit protocol and Automatic Transaction Enlistment to help you follow those basic transaction-processing rules. Once you have a firm grasp of the fundamentals, you write a transactional component by using C# and the .NET `ServicedComponent` class. Along the way, you see some pitfalls and other things to avoid when developing components in C#.

ACID Requirements

Any transaction, whether it is a COM+ transaction or not, must have four basic characteristics to be a transactional system. These rules may seem academic and not worth your attention, but a solid understanding of them helps you understand why COM+ does certain things. A transaction must be: atomic, consistent, isolated, and durable.

Atomic

A transaction represents a unit of work that either completely succeeds or completely fails. A transaction, particularly a COM+ transaction, may have many subtasks to perform in order to execute. For instance, an order-processing application may need to validate data from a customer, decrement the customer's account from one database, and submit the order to another database or to a message queue. Suppose the customer does not have enough credit for the purchase; you don't not want the order to be submitted in that case, correct? The *atomic* rule states that if you decide to abort the transaction because of a lack of customer credit, the order is not submitted. In other words, all the subtasks of a transaction must complete successfully or none of them do.

Consistent

The *consistent* rule states that a transaction must start with data in a consistent state and end with data in a consistent state. Consider a scenario where your application is updating two databases. If the first update is successful and temporarily commits data but the second update fails, the first update must rollback its data to the state it was in before the transaction started. By undoing any temporary changes, a transactional system is able to maintain the consistency of the data during an abort. Conversely, if the transaction succeeds, the committed data must not violate any of the business rules surrounding the data.Consistency is something you need to consider in your application design. For instance, if you have a decimal field in your data that contains three decimal places, you should not round the field to two decimal places during the transaction. Consistency is supported in COM+ only to the extent that data changes can be committed and rolled back. Respecting business rules is up to you.

Isolated

The *isolated* rule states that transactions occurring simultaneously must not see each other's work. If transaction *A* is updating a database table and transaction *B* attempts to query the same table, transaction *B* must not see the data transaction *A* is updating until *A* either commits or aborts. Usually, the isolated rule leads to some pretty hefty locks on database tables, particularly in COM+.

Table locks restrict the level at which another application can view data currently being used by another application.Table locks essentially come in two flavors: read locks and write locks. *Read locks* allow other programs to read data from the table, but do not allow another program to write data to the table.This allows the application that established the lock to get a clean read from the table without seeing another application's partially finished work. Read locks are usually used when an application needs to select data from a table. *Write locks* prevent other applications from reading or writing to the table.Write locks are more restrictive than read locks since they put a greater limitation on the types of activities that can be performed with the table. Write locks are generally used when an application needs to update or insert data into the table.

The level of locking a database applies inside of a transaction is the *isolation level.* Isolation levels can be adjusted to improve performance by decreasing the level of isolation, or they can be adjusted to increase the level of isolation. If decreasing the isolation level improves performance, and increasing the isolation level decreases performance, why would anyone ever want to increase the isolation level? It turns out that increasing the isolation level reduces the chance that another application can modify data while you are still in the middle of a transaction. There are four possible levels of isolation inside of a transaction. Table 4-1 lists and describes each of the possible isolation levels.

TABLE 4-1 ISOLATION LEVELS

Isolation Level	Description
Read uncommitted	This is the lowest isolation level (best performer). This will allow you to read a table that is currently being updated by another application. You run the risk of seeing data that has not been completely updated. This is known as a dirty read.
Read committed	This is a step higher than read uncommitted. An application using this level will wait until any write locks are released. This is a slightly slower performer since the application must wait on other applications to release their locks.
Repeatable Read	This level prevents other applications from establishing write locks. Other applications will be able to establish a read lock, but will not be able to establish a write lock.
Serializable	This level establishes a read or write lock (depending on the task) over the entire range of rows affected by the transaction. For example, if the application is doing a `select *` from a table, then a write lock will be established on all the rows in the table.

A COM+ transaction that runs against Microsoft SQL Server applies an isolation level of serializable. This isolation level is the most restrictive, and it usually leads to table-level locks. Unfortunately in COM+, on Windows 2000 the isolation level is not configurable.

Durable

The *durable* rule states that once a transaction has been committed, its data must be stored in a permanent state that can survive a power outage. If the computer running the transaction should crash and restart immediately after committing the transaction, then the data involved in the transaction should be stored in a permanent location. Put another way, once the transaction commits, the data should be stored in the database and saved to disk by the database engine. Also, for transactions in progress, durability requires that transactions can pick up where they left off after a system interruption such as a power outage. Usually, logs are updated as a transaction is taking place that allows a transaction to be rolled back or restarted after an interruption. If a system interruption occurs during the middle of a transaction, then these log files will be read to determine whether the transaction should be committed or aborted. Transaction managers are responsible for maintaining these types of log files and determining if their part of the transaction should be committed or aborted. Transaction managers are covered in the Physical Transaction Lifecycle section later in this chapter.

Understanding the COM+ Transaction Process

As I mention in the introduction to this chapter, COM+ provides the glue that makes transactional components work. The glue – or underlying transaction architecture – is not something a typical component developer needs to be terribly concerned with on a daily basis. However, a good understanding of how the underlying architecture works helps you design your transactional components and applications.

In COM+, a transaction is divided into two parts: the logical transaction and the underlying physical transaction. Transactional components run inside the logical transaction, which the COM+ runtime hosts. Physical transactions, however, are initiated based upon actions taken inside the logical transaction. Take a look at each of these parts in detail to see how they interoperate to form the complete COM+ transaction.

Logical Transaction Lifecycle

A logical transaction starts when the client makes its first method call against a transactional component. Your components run inside the logical transaction and interact with it through their contexts. The logical transaction drives the underlying physical transaction. Let's break down the lifecycle of the logical transaction to see how this works.

In Chapter 2, I briefly introduce *contexts*. I explain contexts in relation to apartments in that each apartment may be broken down into multiple contexts. Contexts are of particular importance to transactional components. Each component in COM+ gets a context associated with it when it is created. When a client instantiates a transactional component, COM+ looks to see if the client is already participating in a transaction. If the client is running in a transaction (a client can be another transactional component) and if the component supports running in another's transaction, the component is created, and it inherits the context of the client. Think of the context as a sort of property bag that contains runtime-relative information that COM+ and the component use to talk to each other.

Unmanaged components – those written with Visual Basic 6, for example – manipulate the context through properties and methods of the `ObjectContext`. .NET components use a similar object called `ContextUtil`. `ContextUtil` resides in the `System.EnterpriseServices` namespace. If you compare the two APIs, you notice many similar methods and properties.

DECLARATIVE TRANSACTIONS

COM+ supports declarative transactions. *Declarative transactions* allow the developer to manipulate a component's transactional characteristics through attributes. The transaction attribute for a component is stored in the COM+ catalog. You can think of the COM+ catalog as a small database that stores all the information COM+ needs to instantiate and run your component properly. COM+ supports five settings for the transactional attribute:

- `Disabled`: Components never run inside a COM+ transaction. Components with this attribute are nontransactional.
- `Not Supported`: This is the default value for components running in COM+. This attribute tells the runtime that the component does not support transactions. If the component votes on the transaction (see "Casting the Vote" that follows) by calling `ObjectContext.SetComplete` or `ObjectContext.SetAbort`, these votes do not count toward the outcome of the transaction. Components that have this attribute are nontransactional.
- `Supported`: A component that has this attribute can be created within the client's transaction. If the client is not running in a transaction, the component does not run in a transaction. Components that have this attribute are transactional.
- `Required`: This component is required to run in a transaction. The component runs in the caller's transaction if one exists. If the caller is not running in a transaction, a new transaction is created.
- `RequiresNew`: The component must always be created in a new transaction, regardless of the caller's transaction status.

Normally, these attributes are specified in a component's type library. When a component is installed into a COM+ library or server application, the attribute setting is read from the type library and applied to the component. Afterward, these settings can be changed at any time. When you write components with C# or with any other language that supports the CLR, these attributes are inserted directly into the source code through the `System.EnterpriseServices.Transaction` attribute. When the component is compiled, these attributes show up in the assembly's metadata. As you see later in this chapter, this attribute is read from the metadata and applied to the component when it is installed into a COM+ application.

JUST IN TIME ACTIVATION

I state previously that the logical transaction starts when the caller makes its first method call on a transactional component. The logical transaction starts when the component is created. Both statements are true due to a concept called Just In Time Activation (JITA). JITA can be either enabled or disabled for a component. However, for a transactional component, JITA is required. In fact, when you choose a transaction attribute of `Supported`, `Required`, or `RequiresNew`, this attribute is checked and disabled for you. Refer to Figure 4-1 to see what this looks like in the Component Services Explorer.

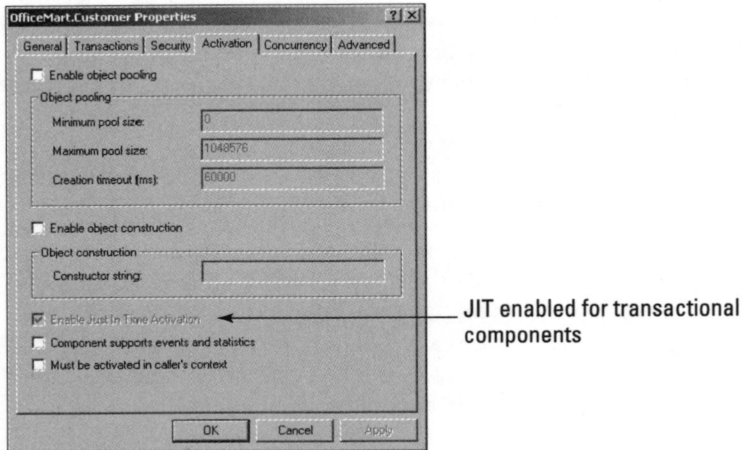

Figure 4-1: JITA is required for a transactional component.

When the client makes a creation request, COM+ intercepts the call and returns a reference of the component to the client without creating the component. As soon as the client calls a method on the component, COM+ activates the component and calls the method. Assuming the component sets its *done* bit to true, the component is destroyed once the method returns.

The done bit is a flag in the context that the component uses to tell COM+ when its work is done. When a method returns, COM+ examines the component's done bit to determine if the component should be destroyed. By default, this setting is set to false when a method is first called. In C#, `ContextUtil.SetComplete` and `ContextUtil.SetAbort` both set this done bit to true. Conversely, `ContextUtil.EnableCommit` and `Context.DisableCommit` set this bit to false. If you have written COM+ components using Visual Basic 6, then these methods of the `ContextUtil` class should look familiar. The `ObjectContext` component used in Visual Basic 6 supports the same set of methods, which incidentally perform the same functions as those from the `ContextUtil` class.

COM+ supports an attribute called `autodone`. This attribute is applied to a method by using the Component Services Explorer. The Auto-Done attribute changes the done bit's default value from false to true when a method is first called. The .NET Framework provides this support through the `AutoComplete` attribute, which you encounter later in the chapter. Figure 4-2 shows a method in the Component Services Explorer that has Auto-Done turned on.

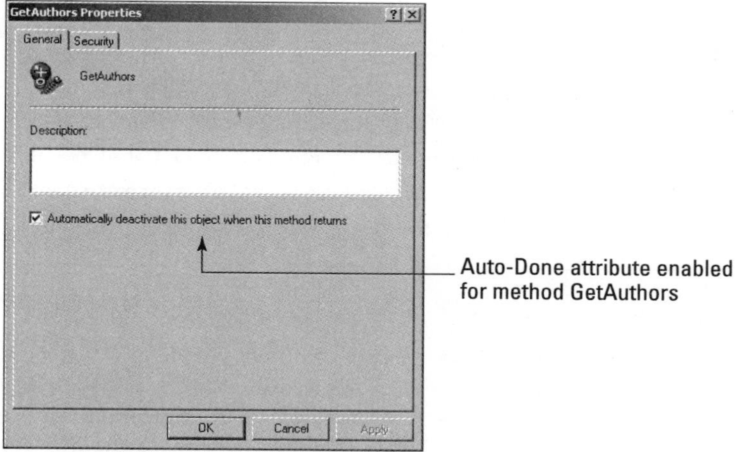

Figure 4-2: Auto-Done attribute turned on for a component's method

The .NET Framework supports the COM+ `AutoDone` attribute through the `AutoComplete` attribute in the `System.EnterpriseServices` namespace. This attribute is applied at the method level and is automatically set in the COM+ catalog when a component is installed.

The JITA model is well suited for transactional components. Transactional components work best when each method call does an atomic unit of work, then exits and is destroyed. If COM+ is allowed to destroy the object after each small unit of work, there is no chance the component's data can corrupt the transaction later. Without JITA in this model, a client has to create the object after each method call. As you might imagine, this can become rather tedious. Because JITA creates the object each time on the client's behalf, the client does not need to worry whether its reference to the component is still valid.

CASTING THE VOTE

As you may have guessed, each component gets a vote in the overall outcome of the transaction. The vote is cast by setting the "consistent" flag on the context to true or false. Methods from the `ContextUtil` object such as `SetComplete` and `EnableCommit` set this bit to true. The `SetAbort` and `DisableCommit` methods set this bit to false. If the component is in a consistent state, it is able to commit the transaction, so its vote is to commit. Conversely, if the object is in an inconsistent state, the component cannot commit its data, so it votes to abort the transaction. Initially, this bit is set to true.

The combination of the done bit and the consistent bit for the logical transaction are used to decide whether to commit or abort. Setting the done bit to true forces COM+ to examine the component's consistency bit. If the done bit is true and the consistent bit is true, the object's final vote is to commit the transaction. If the done bit is true and the consistent bit it false, the transaction aborts regardless of any other object's vote in the transaction.

In addition to JITA, synchronization is required for transactional components. Synchronization keeps two clients from calling a method on the same component at the same time. Synchronization is important for transactional components; without synchronization, one client can enter a component another client is using. This violates the ACID rules of atomicity and isolation.

UNDERSTANDING A TRANSACTION'S SCOPE

Developing transactional components this way is deceptively simple. All you need to do is write your data access logic and business logic, call `SetAbort` if there is a problem, and otherwise call `SetComplete`. The complexity is understanding the scope of the transaction. I have been burned by not completely understanding the scope of my transactional components. To understand the scope of a logical transaction, walk through an example.

Assume you have a GUI application that your end user is using to enter sales orders. Typically, sales orders consist of some header information such as the customer's name, account number, and so on, as well as line-item data. When the user submits the sales order, the GUI application creates your remote transactional component and begins to call methods on the component to submit the sales order to the database. Remember that each method call results in four actions:

- COM+ activates the component.
- The component's method is called.
- The component votes on the transaction.
- COM+ destroys the object.

Here's the tricky part. If the GUI client is responsible for calling methods on the component, a new transaction starts for each method call because the component is created and destroyed each time. If the first method call succeeds and the second fails, the sales order could be left in an inconsistent state in the database.

There are two work arounds for this problem. The first solution is to use the `TransactionContext` object. This object allows nontransactional clients, such as the GUI application mentioned previously, to control or coordinate the transaction. `TransactionContext` has methods to commit or abort the transaction and to create other objects that must participate in the transaction. However, this approach has a couple of drawbacks:

- It requires the client to have the Transaction Context library installed.
- Nontransactional components do not benefit from the automatic transaction services of COM+. If nontransactional components fail, the transaction may or may not be aborted.

The second solution is to create another transactional component that consumes other subtransactional components. This model is preferred because all the work of a transaction can occur within the protection of the COM+ runtime. If we modify the previous example, the GUI client can call one method on the coordinating component and can pass it all the sales-order data at one time. The coordinating component can be responsible for instantiating subcomponents and calling methods to do the database work. This is also a nice way to separate business logic and validation logic from database-access logic. The coordinating component can implement the application's business rules. Assuming the business rules are met, data can be entered through the subcomponents. If you pass all the data into the coordinating component in one method call, you get the added bonus of reducing the number of network trips needed to complete your transaction.. Now, instead of taking a network performance hit each time you make a method call, you need to take only one hit for the entire transaction.

In this scenario, the coordinating component has a `Requires` or `RequiresNew` transaction attribute. The coordinating component acts as the root component of the transaction. When the client calls the first method on an instance of this component, the transaction begins. Once the component has set its done bit to true, the logical transaction ends.

Physical Transaction Lifecycle

In this section, you see what happens behind the scenes during the logical transaction and what happens to the physical resources involved in the transaction after the logical transaction ends.

AUTOMATIC TRANSACTION ENLISTMENT

The physical transaction begins when a transactional component makes a connection to a resource such as a database server or queue manager. In most cases, when a transactional component requests a connection, the connection is dispensed from a resource dispenser. Resource dispensers are responsible for maintaining a pool of volatile resources such as database connections and threads. Resource dispensers are also responsible for registering the connection with the local transaction manager. The process of registering a connection with the transaction manager is *Automatic Transaction Enlistment.* Figure 4-3 illustrates the process that occurs when a transactional component requests one of these resources.

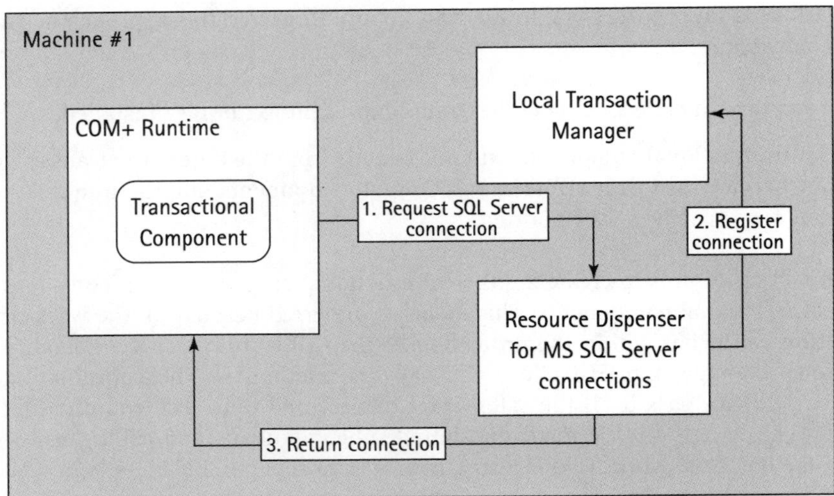

Figure 4-3: Automatic Transaction Enlistment

For example, when a component uses ADO (or ADO.NET, for that matter) to open a connection to a SQL Server database, the request goes to the resource dispenser implemented inside the OLEDB framework. The resource dispenser looks at the connection string passed to ADO to determine if that type of connection exists within the resource dispenser's pool. If a connection exists in the pool that has the same connection string as the one being requested (for example, the same SQL Server, driver, and user ID), the resource dispenser registers the connection with the local transaction manager and returns the connection to the client. If the connection does not exist, one is created and added to the pool.

TRANSACTION MANAGERS

Transaction managers are responsible for tracking activities between components and resource managers. Resource managers manage data resources. Resource managers know how to store data to the database and how to rollback their data in the event of a transaction failure.

In a typical COM+ transaction, at least two machines are involved: one machine the component runs on and another machine the database runs on. Each machine must have a transaction manager to participate in a COM+ transaction. With Microsoft products, the Distributed Transaction Coordinator service implements transaction managers. Windows 2000 and SQL Server both ship with this service.

When the physical transaction starts, the transaction manager running on the same machine as the component is designated as the coordinating transaction manager. The coordinating transaction manager is responsible for initiating the Two-Phase Commit protocol.

TWO-PHASE COMMIT PROTOCOL

Once all of the components in the logical transaction have finished their work and each of their done bits is set to true, COM+ evaluates the transaction to determine if the transaction should commit or abort. If each object's consistent flag is set to true, COM+ instructs the local transaction manager to commit the physical transaction. The physical transaction is committed through the *Two-Phase Commit protocol.*

In phase I, the coordinating transaction manager asks the subordinate transaction managers if they are ready to commit the transaction. Each subordinate transaction manager responds with a vote to commit or abort the transaction. A vote to commit the transaction is a commitment to the coordinating transaction manager indicating that the resources can be committed and made durable. Any vote the transaction managers make to abort dooms the transaction.

In phase II, the coordinating transaction manager tallies the votes from the subordinates. If all subordinates have voted to commit, the coordinating transaction manager sends an instruction to the subordinates to commit their resources. If the transaction is to be aborted, the coordinating transaction manager sends an instruction to the subordinates to rollback the transaction. During this phase, each transaction manager instructs its local resource manager to commit or rollback the transaction. Usually, resource managers maintain some sort of protected log file throughout the transaction to provide this capability. Incidentally, this log allows a transaction to restart in the event of system failure.

Figure 4-4 shows the process a coordinating transaction manager undergoes during a Two-Phase Commit protocol.

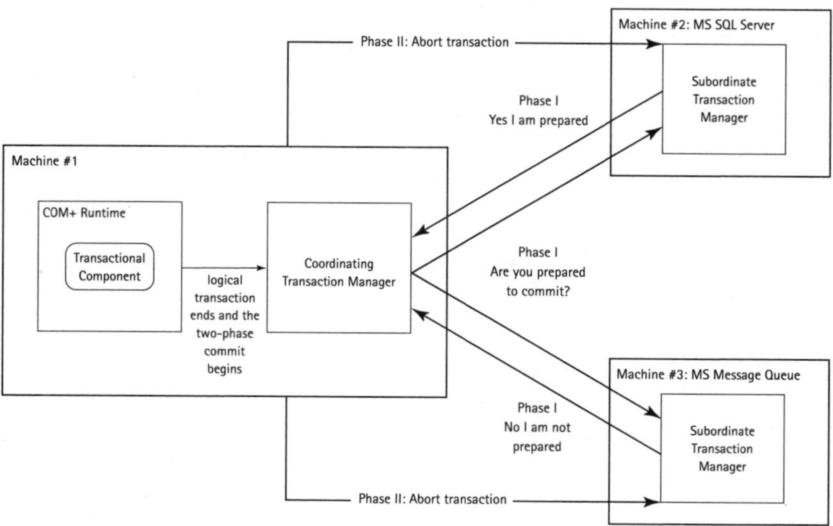

Figure 4-4: Two-Phase Commit protocol

Writing Transactional Components in C#

In this section, you write a transactional component that gets its transaction ID from the `ContextUtil` class and logs it, along with its class name, into a database. You use attributes that provide component support for synchronization, JITA, and automatic completion of methods. In addition, you learn to register a class into a COM+ application.

ServicedComponent Class

Throughout this book, you become intimately familiar with the `ServicedComponent` class. It provides all of the COM+ services such as transactions, object pooling, and automatic registration into COM+ applications. Any C# class that wishes to use COM+ services must inherit from this class.

The `ServicedComponent` class exists in the `System` namespace. To get access to this namespace from your code, implement a `using System` statement within your code. Normally, you must make a reference to an assembly containing the namespace you wish to use. The C# compiler is kind enough to include a reference for each component or application automatically because the `System` namespace is so frequently used.

.NET uses namespaces to organize classes, interfaces, methods, and so on that implement similar or complementary functionality. For example, the `System.EnterpriseServices` namespace implements many attributes, interfaces, and classes you use to interoperate with COM+.

Defining a C# class that inherits from the `ServicedComponent` is relatively simple.

```
Namespace ComTransaction {
using System;
using System.EnterpriseServices;
  public class CRoot : ServicedComponent {
    // add some methods here
  }
}
```

The preceding code consists of four important tasks you must complete to make a C# class a COM+ component:

- Defining the namespace – `ComTransaction` – for your component
- Declaring that you are using the `System` namespace via the `using` statement
- Making the class public
- Inheriting from the `ServicedComponent` class via `: ServicedComponent`

When this class is installed in a COM+ application, it is available for use from managed and unmanaged components alike. Remember from Chapter 3 that a .NET class must be public if you want to use it from an unmanaged COM-based client.

Attribute-based Programming

Next, add a method to the component (Listing 4-1).

Listing 4-1: Transactional Component

```
Namespace ComTransaction {
using System;
using System.Data.SQL;
using System.EnterpriseServices;

[Transaction(TransactionOption.Required)]
public class CRoot : ServicedComponent {

  public void LogTransactionId() {
    SQLConnection cnn = new
SQLConnection("server=localhost;database=Transactions;uid=sa;pwd=");
    SQLCommand cmd = new SQLCommand();
    cnn.Open();
    cmd.ActiveConnection = cnn;
    cmd.CommandText = "insert into TransactionId values('CWorker1',
'" + ContextUtil.TransactionId + "')";
    cmd.ExecuteNonQuery();
    cnn.Close();
  }
}
}
```

We have added a method called `LogTransactionId`. This method creates a command and connection object and inserts the class name and the component's transaction ID into the database. The `ContextUtil` object is used to get the `TransactionId` of the transaction. Also, we have declared this component to require a transaction through the `[Transaction(TransactionOption.Required)]` attribute.

This attribute model is rather different from the COM+ attribute model. Traditional unmanaged COM+ components do not store their attributes inside their code base. Attributes are stored in the COM+ catalog. This results in a dislocation of the attributes from their corresponding components. The architects of the .NET Framework have altered this model by storing the attributes directly inside the code. At compile time, the attributes are converted into metadata and stored in the assembly. This allows the component and its attributes to be in the same file.

Attributes can be applied at the assembly level. Specific to COM+, an assembly can be attributed to affect the name of the COM+ application, the description, and whether the classes are installed in a library or server application. The `ApplicationName` attribute, the `Description` attribute, and the `ApplicationActivation` attribute are all in the `System.EnterpriseServices` namespace and can be used to specify the name of the COM+ application, its description, and the library or server setting, respectively.

COM+ applications can be installed as either library applications or server applications. Library applications run in the same process as their clients, but server applications run in a host process outside of their client's process. The host process on Windows 2000 is `dllhost.exe`.

Installing a Class into a COM+ Application

Now that you have a complete transactional component that does some work, you can install it in a COM+ application. There are two ways to install a C# class in a COM+ application: using lazy registration at runtime or using the `Regsvcs` command-line tool that ships with the .NET Framework SDK.

Lazy registration eliminates the need to install a component manually into an application. When a managed client creates an instance of a class that inherits from `ServicedComponent`, the .NET runtime is intelligent enough to know that the class must be registered with COM+. Of course, once the class is registered, the runtime does not register it. Lazy registration allows you to skip the administrative burden of creating COM+ applications and installing your components. There are, however, several downsides to this feature:

- Lazy registration works only for managed clients. Because the class is not registered ahead of time, an unmanaged client is not able to find the class in the registry.
- Problems registering a component are not caught until runtime. If the component fails to install, the client is out of luck.
- The process that registers the class must run under administrative privileges to create the COM+ application. If the process is running in the security context of the end user, the end user must have administrative privileges.

The Regsvcs command-line tool registers a ServicedComponent class prior to execution. It takes the name of an assembly file as input and creates the COM+ application. All of these ServicedComponent classes inside the assembly are registered into the same COM+ application. The name of the assembly is used for the name of the COM+ application unless it has been overridden using assembly-level attributes. This tool has a number of arguments that can be passed in. Table 4-2 contains some of the more useful arguments I have used in dealing with this tool.

TABLE 4-2 USEFUL REGSVCS ARGUMENTS

Argument	Description
/c	Forces the COM+ application to be installed
/fc	Looks for the application already installed in COM+
/reconfig	Reconfigures the application and components. This is similar to right-clicking the components folder in the Component Service console and clicking Refresh.

The Regsvcs command-line tool and lazy registration both go through the same four-step process to register the class into an application:

1. Load the assembly.
2. Generate and register a type library (similar to the process described in Chapter 3).
3. Create the COM+ application.
4. Read the class metadata to apply the appropriate attributes.

JITA, Synchronization, and AutoComplete

You have learned how a class is declared as transactional through the Transaction attribute. The way you declare JustInTimeActivation support, Synchronization support, and AutoComplete support is not much different. All of these attributes are in the System.EnterpriseServices namespace. In Listing 4-2, we attribute the CRoot class and its method with these attributes.

Listing 4-2: Transactional Component Using AutoComplete

```
Namespace ComTransaction {
using System;
using System.Data.SQL;
using System.EnterpriseServices;

[Transaction(TransactionOption.Required)]
[JustInTimeActivation(true)]
[Synchronization(SynchronizationOption.Required)]
public class CRoot : ServicedComponent {

  [AutoComplete]
  public void LogTransactionId() {
    // database work here
  }
}
}
```

The `JustInTimeActivation` attribute has two constructors. The default constructor (the one with no parameters) sets the `JustInTimeActivation` support to true. The second parameter takes a boolean value that can enable or disable `JustInTimeActivation` support. Notice that this attribute is applied on the class level. The `Synchronization` attribute is similar to the `JustInTimeActivation` attribute in that it has two parameters. The default constructor defaults the `Synchronization` support to `Required`. The `Synchronization` attribute also has a parameter that takes a `SynchronizationOption` enumeration that can be used to set the support to any of the required levels: `Disabled`, `Not Supported`, `Supported`, `Required`, or `RequiresNew`. Finally, the `AutoComplete` attribute is applied at the method level as you would expect. If the method throws an exception, the transaction aborts; otherwise, it votes to commit. When the AutoComplete attribute is applied to a method, the `AutoDone` attribute is applied in the COM+ catalog.

Developing the Root and Worker Objects

Previously in this chapter, I recommend a design pattern for transactional components. The pattern involves a root object that coordinates the work of other subcomponents. The root object starts the transaction, and the subcomponents do the work. Let's extend our preceding example to use this design pattern. Listing 4-3 shows a namespace called `ComTransaction` that implements the root object and two worker objects.

Listing 4-3: Root and Worker Classes

```
namespace ComTransaction
{
  using System;
  using System.Data.SQL;
  using System.EnterpriseServices;

  [Transaction(TransactionOption.Required)]
  public class CRoot : ServicedComponent
  {
      public void LogTransactionId()
      {
         /* log class name and transaction id to database */

         CWorker1 worker1 = new CWorker1();
         CWorker2 worker2 = new CWorker2();
         worker1.LogTransactionId();
         worker2.LogTransactionId();

      }
  }

  [Transaction(TransactionOption.Supported)]
  public class CWorker1 : ServicedComponent
  {
      public void LogTransactionId()
      { /* log class name and transaction id to database */ }
  }

  [Transaction(TransactionOption.Supported)]
  public class CWorker2 : ServicedComponent
  {
      public void LogTransactionId()
      { /* log class name and transaction id to database */ }
  }
}
```

For the sake of clarity, I have omitted the database logic. First of all, notice that on the two `CWorker1` and `CWorker2` objects, I have set the transaction support to `TransactionOption.Supported`. This allows each worker object to participate in the root's transaction. The `CRoot` object uses these two classes as though they are any other class from a namespace. Table 4-3 represents the output made to the database after a client creates the CRoot object and calls its `LogTransactionId` message.

TABLE 4-3 DATABASE OUTPUT

ClassName	TransactionId
CRoot	FF208BBB-D785-4c59-9EA1-D3B6379822FB
CWorker1	FF208BBB-D785-4c59-9EA1-D3B6379822FB
CWorker2	FF208BBB-D785-4c59-9EA1-D3B6379822FB

Notice that the transaction IDs are identical for each object. This proves that each object has indeed run in the same transaction.

Summary

In this chapter, you have learned how the ACID requirements (atomicity, consistency, isolation, and durability) drive the transactional features of COM+ and the underlying transaction managers. These requirements force the underlying architecture to lock resources while they are in use. Often, these locks can prove to be a bottleneck for transactional applications if their impacts are not properly understood. The basic rule of thumb when designing transactional components is to let them do their work, vote, exit quickly, and release their resources.

You have learned some new concepts the .NET Framework has introduced. Attribute-based programming is not new to the COM+ developer, but including attributes directly into source code is. This technique is a convenient way to keep the attributes and their components in one location. This technique also helps to simplify deployment of your components. Finally, you have seen how the `ServicedComponent` class is used in a C# application through inheritance. The combination of the `ServicedComponent` class and attributes from the `System.EnterpriseServices` namespace gives you COM+ support for your C# classes.

In Chapter 5, you learn how .NET provides support for the role-based security feature of COM+.

Chapter 5

Security

IN THIS CHAPTER

- Understanding Windows security
- Authenticating over the wire
- Using COM+ security in C#

THE COM+ SECURITY MODEL provides mechanisms for both declarative security and programmatic security. Declarative security allows a component to be configured at the time it is deployed through the use of attributes recorded into the COM+ catalog. At runtime, these attributes affect the accessibility of the component, its interfaces, and its methods. Programmatic security allows a component to control its accessibility at runtime. In fact, declarative security and programmatic security are interrelated. For a component to use programmatic security, the proper attributes must be set in the COM+ catalog.

In Chapter 4, you encounter one of the central themes of the .NET development model: attribute-based programming. You see that when you write transactional components in C#, you specify, in code, the COM+ catalog settings you desire for your components. This is a significant shift from the traditional way of developing components for COM+. In the traditional development model, you develop your component, install it into a COM+ application, and set the appropriate attributes. The problem with this development model is that you rely typically on an administrator to set these attributes properly. The .NET development model puts this power (and responsibility) into the hands of the developer. As you see in this chapter, .NET Framework security attributes can be a powerful tool for setting every security-related attribute inside the COM+ catalog. The attribute-based programming model in .NET can help you ensure that your application's security settings are correctly configured since the security settings are read from the assembly's metadata at the time they are registered in the COM+ catalog.

In this chapter, you encounter various aspects of the COM+ security model: authentication, authorization, and role-based security. Also, you see how the .NET Framework attributes are used in C# to configure your components properly. Along the way, you learn how authentication is performed *over the wire* from one machine to another. However, before you explore these details, it is important to understand how the security services provided in COM+ are leveraged from the underlying Windows Security Architecture.

Understanding Windows Security

If you have ever looked at the Windows Security API or any of its related documentation, you have realized what a complex topic it is. Fortunately, COM+ programmers need only to know the basics.

Any security system, no matter how complicated, ultimately comes down to a two-step process: authenticate the user, and authorize his or her access. *Authentication* is the process a user goes through to prove his or her identity. *Authorization* verifies that the user has rights to do what he or she is attempting.

Authentication

When you log on to your computer in a Windows domain, you supply your user ID and password to prove that you are who you say you are. Of course, there are more sophisticated techniques for authentication, such as smart cards and various biometric technologies. The goal, however, is to establish your presence on the network so that you can use various resources.

But what happens when a user logs on to his or her computer? Let's break it down. The logon sequence starts when the user presses Ctrl-Alt-Del. This key sequence sends a message known as the *Secure Attention Sequence (SAS)* to the Net Logon Service. The Net Logon Service starts a graphical user interface program known as the *Graphical Identification and Authentication (GINA)*. The GINA is responsible for displaying the user ID and password dialog box you see when you log in to your Windows workstation. If, for example, the user is using a smart card, the GINA is responsible for reading data on it.

Once the user has entered his or her user ID and password (and optionally the domain to log in to) the GINA passes the credentials to the *Local Security Authority (LSA)*. The LSA is responsible for authenticating the user based on the user ID and password provided. In fact, the LSA hands off the user's credentials to yet another component called the authentication package. The authentication package verifies the user's credentials against a database and either authenticates the user or rejects the credentials. If the user is logging in to the workstation by using a Windows user ID and password, the authentication package verifies the credentials against the local *Security Accounts Manager (SAM)* database. In the case of a domain login, the authentication package looks at the directory database for the domain. Directory databases reside on domain controllers in an Active Directory network. The directory database is conceptually similar to a local computer's SAM database except that it stores additional data such as configuration data for the topology of the network, and schema data. Schemas act as a sort of template that defines what properties an object such as a user account or computer account will hold in the directory.

If the authentication package is able to authenticate the user, it reports its success to the LSA. At this point, the LSA does two things: generates a logon session and generates an access token. Logon sessions map one-to-one with the particular user currently logged on to the workstation. Generally, a user cannot have two logon sessions running on the same computer.

The access token is of particular interest here. It defines the user as *the user* in the system. It is a type of data structure that contains all the information about the user, such as the *Security Identifier (SID)*, which uniquely identifies the user, as well as the SIDs of any groups the user belongs to. The access token also contains an ID that represents a user's current logon session.

Windows security subsystems use SIDs in a similar fashion to the way globally unique identifiers (GUID) are used in COM. Just as a class identifier (CLSID)or type library ID are unique across time and space, so are SIDs. SIDs not only represent a user's account but represent just about every other entity that can be secured or identified, such as computers and groups.

Once the user's logon session and access token have been established, the operating system starts the Windows shell. As the user launches applications, such as Internet Explorer, the access token is copied from the shell's process space into the application's process space. Now there are two access tokens, both pointing back to the user's logon session.

Authorization

When a user begins to access secured resources, such as a file or even a component, Windows checks the user's access token against the *Security Descriptor (SD)* for the item being accessed. The SD is a list of all the users and groups who have access to the resource. The SD defines which users have which privileges for the resource.

The SD is a runtime data structure composed of two items: the *System Access Control List (SACL)* and the *Discretionary Access Control List (DACL)*. Windows uses the SACL for auditing purposes. The SACL is of little importance to a COM+ developer because it does not play a role in COM+ security. The SACL is used for Windows auditing, not for COM+ programmatic security auditing, which you encounter later in this chapter.

The DACL maps a user's or group's SID to access rights such as read, execute, delete, and so on. At runtime, Windows examines the SIDs located in the user's access token and compares them to the SIDs in the DACL. If none of the SIDs in the access token match those in the DACL, the user gets the familiar "Access Denied" message. In the case of COM, this can lead to the `E_ACCESSDENIED HRESULT`.

The DACL maps user and group SIDs to access rights through *Access Control Entries (ACEs)*. Each ACE contains a user or group SID and the corresponding access rights for that user or group. In any DACL, there can be two types of ACEs: an access-allowed ACE and an access-denied ACE. Windows searches the list of ACEs in a DACL to determine the user's effective rights on the resource. If Windows encounters an access-denied ACE that can be applied against the user's access token, the user is denied access regardless of any access-allowed ACEs. If no access-denied ACEs are found, the user is granted the sum of all access rights pertaining to all ACEs for the token.

Special Accounts

When the Windows operating system is installed, the installer program creates a number of special groups and user accounts. COM+ uses some of these accounts, such as Everyone, Authenticated Users, and the Interactive User, at various times. Other accounts, such as the System account, are utilized by the underlying services and subsystems COM+ benefits from.

If you are like me, you have often used the Everyone account to overcome some of those annoying security features of Windows during the development of your applications. But what is this account, really? The *Everyone* account is a runtime group account that all authenticated users belong to. In fact, when you log on to Windows, the Everyone SID is placed in your access token. Because the Everyone group is a runtime group, no users can be explicitly placed in it. I have often given the Everyone group full access to files during application development to by pass security (temporarily, of course) and to focus on a different issue. But what happens when you give the Everyone group full control on a file? In this situation, the DACL for the file is set to null. I want to make a distinction here between a null DACL and an empty DACL. DACLs are empty if they contain no ACEs. Any user who attempts to access a resource that has an empty DACL is not granted access. On the other hand, if the same user attempts to access a resource that has a null DACL, he or she is granted access.

Windows provides another special group called *Authenticated Users*. This group is similar to the Everyone group in that it is a special runtime group the operating system maintains. Any user who has been authenticated is a member of this group. The key difference between Everyone and Authenticated Users is that Authenticated Users cannot contain guests. *Guests* are users who cannot be authenticated but who can still access certain resources.

The Guest account is disabled by default when Windows is installed. If Guest is enabled, it allows users who cannot be authenticated to access resources.

The *Interactive User* is yet another special runtime account that represents the currently logged-on user. COM+ uses this account as the default identity for server applications. COM+ server applications that run under the Interactive User account inherit the access token of the user currently logged in to the workstation. Usually, this setting works just fine for development purposes, but it can pose a real problem when you move your component into a production environment. In a typical production environment, nobody is logged in to the server hosting your components. If nobody is logged in, the Interactive User account cannot represent anyone. (Well, this is almost the case.) In a scenario where your component is running "lights out" on a server, a virtual desktop is created when your component is accessed. The Interactive User can take on the rights of this virtual desktop assuming that the "Logon as Batch Job" and "Access this Computer from the Network" rights are granted to the Interactive User. The problem with this approach manifests itself in two ways. First, when an administrator logs in to the console, COM+ applications start to run under the rights of the administrator. This is bad for obvious reasons. Second, if someone who does not normally have these rights logs in to the server console, you indirectly give that person these rights. The Interactive User account is really intended for COM+ applications that are part of a GUI application running on a user's workstation. The Interactive User account works in this type of scenario for two reasons: someone is logged in, and you likely want your COM+ application to run under that user's credentials.

Impersonation

Up to this point, you have encountered security within the bounds of a single user interacting with secured resources on his or her machine. However, in a distributed computing environment, a user needs to interact with remote resources. For a client to be able to do this, he or she must be able to pass his or her identity (or access token) across the network to the destination machine. At that point, the destination machine must be able to access resources on behalf of the client by using a copy of the client's access token. This process is *impersonation.*

When a client connects to a remote server process to create a component, for example, part of the negotiation process involves establishing the level at which the server can impersonate the client. The impersonation level can be one of four values, as shown in Table 5-1.

TABLE 5-1 IMPERSONATION LEVELS

Impersonation Level	Description
Anonymous	The server cannot see the client's access token. In this case, the server is not able to identify or impersonate the client.
Identify	The server can read the client's access token for the purposes of reading its SID and determining its access rights. However, the server cannot impersonate the client.
Impersonate	The server can impersonate the client and access local resources. The server is not able to access other remote resources by using the client's credentials.
Delegate	This includes all of the rights to the token that the Impersonate level grants, plus the bonus of being able to pass on the client's token to other remote servers.

Be aware of a couple of issues regarding these levels. First, the client gets the only say in the impersonation level. It is not a true negotiation, as the server does not get a vote. Second, as you see later in this chapter, an impersonation level can be set on a COM+ package. This setting has no effect on the impersonation level clients use to call into a COM+ application. The impersonation level setting of the COM+ application applies only when a component in the COM+ application acts as a client itself.

Authenticating over the Wire

Instantiating a remote component and calling its methods is *remoting*. Traditionally, the Microsoft remoting model has used *Distributed COM (DCOM)*. DCOM uses the *Remote Procedure Call (RPC)* protocol as its underlying communication mechanism. There are two limitations in using DCOM, however. First, both client and server must run the COM runtime. Usually, this is ok when parts of your application must talk to each other over the Internet, where you are likely to have a Windows client talking to a Windows server. But this model breaks down when the client is on the Internet. Generally, you cannot be assured that a client on the Internet is configured to use COM. In addition, a client on the Internet may have to communicate back to the server through firewalls and even network routers that perform *Network Address Translation (NAT)*. The details of overcoming DCOM issues through firewalls and NAT tables aren't necessary here, but these can be particularly nasty problems to overcome, especially if you do not anticipate them in the design of your application. Server farms can provide a hurdle for your components that use DCOM. Server farms, or clusters, combine several identical Web or application servers into a single virtual server. Clients connect to a cluster based on the cluster IP address that is shared across all servers in the cluster. When a request from a client comes into the cluster, one of the available servers processes the request. For DCOM to work over a cluster, the client's method calls must always return to the original server that instantiates the component. This is known as *affinity*. Affinity can reduce the potency of a cluster by hampering how evenly the work is distributed across the servers that make up the cluster.

Because of these problems with DCOM, the trend Microsoft has taken with remoting is to route method calls through HTTP. *Remote Data Services (RDS)* was the first Microsoft technology to provide remoting over HTTP. RDS is provided as part of the *Microsoft Data Access Components (MDAC)*. With RDS, you can instantiate remote components and even make SQL calls from the client to a database. Because RDS goes through the Web server, it can get you over the affinity hump. But you still have client dependencies because the client must have MDAC installed.

The current trend in remoting uses a technology called the *Simple Object Access* Protocol *(SOAP)*. SOAP uses XML to encode method-invocation requests, and it uses HTTP to transport those requests to the component. SOAP gets you around client dependencies because an XML parser and a networking component that can formulate HTTP requests are the only requirements. The implementation of the XML parser and the HTTP component are completely irrelevant to the SOAP protocol. As you see in Chapter 9, the .NET Remoting architecture uses SOAP extensively.

Both SOAP and RDS use endpoints to instantiate a component and call its methods. SOAP typically uses an Active Server Page (or ASP .NET Web Service page) as its endpoint. RDS uses a Web server extension dll as its endpoint. The process is as follows. The client makes a method call on some kind of proxy object. The proxy object is responsible for encoding the method call and submitting the HTTP request to the Web server. Part of the HTTP request is the URL to the endpoint. When the HTTP request reaches the endpoint, the Active Server Page or extension dll acting as the endpoint unpacks the call, instantiates the COM+ object, and makes the requested method call.

Understanding Authentication in IIS

In light of the HTTP remoting trend Microsoft has adopted, it is particularly relevant to discuss how Microsoft Internet Information Server (IIS) handles authentication and how it impersonates the client. IIS is Microsoft's Web server that ships with Windows 2000. This section explains how IIS and Windows security work together to authenticate a client application making HTTP requests.

By default, IIS runs under the System account. Most native operating system services run as this account by default. When a request for an Active Server Page, or, in our case, a method call for a component, comes into IIS, IIS dispatches a thread to execute the request. In fact, to optimize performance, IIS maintains a pool of worker threads to service requests. Because the System account has so many privileges, IIS does not like to run these worker threads under this account. Instead, it prefers to use either the client's user account (assuming the client has been authenticated) or the default account created when IIS is installed. The default account is named based on a concatenation of IUSR_ + Server Name. For example, if a Web server is named WWW1, the default user account is named IUSR_WWW1.

If each request looks like it is coming from IUSR, this defeats the purpose of using COM+ security. Because COM+ security is derived from Windows security, there must be a way to map a client's credentials from a remote method call to a COM+ component. The answer lies in securing the endpoint that may be implemented. Once the endpoint is secured with the proper user and group accounts and access permissions, IIS prompts the user for his or her credentials. If the user supplies the proper credentials and has access to perform the requested operations against the endpoint, IIS dispatches one of its worker threads to handle the request. The worker thread impersonates the client by using a special access token called an *impersonation token*. As a COM+ developer, all you really need to know about an impersonation token is that it authenticates against a component as if the impersonation token were the client's own access token.

IIS provides four methods for authenticating a user:

- Anonymous access
- Basic authentication
- Digest authentication
- Integrated Windows authentication

Anonymous access should be used for pages or endpoints that do not need to be secured. In this scenario, IIS impersonates the IUSR account with one of its worker threads. The next step up from Anonymous access is Basic authentication. You can think of this as the default authentication method for HTTP. The big problem with Basic authentication is that the client's user ID and password are transmitted across the network in clear text. Digest authentication and Integrated Windows authentication, on the other hand, do not transmit the user's credentials in clear text. In both of these modes, the client generates a hash based on its credentials. The hash is sent over the network, and analyzed by the server. This technique is more secure than Basic authentication, but it does introduce client dependencies. This may be something you are trying to avoid if you wish to run your application on the Internet. Digest authentication applies only when a Windows 2000 client (workstation or server) needs to talk to another Windows 2000 server. Digest authentication requires a domain server to issue a certificate used during the transmission of data. Integrated Windows authentication is used when at least one party runs Windows NT.

Using the COM+ Security Model

You learn at the beginning of this chapter that the .NET Framework security attributes put the power of configuring an application into the hands of the developer. As you will see in this section, the .NET Framework provides a corresponding attribute for each of the declarative security attributes defined in the COM+ catalog. Unless otherwise stated, all of the .NET security attributes described in this section can be found in the `System.EnterpriseServices` namespace.

Authentication & Authorization

The first step toward configuring security in COM+ is to set the authentication level. Authentication is either turned on or off at the package level. The degree to which the client is authenticated is also set at the package level. Figure 5-1 shows the security tab for a server application.

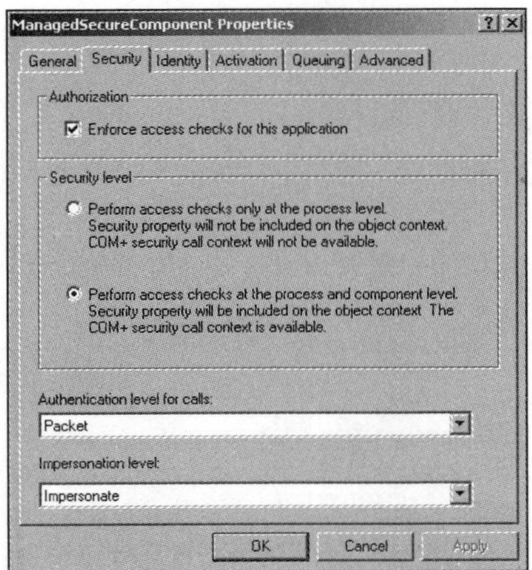

Figure 5-1: Server application security tab

The first attribute on this tab is Authorization. When checked, this attribute turns on role-based security for all components in the application. For a server application, this attribute has the additional effect of enabling the authentication level to be enforced.

The attribute below Authorization is the security level. As you can see from Figure 5-1, the security level is one of two values: process level or process level and component level. The default value for this attribute is to perform authorization at the component and process levels (second bullet in the group). This value must be used if you wish to perform programmatic security in your components. COM+ does not initialize a security context for components in applications that perform only access checks at the process level (first option in the group).

The .NET Framework includes an attribute called ApplicationAccessControl. C# applications use this attribute to set the security level of an application. Because the security level is set on an application, the ApplicationAccessControl attribute must be defined for an assembly. The ApplicationAccessControl attribute has several properties that correspond to the various COM+ attributes on the Security tab. To set the security level of a COM+ application, use the AccessChecksLevel property. The code sample that follows shows how to use this property and how to apply the AccessChecksLevel property to an assembly.

```
using System;
using System.EnterpriseServices;
[assembly: ApplicationAccessControl(
    AccessChecksLevel = AccessChecksLevelOption.ApplicationComponent
   )
]
public class SecuredComponent : ServicedComponent {
    // some method implementations
}
```

Notice that I use the assembly keyword inside the attribute tags. This tells the C# compiler that the attribute is assembly level. Inside the attribute declaration, I have set the AccessChecksLevel property to application and component by using the AccessChecksLevelOption enumeration.

Performing access checks at the process level ensures that the caller has permission to execute the application. If this is the case, the caller can instantiate and consume any of the components in the application. If your application is a server application, you are relying on dllhost.exe (the COM+ host exe for server applications) to perform access checks. However, if you are developing library applications, you are relying on some other host to perform those checks. This is not likely to be an acceptable scenario if you are using programmatic, role-based security. If authentication occurs only at the process level, COM+ does not initialize the security context for components. Without a security context, components are not able to see who is trying to access the component and what roles users may be in.

The Authentication attribute defines how stringently COM+ verifies the identity of the caller. The caller can be authenticated based on one of six possible values, as in Table 5-2.

TABLE 5-2 AUTHENTICATION LEVELS

Authentication Level	Description
None	The client is never authenticated when it calls into a component. Setting the authentication level to none has the same effect as turning off authorization for the application.
Connect	Authentication is performed when the caller connects to the application.
Call	Authentication occurs at every method call.
Packet	Packets are analyzed to ensure that all have arrived and that they have all come from the client. This is the default authentication level.
Packet Integrity	Packets are analyzed to verify that none have been modified in transit.
Packet Private	Packets are encrypted for transport over the network.

Authentication levels become more stringent, or more protective, the farther you go down the list. For example, `Call` ensures a higher authentication standard than `Connect`; `Package Packet` ensures a higher standard than `Call`, and so forth. Keep in mind, however, that the higher the level of authentication you choose for your application, the greater the likelihood that performance will be affected.

In the .NET Framework, the authentication level is defined at the assembly level by using the `ApplicationAccessControl` attribute. The property of this attribute that controls the authentication level is called, logically enough, `Authentication`. The `Authentication` property uses the `AuthenticationOption` enumeration to set the property to one of the corresponding authentication levels. I have added this property to the preceding code example.

```
using System;
using System.EnterpriseServices;
[assembly: ApplicationAccessControl
  (
    AccessChecksLevel = AccessChecksLevelOption.ApplicationComponent
    Authentication = AuthenticationOption.Connect
  )
]
public class SecuredComponent : ServicedComponent {
    // some method implementations
}
```

The authentication level is negotiated between the caller and the application. Whoever requests the higher authentication level wins. For example, if the caller requests `Packet`, and the application requests `Packet Integrity`, the authentication level is `Packet Integrity`. This behavior allows each party to specify a minimum level of authentication. It is important to understand that this negotiation occurs between two processes. Because library applications do not run in their own process but rather in their caller's process, setting this attribute is not an option for library packages.

The discussion about Windows security in this chapter leads us into impersonation. Remember that impersonation is the level at which a client allows another process or thread to use its identity. In COM+, impersonation applies when a component in a server application acts as a client itself. At the bottom of the security tab in Figure 5-1, you can see the impersonation list box. Each of the four impersonation levels is available to a COM+ application.

- Anonymous
- Identify
- Impersonate (default)
- Delegate

If you are developing server applications that use components in other applications implementing role-based security, you must choose an impersonation level other than `Anonymous`. This setting effectively hides the caller's identity from the application you are trying to use.

Once again, use the `ApplicationAccessControl` attribute in .NET to determine this level at the time of deployment. The `ImpersonationLevel` property allows you to specify the impersonation level by assigning one of the values from the `ImpersonationLevelOption` enumeration. If you add an impersonation level of `Delegate` to the preceding code, you get the following code snippet.

```
using System;
using System.EnterpriseServices;
[assembly: ApplicationAccessControl
  (
    AccessChecksLevel=AccessChecksLevelOption.ApplicationComponent,
    Authentication=AuthenticationOption.Connect,
    ImpersonationLevel=ImpersonationLevelOption.Delegate
  )
]
public class SecuredComponent : ServicedComponent {
    // some method implementations
}
```

Role-based Security

Roles are used to group together users and groups that need to perform similar functions within an application. Roles are defined at the application level. Role-based security can be performed on the component, interface, and even the method level. Both server and library applications can implement roles and apply them to their components.

Figure 5-2 shows the expanded list of roles for one of the applications on my computer. Notice that I can specify multiple roles within one application. In addition, within each role, I can add multiple users and groups. For instance, in the Authors role, I have added the user Nick and the group HMI Authors.

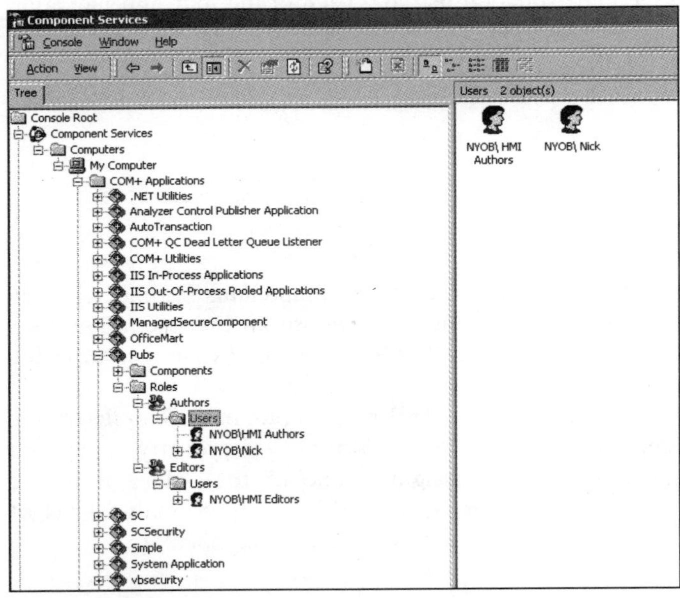

Figure 5-2: Application roles

Once you have defined the roles for your application, you can apply them to components, interfaces, and methods. Security in COM+ is inherited downwards. If you define a role for a particular component, that component's interfaces inherit the role. Figure 5-3 shows the security tab for a component called CAuthors. As you can see, both the Authors and Editors roles are listed. However, access to this component I limited to those users in the Authors role.

Because Nick is a member of the authors group, he is able to access the `CAuthors` component. When a caller accesses a component, COM+ builds an SD from the users and groups in the Authors role. In the example, the security descriptor contains Nick's SID, as well as the SID of the `HMI Authors` group. If Nick's SID is in the SD, he is given access; if not, he gets an "Access Denied" error.

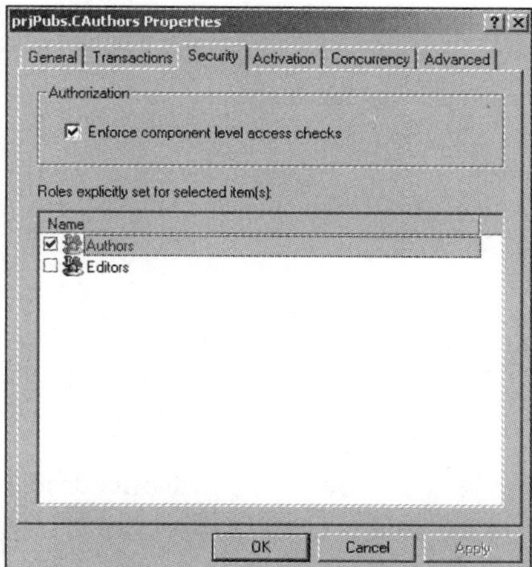

Figure 5-3: Security tab for CAuthors component

Security roles can be defined by your C# classes and assemblies through the `SecurityRole` attribute. This attribute can be defined on the assembly level just as the `ApplicationAccessControl` attribute. This attribute can also be applied to a class. When it is applied to a C# class, it has the effect of applying that role to the class. When you use the `SecurityRole` attribute, you have your choice of two constructors. The first constructor takes one parameter: the name of the role you wish to create or apply to the class. The default behavior of this constructor places the special Everyone group into this role. The second constructor, which I have chosen to implement, takes the role name (string data type) as the first parameter and boolean parameter to specify whether or not the Everyone group is added to this role. Aside from adding the Everyone group to a role, you must rely on an administrator to add users and groups to your roles by using the Component Services Explorer.

The `SecurityRole` attribute does not enable authorization for the component. For that, you need to use the `ComponentAccessControl` attribute. This attribute is applied only at the class level. The default constructor (parameterless) enables authorization for the component. Also, there is a constructor for this attribute that takes a boolean parameter. With this parameter, you can either enable authorization (by passing in true) or disable authorization (by passing in false).

I have added the `SecurityRole` attribute and the `ComponentAccessControl` attribute to our `SecuredComponent` class. I have added a new role called `customers`, and I have given the Everyone group access to this component.

```
using System;
using System.EnterpriseServices;
[assembly: ApplicationAccessControl
  (
```

```
        AccessChecksLevel=AccessChecksLevelOption.ApplicationComponent,
        Authentication=AuthenticationOption.Connect,
        ImpersonationLevel=ImpersonationLevelOption.Delegate
    )
]

[SecurityRole("customers", true)]
[ComponentAccessControl]
public class SecuredComponent : ServicedComponent {
    // some method implementations
}
```

The `ComponentAccessControl` attribute may look a little peculiar. Notice that I have not included the parenthesis for this attribute. The C# compiler interprets this to mean that I wish to use the default parameterless constructor for this attribute.

When this class is compiled and registered with COM+ using the `RegSvcs` tool, the customers role is created, and the Everyone group is added to this role. Effectively, this means that anyone who can be authenticated is allowed to use this component. Figure 5-4 shows what the security tab for the `SecuredComponent` class looks like once it has been installed into COM+.

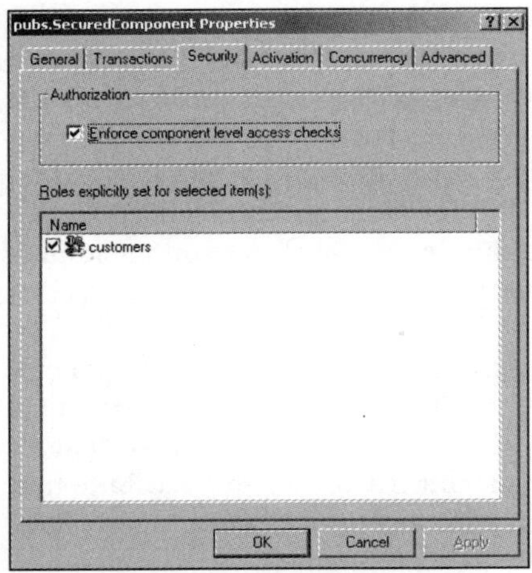

Figure 5-4: Security tab for SecuredComponent class

Understanding Security Scope

You must consider several issues when deploying your components into COM+ applications. You have already encountered several issues. For instance, if your application needs to enforce an authentication level or an impersonation level, you are best off deploying your components in a server package. Another issue deals with the chain of calls that can arise when the base client (the user's process) calls into a component and that component calls another component and so on. COM+ enforces role checking based on the SID of the direct caller. Let's walk through anexample to see how this may affect deployment decisions. Let's say our user, Nick, opens his browser and navigates to the URL of one of our secured ASP .NET pages. Because the page is secured, he is prompted for his user ID and password. When Nick successfully authenticates to the page, IIS assigns one of its worker threads to process the page Nick has requested. This thread operates under a copy of Nick's access token. When the worker thread hits a section of code in the ASP page that creates a new managed COM+ object running in a server package, an instance of dllhost is started (assuming there is not already a running instance). Likely, the instance of dllhost is running under a generic user ID, as we now know the Interactive user is not a good choice for server-based deployment. When Nick's worker thread tries to access the component, the SIDs in Nick's access token are compared to the SIDs in the component's SD. If two matching SIDs are found, Nick is granted access. So far, everything seems ok, right? Well, what happens if the component the Active Server Page is using accesses another component in another COM+ package? The answer is that the SID from the access token for the dllhost process is used for role authentication on the second component. In this scenario, Nick's access token is not used for authenticating to the second component. Figure 5-5 illustrates this process in detail.

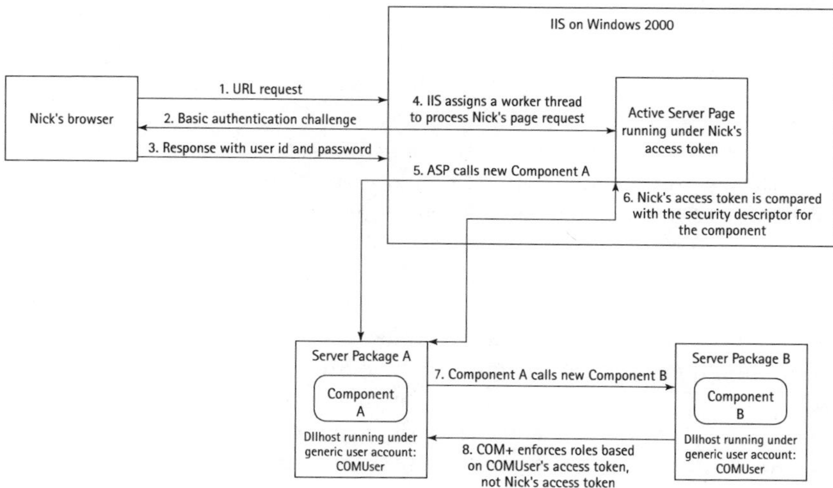

Figure 5-5: Call chain security

The point of all this is that the direct caller may or may not be the actual user. The list of all user accounts calling components in an application is the *call chain.* It is important to understand how the call chain affects security because it may cause you to inadvertently to give or deny a user access to one of your components. If you get into this scenario in your applications and you wish to enforce security on a user somewhere up in the call chain, you must do it programmatically.

Fortunately, .NET provides a collection class that gives you access to each of the users in the call chain. The SecurityCallers class represents each of the users in a call chain. Each item in the SecurityCallers collection represents a SecurityIdentity class. This class contains information such as the user's account name and impersonation level. To gain access to the SecurityCallers collection, you must call the CurrentCall property of the SecurityCallContext class. The CurentCall property of the SecurityCallContext class is a static property that returns the security-context information for a component. Using this property, you can gain access to the Callers property of SecurityCallContext. The Callers property returns an instance of the SecurityCallers collection. In the code that follows, I have extended the SecuredComponent class from our previous examples to give you a flavor of how these classes are used together.

```
[SecurityRole("customers", true)]
[ComponentAccessControl]
public class SecuredComponent : ServicedComponent {
  public void ShowCallChain(){
    SecurityCallContext sc=SecurityCallContext.CurrentCall;
    SecurityCallers scs=sc.Callers
    Foreach (SecurityIdentity si in scs) {
      Console.WriteLine(si.AccountName);
    }
  }
}
```

There is one last point I wish to make about the scope of security in COM+. Security is performed on the application boundary. In the preceding scenario, Nick has been denied access to component *B* because the call chain crossed application boundaries, which forced the direct caller's (COMUser) role membership to be verified. If component *B* were in the same COM+ application as component *A*, Nick would be granted access even though he technically is not in any of the roles assigned to component *B*. If you encounter this scenario, it may be useful to determine programmatically if the caller is in the role you wish. The SecurityCallContext class implements a method called IsUserInRole. This method takes the name of the role and the user's account name as input parameters and returns true if the user is in the role or false if the user is not in the role. To get the user's account name, use the SecurityIdentity class's AccountName property.

```
[SecurityRole("customers", true)]
[ComponentAccessControl]
public class SecuredComponent : ServicedComponent {
  public void ShowCallChain(){
    SecurityCallContext sc = SecurityCallContext.CurrentCall;
```

```
    SecurityCallers scs = sc.Callers;
    Bool CustomerInCallChain = false;
    Foreach (SecurityIdentity si in scs) {
      If (sc.IsUserInRole(si.AccountName, "customers")) {
        CustomerInCallChain = true;
        break;
      }
    }
    if (!CustomerInCallChain) {
      throw new UnauthorizedAccessException("no customers found in
call chain");
    }
  }
}
```

In the preceding example, if you do not find a customer anywhere in the call chain, throw an `UnauthorizedAccessException`. This is an exception class found in the `System` namespace. The .NET runtime raises this exception anytime a caller does not have access to a component, interface, or method.

Summary

Whew! We have certainly covered a lot of ground in this chapter. Security is probably one of the most difficult topics to understand in all of computer science. Understanding how role-based security works in COM+ becomes much easier if you are at least familiar with how Windows security architecture implements those services. In light of the current trend in remoting, namely the use of HTTP for method calls (Web services), I think it is particularly relevant to discuss how IIS authenticates users and how a user's access token is used at different points in the call chain. Above all, I hope you have been able to see how the attributes and classes in the .NET Framework help to simplify development and deployment of your components.

In Chapter 6, you encounter the COM+ event model. Also, you encounter to the .NET event model and compare the two.

Chapter 6

Events

IN THIS CHAPTER

- Understanding the need for LCEs
- Understanding the LCE Architecture
- Writing LCE Components in C#

EVENT-BASED PROGRAMMING has been the primary development model for graphical user interface applications for many years. In many Windows user interface applications, a button click or a mouse movement triggers an event. When the event is raised, another part of the application can respond and react accordingly. This development model works well when the source of the event, the event itself, and the piece of code responding to the event are all contained in the same application. This type of event model is a *Tightly Coupled Event (TCE)*. As you'll see in this chapter, this development model does not work so well for distributed applications.

Because of the limitations of TCEs for distributed or server-based applications, COM+ supports an event system known as a *Loosely Coupled Event (LCE)*. In this chapter, you delve into the reasons distributed applications need LCEs. You accomplish this by examining the .NET event model and comparing it to LCEs. Also, you examine the LCE architecture including the limitations and requirements for LCE components. No discussion of a COM+ feature is complete without including the appropriate attributes from the catalog and the framework.

Understanding the Need for LCEs

TCEs include the .NET event model and the COM Connection Point event model. TCEs are primarily used in user interface-based applications where one application contains the entire life of the event. In a TCE, the source of the event (the publisher) and the method or component that handles the event (the event subscriber) are closely tied together. This model has worked well for user-interface applications, but it falls short when you want to implement it in a distributed environment. TCEs suffer from the following general problems when they are used for distributed applications:

- Subscribers must be running when the publisher initiates an event.
- There is no way to filter or intercept events before they reach the subscriber.

- Subscribers must have explicit knowledge of the publisher.
- The publisher has to have a list of all subscribers.

To understand each of these points, run through an example of a .NET TCE.

.NET Event Architecture

The .NET Framework event model shares some similarities with the COM+ event model. The .NET event model has a class that sends events and a class that receives events. The class that sends events can roughly be equated to the publisher in a COM+ event. You can think of the class that receives events as a COM+ event subscriber.

The event class must have some mechanism for sending the event notification and associated information to the event receiver class or classes. This is accomplished through a special type of class called a delegate. *Delegates* are managed pointers to methods. If you are familiar with function pointers in C or C++, you can think of .NET delegates as their close relatives.

As you see in the example that follows, delegates are declared with the C# keyword `delegate`, followed by the return type, delegate name, and parameters. Delegates are defined outside of the definitions of the event source and receiver classes. They are used to tie, or wire, the event source to the event receiver. The event source defines a member variable of the delegate type. Event receivers that wish to subscribe to the event must implement a method that has the same signature as the corresponding method from the delegate. At runtime, the method the event receiver provides is wiredto the delegate the event source defines. This becomes clearer in a moment.

Method signature refers to the return type and the number and data types of a method's parameters. In the case of .NET events, the method the receiver class implements can be given any legal method name. It is only important for the method's signature to match with the delegate's method signature.

The typical signature for a delegate is a void return value and two parameters: object type and an event-arguments type. If you develop WinForms or ASP .NET pages, you see that the signature for various event methods such as a button click or mouse movement is a void return value with object type and event arguments type as parameters. The reason for making this a void function is that many receivers might be receiving events from the event source. A return value is pretty useless in this scenario, as the return value represents only the last receiver to be notified. All other return values from other receivers are lost. The first parameter, and object type, represents the instance of the class that has raised the event. Because the type cannot be known necessarily ahead of time, this parameter type is

System.Object. Usually, the second parameter is a class that contains the event arguments for the event. For example, in a mouse-move event, the event arguments class might contain the *x* and *y* axis positions of the mouse.

Listing 6-1 shows an example of an event source class named EventSource and an event receiver class named EventReceiver. The event class uses the delegate MyEventHandler to define a delegate event member type called EH. The event keyword is a C# construct used to declare a member of a delegate type. This delegate instance is wired to the corresponding event method of the EventReceiver class named EventMethod. Notice that the signature of the EventMethod class matches that of the delegate class, but the signature is not defined as a delegate type.

Listing 6-1: Event source and receiver classes

```
namespace MyNetEvents
{
  using System;
  public delegate void MyEventHandler(string msg);

  public class EventSource
  {
    public event MyEventHandler EH;
    private void OnEvent(string msg)
    {
      EH(msg);
    }
    public void FireEvent()
    {
      OnEvent("hello");
    }
  }

  public class EventReceiver
  {
    public void EventMethod(string msg)
    {
      Console.WriteLine("EventReceiver: " + msg);
    }
  }

  public class CMain
  {
    public static void Main()
    {
      // instantiate the event destination class
      EventReceiver er = new EventReceiver();
```

```
            // instantiate a new event source
            EventSource es = new EventSource();

            // wire the event
            es.EH += new MyEventHandler(er.EventMethod);

            // fire the event
            es.FireEvent();
        }
    }
}
```

After instantiating instances of the two classes, you are able to wire the `er.EventMethod` method to the `EH` delegate by instantiating a new instance of the `MyEventHandler` class. The .NET runtime provides a single parameter constructor for delegates. As you can see, the constructor takes a reference to a method that has the same signature as the delegate. The new instance of the delegate is wired to the `EH` instance by using the += operator. Finally, call the `FireEvent` method on the instance of the event source class. The `FireEvent` method is pretty straightforward. It does calls the private `OnEvent` method of the event source. Normally, the `OnEvent` method is called only if some condition becomes true or if some event happens in the `FireEvent` method. The `OnEvent` method is private; normally, you want the event to fire only if some condition becomes true in the event source class. You do not want clients of the event source class firing events.

The `OnEvent` method fires the event by calling the `EH` delegate. The .NET runtime is responsible for retrieving the list of classes that have wired themselves to the event and for calling their event methods. In your case, the method the runtime calls is `er.EventMethod`.

Comparing TCE Events to COM+ LCE

Now that you have an idea of how tightly coupled events work in the .NET Framework, address the points you encounter at the beginning of this section. The first point is that subscribers must be running in a TCE model before the publisher, or event source, initiates the event. In the preceding code example, before you can wire the event receiver's event method to the delegate and receive events, you must instantiate an instance of the receiver class. In the COM+ event model, classes that receive events (called subscribers) do not need to be activated before the event occurs.

The second point is that there is no way to filter events before they are sent to the receiver(s). The .NET runtime manages the list of receivers and calls their event methods. Unfortunately, it does not provide any mechanism to prevent calls from being made to receivers. Later in this chapter, you encounter methods COM+ provides to filter event notifications.

Essentially, the last two points state that the subscriber and publisher must have explicit knowledge of each other. In the preceding example, the subscriber class is the `EventReceiver` class, and the publisher is the `Main` method of the `CMain` class. The `Main` method instantiates the event receiver class itself and knows which method must be used to wire the event. This requires explicit knowledge of the receiver's method(s) and the number and types of receivers. The COM+ event model stores this information in the COM+ catalog, which the COM+ runtime accesses itself when an event is fired. Because of this service, the publisher does not need to know who its subscribers are or which of the methods must be called for an event.

The LCE Architecture

The COM+ event system is loosely coupled for a number of reasons. First off, the publishers and subscribers do not need to know of each other. Generally, the publisher does not need to know who the subscribers are or how many of them exist. Subscribers can come and go at anytime without breaking the publisher's application. Secondly, the subscribers do not need to be active at the time the publisher initiates the event. As you see in a moment, COM+ activates the subscribers on behalf of the publisher when the publisher initiates an event. These features are quite different from the tightly coupled event architecture described in the first section of this chapter.

The COM+ Event system is a Windows 2000 service that propagates events to subscribing components.

An application that uses LCEs consists of four entities:

- publisher
- event class
- subscriber(s)
- event(s)

Publishers start the process by activating the event class and calling its methods. Each method the publisher calls represents a single event. When the event class is activated, COM+ queries its catalog for a list of interested subscribers. Once this list is determined, COM+ redirects method calls made on the event class to the subscriber classes. Figure 6-1 illustrates this process.

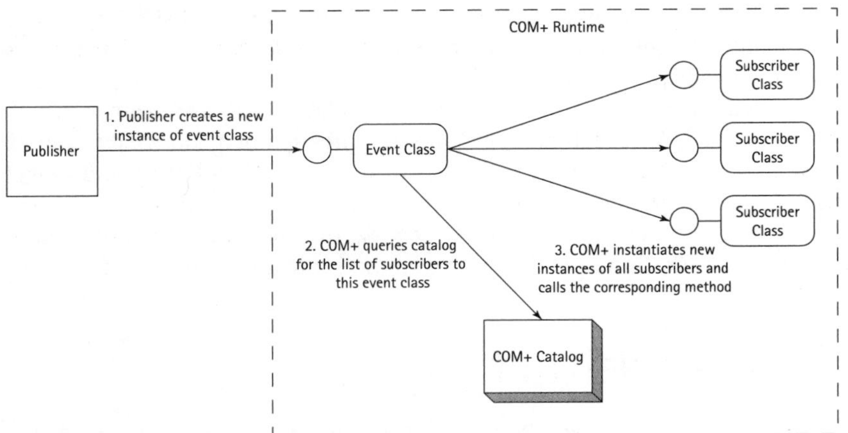

Figure 6-1: Publisher to subscriber call chain

As a rule of thumb, publishers cannot determine the order in which subscribers are notified about an event. The COM+ event system makes this determination. Later in this chapter, you see a couple of techniques for influencing the order in which subscribers are notified.

Subscribers need to implement the method(s) the publisher calls on the event class in order for all of this to work. The event class does not need to implement the methods to which subscribers choose to subscribe. In fact, even if the methods are implemented, they are not called when the publisher initiates the event. Although the publisher thinks it has a simple reference to an event class, it is talking to the COM+ event system, which, in turn, is making calls to subscribers.

For a subscriber to subscribe to an event class's events (methods), it must implement the interface(s) the event class supports. The subscriber does not need to implement all the interfaces of the event class, only interfaces that contain methods from which the subscriber wishes to receive events. Interface identifiers of the subscriber and event class (GUIDs) must also be the identical to each other.

Event classes must meet certain criteria to work properly in the LCE system. One of the criteria is that the class cannot contain implementations of any of its methods. An event class's methods must not contain any output parameters if the event class is to have more than one subscriber. In other words, the event class cannot contain methods that return a value to the publisher as a parameter. If you think about it, this rule makes sense for two reasons. First, if there are multiple subscribers, each of whom changes the value of the output parameter before it reaches the publisher, how does the publisher know if the returned value is correct? The publisher cannot know this. Second, if the publisher does not need to know about its subscribers, it does not necessarily care about actions or return values subscribers take.

An event class must return only success or failure COM `HRESULT`s. This is not something you need to be terribly concerned about if your application runs entirely in managed code. However, you want to know this if you are writing managed event classes unmanaged subscribers use.

Understanding Subscriptions

COM+ supports two types of subscriptions: persistent and transient. Persistent subscriptions remain in the COM+ catalog until they are physically taken out. These types of subscriptions must be added via the Component Services Explorer snap-in for both managed and unmanaged code. The .NET Framework does not provide attributes for adding subscriptions to the COM+ catalog.

The COM+ Administration API is COM based and supports programmatic administration of the COM+ catalog. All of the functionality (and much more) of the Component Services snap-in can be reproduced through the Admin API.

Transient subscriptions, on the other hand, exist only within the lifetime of the subscriber component. Transient subscriptions cannot survive a restart of the COM+ event system or a reboot of the machine they are running on. They must be added at runtime by using the COM+ Admin API. Unlike persistent subscriptions, which instantiate a new instance of the subscriber, transient subscriptions are added by making a reference to an already instantiated component in the COM+ catalog.

Be aware of one other type of subscription. *Per User* subscriptions allow you to create a subscription when a user logs on to the system. When the user logs off, these subscriptions are disabled. These types of subscriptions work only when the publisher and the subscriber are on the same computer.

COM+ Attributes

The COM+ attributes for a LCE component application really center on the event class. Subscribers and publishers (if the publisher is a COM+ component) do not need event-specific attributes set in order for the event system to work. You examine the event attributes and their values in this section; in the last part of the chapter, you see how these attributes are implemented in the .NET Framework. The COM+ event attributes are as follows:

- Fire in Parallel
- Allow in-process subscribers
- Publisher ID

FIRE IN PARALLEL

The Fire in Parallel attribute affects the way in which the event system notifies subscribers. Figure 6-2 shows this attribute as checked in the Advanced tab in Component Services Explorer. With this attributed checked, COM+ notifies subscribers at the same time. Normally, the event system notifies subscribers in a serial fashion. By default, this attribute is not checked.

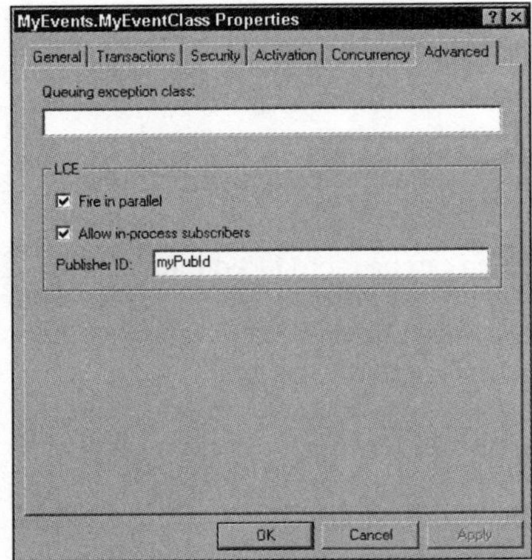

Figure 6-2: Fire in Parallel attribute in Component Services Explorer

This attribute can have a positive effect on the performance of your application because COM+ initiates multiple threads to notify subscribers. If this attribute is not checked, the event system notifies subscribers one by one, and it waits for each subscriber to return before calling the next.

ALLOW IN-PROCESS SUBSCRIBERS

By default, the Allow in-process attribute is selected. When this attribute is turned off, COM+ does not allow subscribers to run in the same address space of the publisher. Even if the subscriber is configured as a library package, COM+ creates a new process for the subscriber. The reason for this default behavior stems from security concerns. Because the publisher does not necessarily know about subscribers, it cannot trust subscribers to behave properly inside its process. If, however, you are writing a publisher application and you feel you can trust the subscribers of your event class, you can enable the Allow in-process subscribers attribute. By checking this option, you are trading stability for performance. This attribute setting can be found on the Advanced tab of the event class's properties. Refer to Figure 6-2 to see this attribute in Component Services Explorer.

PUBLISHER ID

The Publisher ID attribute (also visible from Figure 6-2) provides another way for a subscriber to subscribe to an event class. You have explored one way for a subscriber to subscribe to an event: the CLSID of the event class. Publisher ID allows you to use a more user-friendly method for creating a subscription. Understand that this attribute applies to the event class, not the publisher. The name can be a little misleading, so do not get confused.

Controlling Subscriber Notification Order

COM+ provides two methods that allow you to influence the order in which subscribers are notified of events: publisher filtering and parameter filtering. Publisher filtering is a bit more complicated to implement than parameter filtering, but it allows for a finer degree of control.

PUBLISHER FILTERING

Publisher filtering is a technique that allows publishers to specify a filter component that should be used when events are triggered. The filter component is responsible for making decisions about which subscribers should be notified about an event and in what order they should be notified.

The publisher uses the COM+ Admin API to set the `PublisherFilterCLSID` property for an event class. This is a read/write property that accepts the CLSID of the filter component. The filter is simply another COM+ component that implements either the `IMultiPublisherFilter` interface or the `IPublisherFilter` interface.

When the event class is instantiated, the event system looks at the `PublisherFilterCLSID` property and instantiates the corresponding filter component. When the publisher fires the event on the event class, the event system passes control to the filter object. The filter object's responsibility is to forward events to subscribers. The filter component accomplishes this by retrieving a collection of subscribers and firing the event on each subscriber. The filter component, of course, can elect not to fire an event for a particular subscriber. When the filter component fires an event, the event system takes over and initiates the event on subscribers.

PARAMETER FILTERING

Parameter filtering can be used in conjunction with publisher filtering, or it can be used by itself. The subscriber component, as opposed to the publisher, implements this technique. Through an option in the subscription properties, the subscriber can define criteria that can influence whether the event system fires a method.

Figure 6-3 shows the properties dialog box for a subscription for a subscriber component. The Filter Criteria dialog box on the Options tab defines the parameter filter for the subscription. This particular parameter filter defines a rule that enables the subscription if the parameter named `Symbol` equals "MSFT" and the parameter `Price` does not equal 60. If the condition defined in the filter criteria evaluates as true, the event is processed for that subscriber. In addition, if you define a filter criteria and your subscription is for all methods of that interface, the criteria are applied to all methods. For example, if you define a parameter called `Symbol` and that parameter is not found in one of the interface's methods, your event fails. You see how this works in the last section of this chapter.

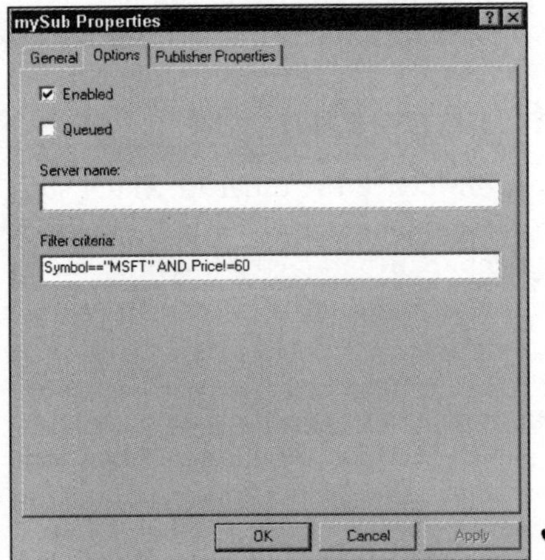

Figure 6-3: Filter Criteria dialog box for a subscription

The operators for the criteria string are rather simplistic. The operators include equality symbols and logical operators such as `AND`, `OR`, and `NOT`. If you need a more sophisticated strategy, you should consider using publisher filtering.

Parameter filtering does not have a direct effect on the order in which subscribers are notified. Parameter filtering can be used to determine if an event fires for a particular subscription based on the values of parameters at runtime. This technique can have the side effect of determining which publishers get notified and possibly in which order.

Writing LCE Components in C#

In the last part of this chapter, you see how to write different event and subscriber classes. The first set of classes is an introduction to writing components that use LCE. This example consists of a subscriber component that uses a static subscription to the event class. The second and third examples use some of the other features of COM+, namely object pooling and transactions. For each of the examples, a C# console application is the publisher.

Your First LCE Component

Listing 6-2 shows a single namespace that contains both the subscriber class and the event class. As you can see, the subscriber class is MySubscriberClass; the event class is MyEventClass. Each of these classes implements an interface called IMyEvents. The IMyEvents interface contains one method — PrintName — that prints out the name of the class on which the event is called. In this case, the output of this method, or event, is the name of the subscriber class.

Listing 6-2: A simple LCE component

```
using System.Reflection;

[assembly: AssemblyKeyFile("mykey.snk")]

namespace MyEvents
{
  using System;
  using System.EnterpriseServices;

  [EventClass]
  public class MyEventClass : ServicedComponent, IMyEvents
  {
    public void PrintName() {}
  }

  public class MySubscriberClass : ServicedComponent, IMyEvents
  {
    public void PrintName()
    {
      Console.WriteLine("MyEvents.MySubscriberClass");
    }
  }

  public interface IMyEvents
  {
    void PrintName();
  }
}
```

The first two lines should look familiar. They define the AssemblyKeyFile attribute so that you can install this assembly into the Global Assembly Cache (GAC). Although installing these types of assemblies into the GAC is not strictly necessary, it often helps you deploy your applications. Installing assemblies into the GAC makes considerably more sense for LCE components than for other components, particularly for those assemblies that contain subscriber components. Because the publisher does not necessarily know about the event's subscribers, it does not make sense to assume that you are able to deploy the subscriber assembly into the same directory as the publisher or event class.

Below the declaration of the namespace `MyEvents`, you can see the definition of the event class. The event class, `MyEventClass`, is decorated with the `System.EnterpriseServices` attribute `EventClass`. The `EventClass` attribute tells the installation utility that `MyEventClass` should be installed as an event class, not just as a regular component.

The next class I have defined is the subscriber class called `MySubscriberClass`. This class is simply a normal `ServicedComponent` type that implements the shared interface, `IMyEvents`. When this class is compiled and registered, you are able to create a subscription for the event class. Subscriptions for the event class must be created manually; there is no attribute support for adding a subscription to an event.

Finally, I have defined an interface called `IMyEvents`. Both the subscriber and event classes implement the interface. This interface is really the glue that binds the event class and the subscriber.

Compile and register this assembly just as you do any other assembly containing `ServicedComponents`. The `Regsvcs.exe` tool is smart enough to know, based on the `EventClass` attribute, that the event class must be installed as an event class, not as a regular COM+ component. Figure 6-4 shows what these classes look like in the Component Services Explorer once they are registered. Notice that the `IMyEvents` interface is listed under the "Interfaces" folder for each component.

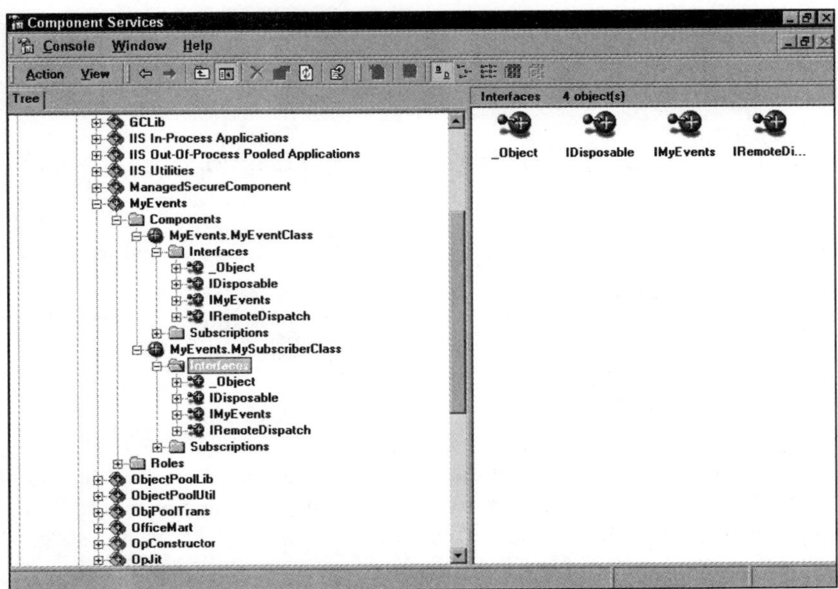

Figure 6-4: Interface listing for subscriber and event class

Figure 6-5 shows the Advanced tab for the event class. I have included this illustration to show you that the event class has indeed been installed as an event class. Notice that the Allow in-process subscribers attribute has been set by default.

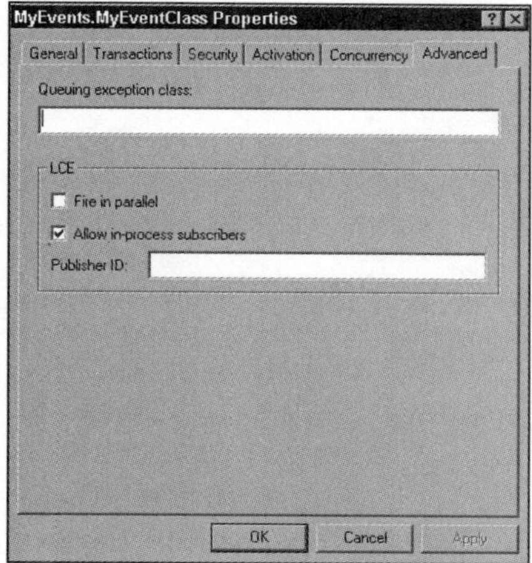

Figure 6-5: MyEventClass LCE properties

Creating Subscriptions by Using Component Services Explorer

Now that you have an event class and subscriber component, the next step is to create the subscription. In Figure 6-4, both classes have a folder called Subscriptions. To create a subscription, right-click the Subscriptions folder for the subscriber component, and click New Subscription. This starts the COM+ New Subscription Wizard, as seen in Figure 6-6. This figure shows all of the interfaces the subscription class supports. The only interface you are interested in here is `IMyEvents`.

The next step toward creating a subscription is to select the event class. After selecting the interface to be used to subscribe to the event, choose the event class to which you want to subscribe. Figure 6-7 shows the `MyEventClass` event class listed as the only available event class that supports the `IMyEvents` interface. Notice that the details box is checked. When you check this box, you are able to see the CLSID and the description for the event class.

The last step in adding a subscription is to give the subscription a name and, optionally, enable it. In figure 6-8, I have checked the "Enable this subscription immediately" check box. Unless this box is checked, events are not sent to this subscriber component. The name for the subscription is simply a user-friendly name you give it.

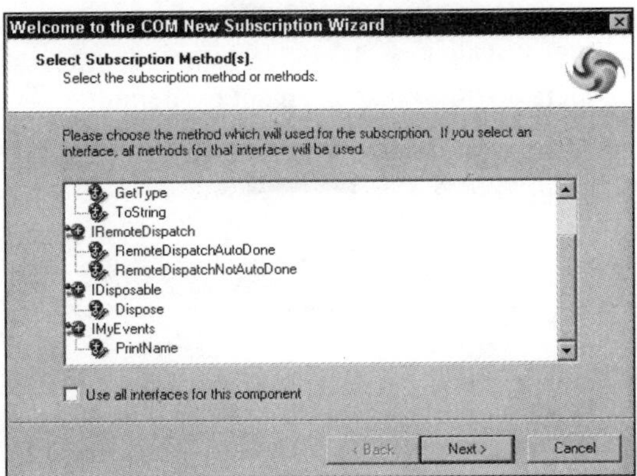

Figure 6-6: COM+ New Subscription Wizard

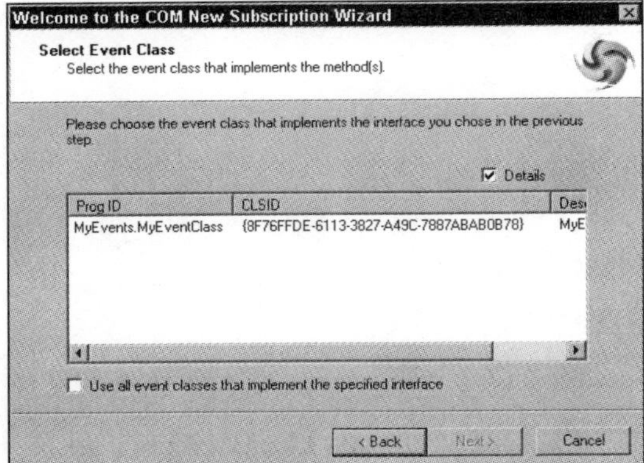

Figure 6-7: Selecting the event class

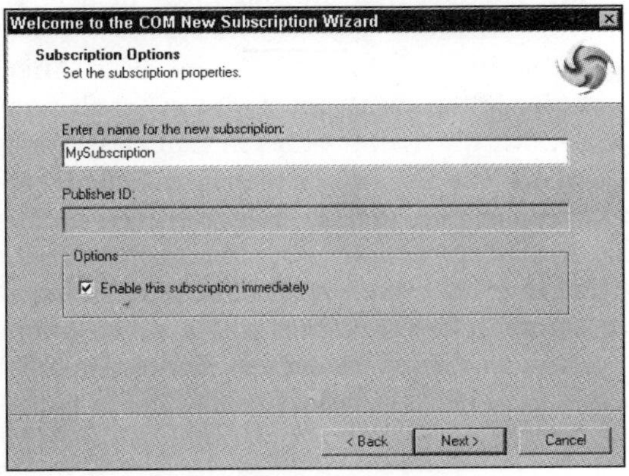

Figure 6-8: Enabling the subscription

Once the subscription is created, you are able to see it listed in the Subscriptions folder. Figure 6-9 shows the new subscription called `MySubscription` listed in the Subscriptions folder for the subscriber class.

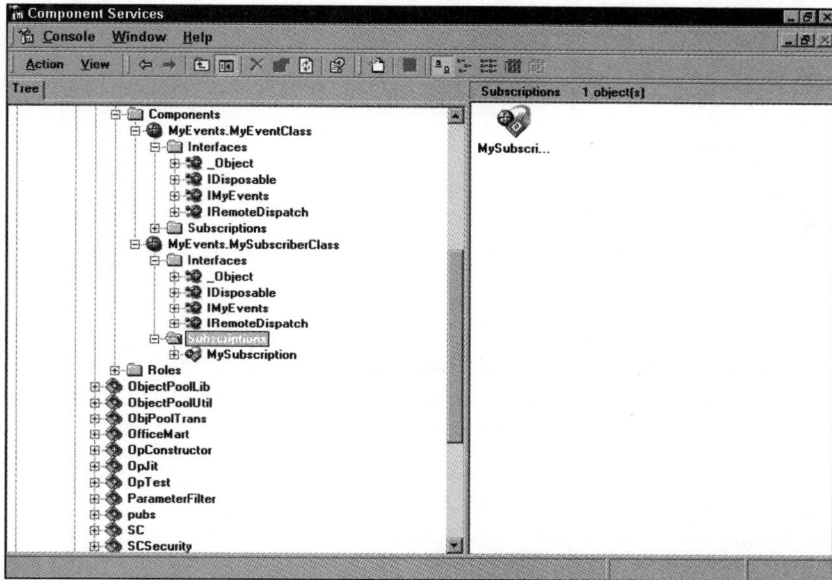

Figure 6-9: Subscriptions listing for subscriber component

.NET Framework EventClass Attribute

Let's take a closer look at the `EventClass` attribute. As you learned previously, this attribute comes from the `System.EnterpriseServices` namespace. Table 6-1 lists the properties this attribute supports.

TABLE 6-1 EVENTCLASS ATTRIBUTE PROPERTIES

Property	Data Type	Description
`AllowInProcSubscribers`	`Bool`	This property allows or disallows subscribers to run in process with the publisher.
`FireInParallel`	`Bool`	Set to true, this property allows the event system to notify subscribers of events in an asynchronous fashion.
`PublisherFilter`	`string`	This string consists of the publisher filter class's globally unique identifier (GUID).

If you take the preceding event class and define these properties, you get something similar to the following code. For the sake of clarity, I have included only the code for the event class.

```
[
  EventClass
  (
    AllowInProcSubscribers=true
    FireInParallel=true
  )
]
public class MyEventClass : ServicedComponent, IMyEvents
{
  public void PrintName() {}
}
```

Once this class is compiled and registered, you can see that the attributes get applied by looking at the Advanced tab for the event class. Figure 6-10 shows the Fire in parallel and Allow in-process subscribers check boxes checked.

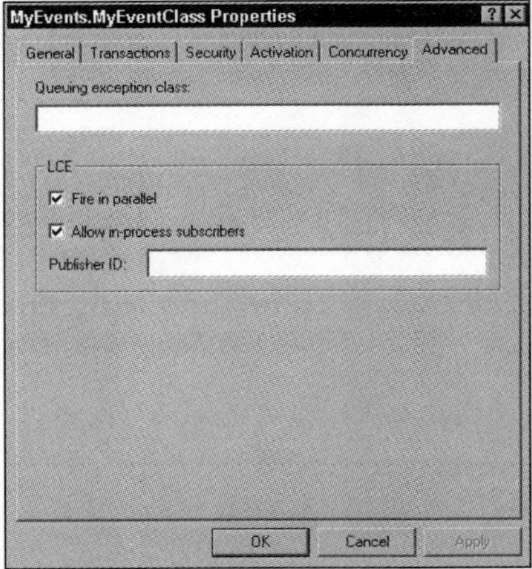

Figure 6-10: EventClass attribute enables LCE properties

Using Transactions with Events

In the final section of this chapter, you learn to write a publisher, event class, and subscriber that use transactions. The purpose of this section is to demonstrate how other services of COM+ are used with events.

To demonstrate how transactions can be used with events, I will modify the preceding code example to include a transactional `ServicedComponent` class called `MyTransactionRoot`. This class is in charge of starting the transaction (through the `TransactionOption.Required` property) and initiating the event by calling the `PrintTransactionId` method on the event class. This method prints out the transaction ID for the current transaction. Before the transaction root component starts the event, it prints out its own transaction ID. The definitions of all the classes and the shared interface are shown in Listing 6-3.

Listing 6-3: Using transactions with events

```
[EventClass]
public class MyEventClass : ServicedComponent, IMyTransactionEvents
{
  public void PrintTransactionId() {}
}

[Transaction(TransactionOption.Supported)]
public class MySubscriberClass : ServicedComponent,
    IMyTransactionEvents
{
  public void PrintTransactionId()
  {
    Console.WriteLine(ContextUtil.TransactionId.ToString());
  }
}

[Transaction(TransactionOption.Required)]
public class MyTransactionRoot : ServicedComponent
{
  public void StartTransaction()
  {
    Console.WriteLine(ContextUtil.TransactionId.ToString());
    MyEventClass ec = new MyEventClass();
    ec.PrintTransactionId();
  }
}

public interface IMyTransactionEvents
{
  void PrintTransactionId();
}
```

In this example, the transaction root component – `MyTransactionRoot` – acts as the publisher. Because this component is activated always in a transaction, the transaction is propagated to the subscriber components.

In fact, if you write a console application that instantiates an instance of the transaction root component and you call the `StartTransaction` method, you see output similar to the following.

```
654675f8-8b76-45f8-9d70-d17bc59046ad
654675f8-8b76-45f8-9d70-d17bc59046ad
```

As you can see, the root component and the subscriber component both display the same transaction ID, meaning they are both running in the same transaction.

Perhaps the subtlest issue here is the lack of declarative transaction support for the event class. Notice that this class is not declared as transactional. Because the event system – not the event class – forwards events to subscribers, the event system can propagate the transaction from the root to the subscribers. Of course, all of the other rules such as Just In Time Activation and the behavior of the transaction attribute apply to the publisher and subscriber.

Summary

In this chapter, you get an introduction to both the .NET event model and the COM+ event model. Trying to understand how events work can be rather tricky, so don't get discouraged!

These two types of events are not competing models but complement each other. In fact, the .NET event model is used heavily throughout .NET user interface applications such as WinForms and ASP .NET pages. There is a time and place for everything. This is certainly true in regards to events. Tightly coupled events work well in an application such as a .NET Windows Forms application or an ASP .NET application. Distributed applications, however, benefit more from the loosely coupled event architecture provided by COM+. In this chapter I compared the COM+ LCE architecture and the TCE architecture used in .NET Windows Forms. I also demonstrated how the attributes and classes of the `System.EnterpriseServices` namespace provide you with a means to write your own LCE event classes and subscribers. By now, you should know how to implement your own event classes and subscribers and where and when to use them.

Chapter 7

Object Pooling

IN THIS CHAPTER

- Understanding object pooling
- Requirements for object pooling
- Object pooling in C#

WHEN I FIRST HEARD that the .NET Framework was going to support COM+ object pooling, I was excited to say the least. Previously, object pooling was the domain of the C++ programmer. No longer! With the introduction of .NET and the `ServicedComponent`, object pooling is now in the arsenal of Visual Basic developers and, of course, C# developers.

In this chapter, you learn what object pooling is all about and what requirements a poolable object must meet. As you will see, object pooling should not be implemented for every object. In some cases, however, object pooling can significantly improve scalability.

Understanding Object Pooling

Simply stated, an *object pool* is a collection of preinstantiated objects that share the same CLSID. By preinstantiated, I mean that the objects' constructors have already been called and are ready for a client to use them. An object pool is homogeneous because each object is a new instance of the same object; thus, each object in the pool has the same CLSID. Figure 7-1 shows the CLSID for a managed component from Component Services Explorer.

Incidentally, the `Regsvcs` registration tool generates CLSIDs automatically for you. `Regsvcs` generates a CLSID based on a hash of the class's method signatures, the assembly's version, and (if available) the assembly's strong name. It is possible to create and install two unique classes by changing the version of the assembly, as seen in Figure 7-2.

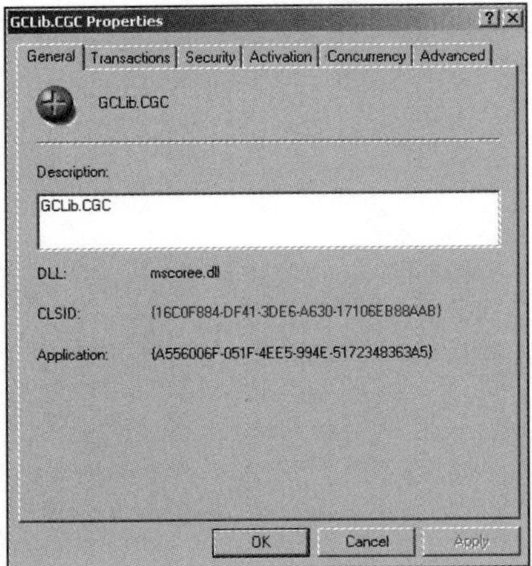

Figure 7-1: CLSID for a ServicedComponent

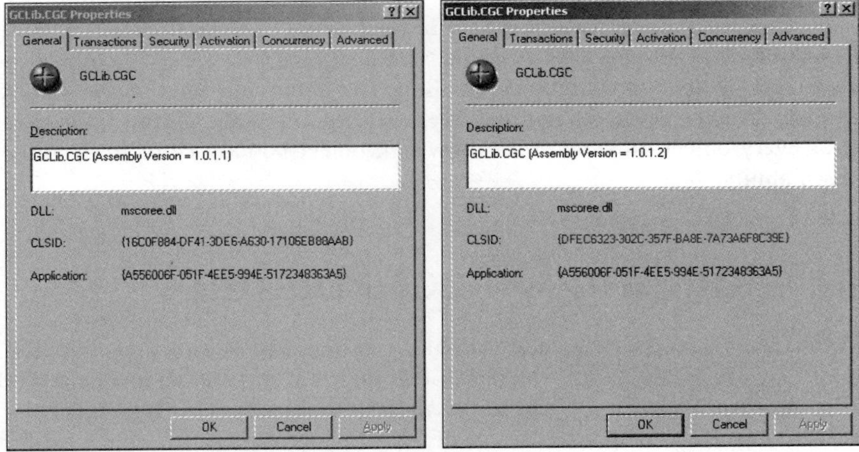

Figure 7-2: Two CLSIDs for a ServicedComponent class

Although these two classes differ only by their revision numbers (1.0.1.1 and 1.0.1.2), each gets its own CLSID. Assuming these are pooled components, COM+ maintains two unique pools.

It is possible to override automatic CLSID generation. The `System.Runtime.InteropServices` namespace provides an attribute called `GuidAttribute` that can be used to decorate a class, assembly, interface, enumeration, structure, or delegate. The code example that follows demonstrates the use of this attribute.

```
using System;
using System.EnterpriseServices;
```

```
using System.Runtime.InteropServices
[GuidAttribute("24B7B5C4-CBEA-4668-AF67-1E3D44F87A68")]
public class CPooledObject : ServicedComponent {}
```

This `GuidAttribute` attribute has one constructor that takes the GUID in the form of a string. Visual Studio comes with a utility called `GuidGen.exe` that you can use to create your unique GUID.

Most of the attributes in the .NET Framework allow you to omit the "Attribute" at the end of the name of each attribute. Generally, this is not a good idea for the `GuidAttribute` attribute. The `System` namespace contains a `Guid` structure. If you are using the `System` namespace, and you are if you are implementing `ServicedComponents`, you run into a naming conflict.

When to Use Object Pooling

So when do you use object pooling? If it improves scalability, shouldn't you use it for every `ServicedComponent`? Well, not exactly. Here are a few guidelines that should help you decide when to use object pooling:

- Use object pooling when your object needs to acquire expensive resources such as database connections.
- Use object pooling when your method calls do a small amount of work, then exit and deactivate the object (that is, set the done bit = true).
- Use object pooling when you need to limit the number of concurrent connections to resources.
- Do not use object pooling when your methods take more time to complete than constructing your objects takes.
- Do not use object pooling for objects that hold client state (after a method call).

Object pooling is intended to spread the cost of an object's initialization across multiple clients. The first client that creates a new object takes a performance hit, but as soon as that client releases the object, the object returns to the pool. Without having to wait for the object to be constructed, the next client that needs an instance of the object gets the instance the first client creates. This is the basis of the first rule in the preceding list. Figure 7-3 demonstrates the concept behind this rule.

The second and third rules of the preceding list go hand in hand. If your component implements only methods that perform a granular amount of work relative to the amount of work performed in constructing the object, your object is a good candidate for pooling. To say it another way, if most of the work a component performs is generic to any client, it may make sense to do the client-independent work in the object's constructor. This allows the component's methods to do a relatively small amount of work. Also, this gives you the opportunity to spread the client-independent work performed in the constructor across multiple clients.

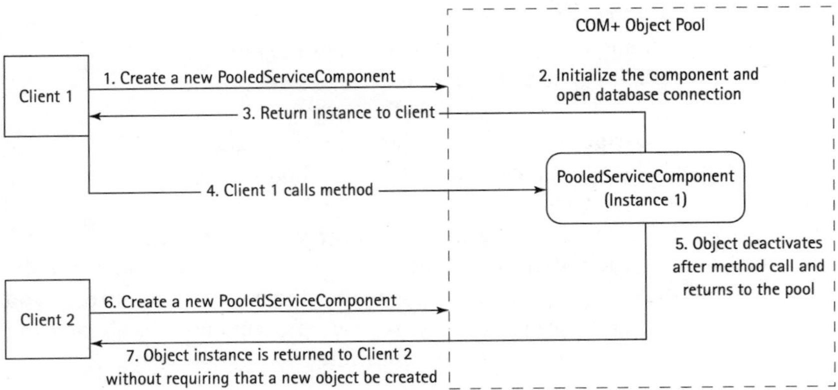

Figure 7-3: Sharing the cost of a database connection

In some scenarios, it may make sense to use object pooling to limit the number of clients that can concurrently access a given resource (a database, for instance). For example, if you have only a 100 concurrent connection license, you can configure your object pool to allow only 100 objects to enter it. The trick here, of course, is to ensure that your clients can get access to the database through the components in your pool only.

When you get into the requirements section later in this chapter, you see why the fifth rule of the preceding list is so important. Poolable components that hold state can be dangerous for a number of reasons.

Object Pooling Attributes

An object pool has three attributes defined by using either the Component Services Explorer or by using the `ObjectPooling` attribute in the `System.EnterpriseServices` namespace. The attributes are as follows:

- `MinPoolSize`
- `MaxPoolSize`
- `CreationTimeout`

When a COM+ application—be it a library or server application—starts up, COM+ instantiates as many components as the minimum pool size requires. As client requests come in, these initial few objects are served to clients. For example, if the minimum pool size is 2, the first two requests are served from objects in the pool. As additional requests for objects come in, COM+ creates new instances up to the maximum pool size. Once the maximum number of objects has been created, client requests are queued until an object becomes available. (Incidentally, you can use the `MaxPoolSize` attribute to control how many concurrent connections you have to a database, just as we discussed in the preceding section.) Clients wait for an object to be returned to them until the creation timeout value has been reached. An object creation request can time out for the following reasons:

- Object construction time is longer than the creation timeout limit.
- A client's request sits in the queue longer than the timeout value does.

Figure 7-4 demonstrates how COM+ uses these attributes to control the pool.

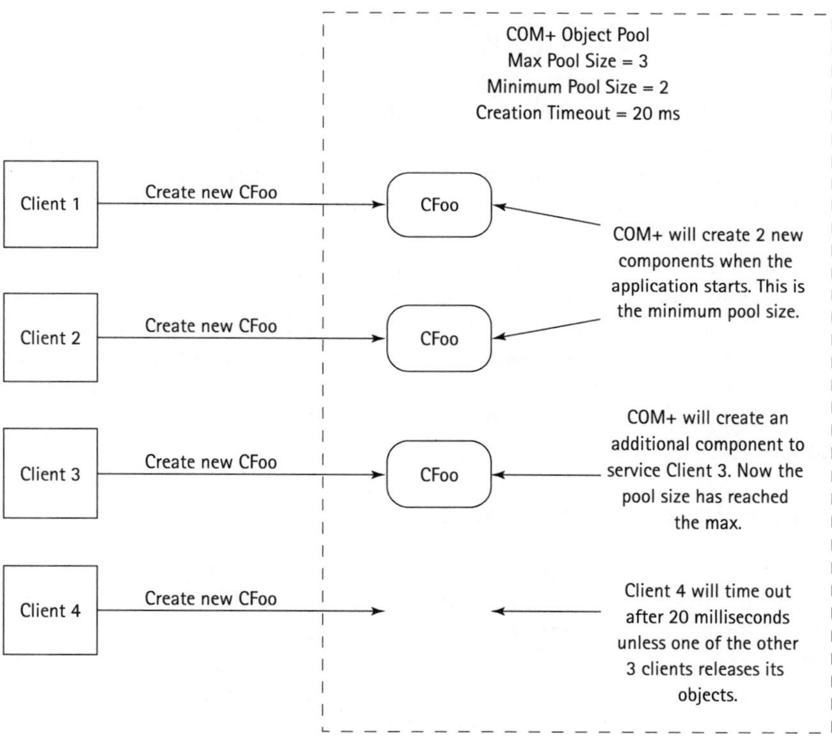

Figure 7-4: Controlling object pooling

Often, determining the optimum level for these settings is a matter of trial and error. It ultimately comes down to how your application works. Here are some things you want to consider when trying to determine the minimum and maximum pool sizes and the creation timeout:

- How long do my methods take to return?
- How long does it take to construct my object?
- How many creation requests can I expect during the busiest times?
- Are my clients doing other work between calls of my methods?

I strongly suggest running some tests to determine how long it takes to construct your objects and how long it takes to run your most expensive method calls. Essentially, you want to set your creation timeout to be at least as long as it takes to construct one of your objects under the worst possible circumstances. You should hope that each client request for an object does not require a new object to be constructed. Most of the time, you should expect requests to be served from objects already constructed and added to the pool. A period of time always exists between your application's starting up and the pool's filling to its maximum level. During this time, new objects need to be constructed, and your clients have to wait for this. Bear this in mind as you consider the duration of your creation timeout.

The third question in the preceding list should influence your thinking about the maximum pool size. You want enough objects available to be able to satisfy requests during the busiest time. The fourth question also should influence the maximum pool size. If your clients typically do other work between method calls, you can take advantage of JITA. Just-in-time activation allows multiple clients to use your component seemingly simultaneously. You explore just-in-time activation and object pooling in greater depth in the next section.

Object pooling represents one of the classic tradeoffs in computer science. When you use object pooling, you are sacrificing memory for performance. The larger your pool size, the more memory you are consuming, and the more clients you can satisfy. At some point, you see the benefits of pooling decrease as you allow your pool to grow. This is why it is so important to stress-test your applications before they go into use. Proper testing gives you a good indication of what your attributes' setting should be.

Object Pooling and Scalability

Developers and architects implement object pooling because they hope doing so will give them greater scalability. Unfortunately, *scalability* is often misused and misunderstood. Take a minute to look at what scalability means.

Scalability is the impact that the addition of resources and users has on an application's throughput. An application is scalable if you can add resources as user load increases and can have a positive effect on throughput.

With COM+ object pooling, you can administratively add components (that is, resources) by increasing the minimum and maximum pool sizes as your user load increases. The more components you allow to be added to your pool, the more clients you can service.

Just-in-time activation (JITA) has an interesting effect on scalability for a poolable object. Remember that JITA allows an object to deactivate after a method call and to activate upon the next method call. Because a client does not have control over the component between method calls, the component is freed back into the pool. Once the component goes back to the pool, it becomes available for other clients. Figure 7-5 shows how JITA allows two clients to use the same instance of an object virtually simultaneously.

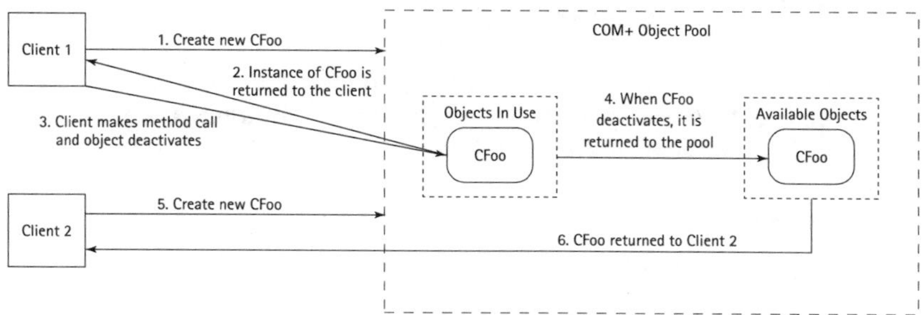

Figure 7-5: How JITA allows scalability in an object pool

In Figure 7-5, client 1 obtains an instance of class `CFoo` from the pool and calls one of `CFoo`'s methods. When the method returns, the object is deactivated and returned to the pool. At this time, client 1 thinks it still has a valid reference to `CFoo`. Next, client 2 requests an instance of `CFoo`. Because an instance of this class has been released back to the pool, client 2 gets the same instance of `CFoo` that client 1 thinks it has. At this exact moment, both clients think they have a valid reference to the same instance of `CFoo`. This is scalability. By using one object to service multiple clients, you can achieve scalability in your applications. As you add objects to the pool, the client base you can support should increase by some factor greater than the number of objects you are adding.

Admittedly, the scenario demonstrated in Figure 7-5 is a rather extreme case. Normally, you do not have only two clients and one object. Also, a client does not necessarily get back the same instance of an object it was previously using. However, the effect of object pooling on scalability remains the same.

I should clear up a point in the preceding scenario. In Figure 7-5, you see the COM+ object pool divided into two sections: objects in use and available objects. Essentially, objects in use are objects in which a client is executing code. Available objects represent objects a client can access. The pool size is always the total number of objects in use plus those available for use. The maximum pool size never exceeds this value.

Object Pooling and Nondeterministic Finalization

Keep in mind that although `ServicedComponents` take advantage of COM+, they still run inside the Common Language Runtime (CLR). This means that pooled objects are still subject to Garbage Collection, which, as you learn in Chapter 1, can occur at any time. Normally, if a class uses expensive resources (for example, database connections, file handles, or network connections), some kind of a `Close` or `Dispose` method should be implemented. However, this solution does not fit well with poolable objects. Because the purpose of writing a poolable object is to spread the cost of acquiring these types of resources across multiple clients, it does not make sense to dispose of these resources after each client is done with the object. The only practical option (that I can think of, at least) is to free these resources in the class's finalizer.

Requirements for Poolable Objects

COM+ insists that poolable objects meet certain requirements. Fortunately, the .NET runtime meets most of these requirements for us. Four requirements all objects must meet if they are to be pooled are the following:

- They must be stateless.
- They must support JITA.
- They must support aggregation.
- They must *not* have affinity to any thread.

Overall, you understand the first two requirements. Statelessness and support for JITA really go hand in hand. I should point out that these requirements are so not much requirements as they are recommendations (very strong recommendations). It is technically possible to write a pooled component that is not stateless and does not support JITA. However, unless you have very strong reasons for not making your components stateless, you should consider these two recommendations a requirement.

All `ServicedComponents` support aggregation. As such, this is not something you need to implement explicitly in your classes. Aggregation involves an inner component and an outer component *morphing* together to form one component. From the client's perspective, the client is dealing only with one component. COM+ provides an outer component that aggregates the inner component, namely, the pooled component. When COM+ aggregates a `ServicedComponent`, it is aggregating the COM Callable Wrapper (CCW). Remember from Chapter 3 that the CCW is responsible for managing the transition between the COM runtime and the .NET runtime. Figure 7-6 shows what a `ServicedComponent` looks like from the point of view of aggregation.

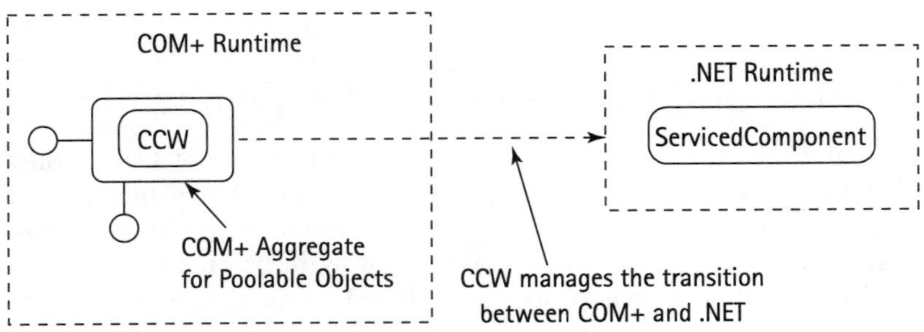

Figure 7-6: Aggregating the CCW

The final requirement for pooled components is that they must not have affinity to any particular thread. Previously in this chapter, you see that multiple clients can use a single component simultaneously. In this scenario, multiple threads are accessing the component. Because any thread may access the component, the component should not rely on data, such as thread local storage, specific to any thread. A good example of this is COM+'s *Shared Property Manager (SPM)*. The SPM is a resource dispenser for a thread's local storage area of memory. Do not use the SPM in your pooled components.

Requirements for Transactional Objects

In addition to the requirements mentioned previously, transactional objects must meet a few additional requirements to be poolable:

- They must manually enlist resources.
- They must turn off automatic enlistment of resource managers.
- They must implement the `IObjectControl` interface.

In our discussion of transactional objects in Chapter 4, you learn that COM+ provides a service known as Automatic Transaction Enlistment. Automatic Transaction Enlistment enables resources (database connections) to enlist into a DTC transaction automatically. Before a database connection can be manually enlisted into a COM+ transaction, the automatic-enlistment behavior must be disabled. This is the basis of the second rule of the preceding list.

Transactions are relative to a particular context. When you open a database connection in an object's constructor, there is no active context, and thus no transaction, for the connection to enlist into. However, if a database connection is opened in a particular context that has an associated transaction and the database connection remains open when the object is returned to the pool, the next client that gets that object may be using a connection that has been enlisted in a different transaction.

To illustrate this point, consider the following scenario depicted in Figure 7-7. Two clients are transactional (not pooled) `ServicedComponents`. Each client requires its own COM+ transaction, and each client represents a unique transaction root. In addition, each component uses a pooled component that supports transactions. To make the point a little easier to understand, say that your minimum and maximum pool sizes are 1. The pooled component opens a database connection on the first call to `Activate` and does not release the connection until the component's finalizer is called. When client 1 calls into the component, the pooled component takes the following actions:

1. It opens the database connection.
2. It enlists the database connection into the first client's transaction.
3. It performs some work on the database connection.
4. The method call executes and COM+ returns the component back to the pool.
5. The client sees there are no errors and commits the transaction.

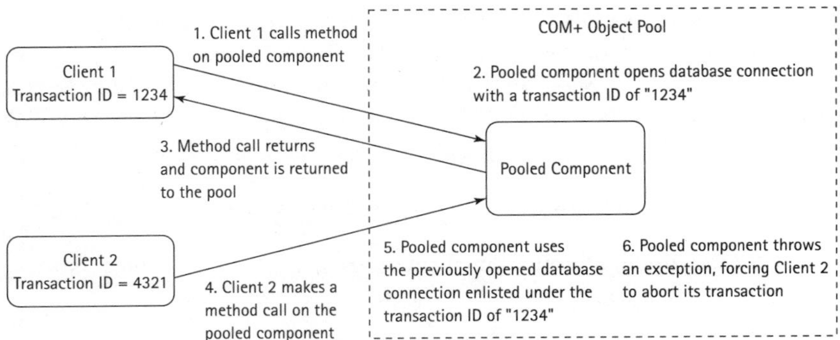

Figure 7-7: Enlisting pooled objects into a transaction

At this point, the transaction is committed, but the database connection still thinks the database connection is enlisted in the first client's transaction. When the second client makes a call into the component, the database connection is not reopened, as it has never been closed in the first place. When the pooled component attempts to do some work on the open connection, an exception is thrown because the database connection is attempting to operate in a transaction that no longer exits.

The final rule that a transactional pooled component must follow is to implement the `IObjectControl` interface. Managed components that inherit from the `ServicedComponent` class do not need to implement the `IObjectControl` interface explicitly. A class that inherits from `ServicedComponent` needs only to override the virtual methods: `Activate`, `Deactivate`, and `CanBePooled`. `Activate` and `Deactivate` allow you to perform context-specific activation and cleanup work. It is not strictly necessary to implement these two methods, but it is generally a good idea. The `CanBePooled` method, on the other hand, must be implemented. If this method is not implemented, COM+ assumes that it returns false. Returning false from `CanBePooled` dooms a transaction. `CanBePooled` gives you a good opportunity to check the state of your component. If you determine that your object is no longer in a consistent state, you can return false from this method, and the object is not returned to the pool.

Before you go on to the next section, consider one additional feature COM+ provides for poolable transactional components. COM+ maintains a subpool for transactional components. If a client is involved in a transaction and the client calls into a pooled component that supports transactions, COM+ examines the object pool to determine if a component exists that previously has been part of that client's transaction. This feature exists to improve performance. Typically, a transactional component that uses another pooled transactional component uses that component in rapid succession. Because COM+ remembers what transaction a pooled component previously has been a part of, it can simply return that instance of the component to the client without having to reinitialize the component into the current transaction. If a pooled component that matches the current transaction is not found, another component from the pool is returned to the client.

Object Pooling in C#

In this section, you run an experiment. You write two `ServicedComponent` classes. One class is a pooled object; the other is a normal JITA-enabled class. Each of these classes contains one method — `ExecuteCategoryQuery` — that performs a simple select against a database called OfficeMart. You create a console application that measures how long it takes you to create new instances of these components and to call the `ExecuteCategoryQuery` method. Because you are concerned only with examining the performance benefits that object pooling can provide, don't worry about getting a result from your query. Discard query results, and assume your query is successful if no exceptions have been thrown.

Pooled and Nonpooled Components

Begin this discussion by examining the classes in the `ObjectPoolLib` namespace in Listing 7-1. To help you better understand where each framework attribute and class comes from, each of the following elements contains a fully qualified namespace.

Listing 7-1: Pooled and Nonpooled Classes

```
[assembly: System.Reflection.AssemblyVersion("1.0.1.1")]
[assembly: System.Reflection.AssemblyKeyFile("mykey.snk")]

namespace ObjectPoolLib
{
  using System;
  using System.Xml;
  using System.EnterpriseServices;
  using System.Data;
  using System.Data.SqlClient;

  [
    System.EnterpriseServices.ObjectPooling
    (
      true,
      10,
      100,
      CreationTimeout=1000
    )
  ]
  [System.EnterpriseServices.JustInTimeActivation(true)]
  [
    System.EnterpriseServices.Transaction
    (
```

```
      TransactionOption.NotSupported
    )
  ]
  public class PooledObject : System.ServicedComponent
  {
    private System.Data.SqlClient.SqlConnection _cnn;
    private System.Data.SqlClient.SqlCommand _cmd;

    public PooledObject() {
      _cnn = new SqlConnection(
          "server=(local);database=OfficeMart;uid=sa;pwd="
        );
      _cmd = new SqlCommand();
      _cmd.CommandType = System.Data.CommandType.Text;
      _cmd.Connection = _cnn;
      _cnn.Open();
    }
    [AutoComplete]
    public void ExecuteCategoryQuery()
    {
      _cmd.CommandText =
        "select CategoryName, Description from Categories";
      _cmd.ExecuteNonQuery();
    }

    // ServicedComponent virtual functions
    public override void Activate()
    {
      // nothing to do here
    }

    public override void Deactivate()
    {
      // nothing to do here
    }

    public override bool CanBePooled()
    {
      if (_cnn.State != System.Data.ConnectionState.Open)
      {
        return false;
      }
      else
      {
        return true;
```

```
    }
  }
}
[System.EnterpriseServices.JustInTimeActivation(true)]
[
  System.EnterpriseServices.Transaction
  (
    TransactionOption.NotSupported
  )
]
[
  System.EnterpriseServices.ConstructionEnabled
  (
    Default="server=(local);database=OfficeMart;uid=sa;pwd="
  )
]
public class NonPooledObject : ServicedComponent
{
  private string _sConnection;
  private System.Data.SqlClient.SqlConnection _cnn;
  private System.Data.SqlClient.SqlCommand _cmd;


  public NonPooledObject()
  {
    // nothing to do here
  }
  [AutoComplete]
  public void ExecuteCategoryQuery()
  {
    _cnn = new SqlConnection(_sConnection);
    _cmd = new SqlCommand();
    _cmd.CommandType = CommandType.Text;
    _cmd.Connection = _cnn;
    _cmd.CommandText =
      "select CategoryName, Description from Categories";
    _cnn.Open();
    _cmd.ExecuteNonQuery();
    _cnn.Close();
    _cmd.Dispose();
  }

  // ServicedComponent virtual functions
  public override void Activate()
  {
```

```
            // nothing to do here
        }

        public override void Deactivate()
        {
            // nothing to do here
        }

        public override bool CanBePooled()
        {
            return false;
        }

        public override void Construct(string s)
        {
            _sConnection = s;
        }
    }
}
```

The first two lines of Listing 7-1 should look familiar. They define the assembly version and the key file you use to sign the assembly. Remember that you need to add a key file to your assembly so that you can give it a strong name and install it into the Global Assembly Cache. It is not absolutely necessary to sign your assembly. I personally prefer to sign my assemblies that run in COM+ server applications. Because server applications run as the `dllhost.exe` process, the .NET runtime's assembly resolver looks for the assembly in `\winnt\system32`, as this is where `dllhost.exe` has been loaded. Unless you want to install your server application assemblies under `\winnt\system32`, you need to add them to the Global Assembly Cache or define a location for them in your application configuration file. It is really just a matter of personal preference.

The first class defined in the namespace is `PooledObject`. The first attribute that decorates this class is `ObjectPooling`. Tables 7-1 and 7-2 list the constructors and properties, respectively, for the `ObjectPooling` attribute.

TABLE 7-1 OBJECTPOOLING ATTRIBUTE CONSTRUCTORS

Constructor Signature	Arguments	Description
`ObjectPooling()`	no arguments	Enables object pooling. Default minimum and maximum pool sizes are 0 and 1048576, respectively. Default creation timeout is 60000 ms.

Constructor Signature	Arguments	Description
`ObjectPooling(bool)`	enabled	Either enables (true) or disables (false) object pooling. Defaults are the same as the preceding.
`ObjectPooling (int, int)`	minimum, maximum pool size	Enables object pooling with the minimum and maximum pool sizes. Default creation timeout is 60000 ms.
`ObjectPooling (bool, int, int)`	enabled, minimum, maximum	Enables or disables object pooling with the minimum and maximum pool sizes.

TABLE 7-2 OBJECTPOOLING ATTRIBUTE PROPERTIES

Property Name	Data Type	Description
`CreationTimeout`	`int`	Specifies the time in milliseconds a client waits for an object to be returned from a call to the C# keyword `new`
`Enabled`	`bool`	Specifies whether object pooling is enabled
`MaxPoolSize`	`int`	Maximum number of objects COM+ allows in the pool
`MinPoolSize`	`int`	Minumum number of objects in the pool at any given time

When the application first starts, COM+ creates `MinPoolSize` number of objects.

You have examined the next two attributes — `JustInTimeActivation` and `Transaction` — in previous chapters, so we don't need to go into them here.

In the constructor for the `PooledObject` class, I am initializing instances of `qlConnection` and `SqlCommand` objects. The types in the `System.Data.SqlClient` namespace are intended for use with Microsoft SQL Server databases only. If you need to access another database (such as Oracle) that supports Microsoft's OLE DB specification, you should use types from the `System.Data.OleDb` namespace.

Probably the most important task you perform in the constructor is opening the database connection. This allows you to share the connection with multiple clients. Opening the connection in the constructor is about the only thing that differentiates the `PooledObject` and `NonPooledObject` classes.

In Listing 7-1 you see the ExecuteCategoryQuery method defined below the definition of the constructor. This method is decorated with the AutoComplete attribute. You need to set the AutoComplete attribute for this method because you want the object to be deactivated after the method call and returned to the pool. Remember that this attribute automatically sets the object's done bit to true when a thread enters the method. The implementation of this method sets the command text of the SqlCommand class to your SQL select statement and executes select against the database. Because you are not concerned with getting data back from the database, use the ExecuteNonQuery method, which, in this case, discards query results.

The last three methods in this class represent the IObjectControl interface methods. The ServicedComponent class defines these methods as virtual. Because the object inherits from the ServicedComponent class, you do not need to implement IObjectControl.

C# supports both the virtual and abstract keywords. These keywords are close cousins of each other, but they do implement slightly different behaviors. The virtual keyword can be used to decorate methods and properties in a class. The abstract keyword, on the other hand, can be used to decorate classes as well. The child class does not necessarily need to implement methods defined as virtual. This is the case for the methods Activate, Deactivate, and CanBePooled in the ServicedComponent class. The child class must implement abstract methods.

Because you are not doing any context-specific work in the NonPooledObject class, you have nothing to do in the Activate and Deactivate methods. They are here to show you how they are declared in a ServicedComponent-derived class. The CanBePooled method shows how you can use it to examine the state of the object and to decide whether or not to return it to the pool. In your example, look to see if the connection is still open before returning it to the pool.

The NonPooledObject class comes next in the code listing. The work this class performs is essentially the same as the work done in the PooledObject class. You do only two things differently in the NonPooledObject class. First of all, because the NonPooledObject class is not a pooled component, you do not open the connection in the constructor. Instead, you open it in the ExecuteCategoryQuery method.

Also notice that this class contains a new attribute: ConstructionEnabled. This attribute allows COM+ to pass in a string when your component is activated. This string can be anything you want, but in your case, you are passing in the connection string for your database. The Default property defines the construction string added to the catalog when you register your component. Figure 7-8 depicts the Activation tab for this component. Notice that the "Enable object construction" check box is checked and the connection string has been added to the text field.

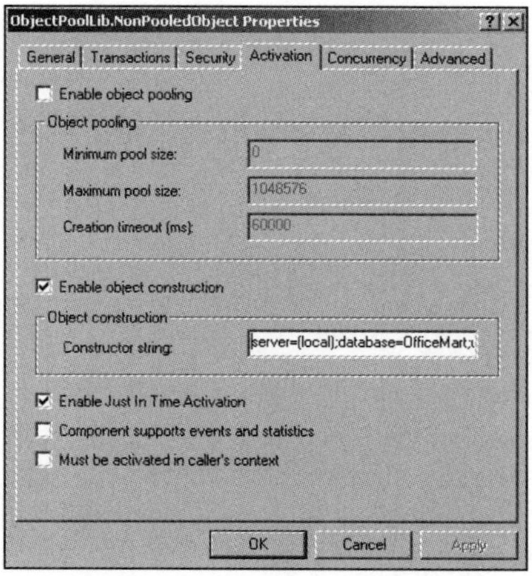

Figure 7-8: Activation tab for a construction enabled component

Override the virtual method, `Construct`, from the `ServicedComponent` class so you can get access to the constructor string. Normally, if you are developing a unmanaged component, you have to implement the `IObjectConstruct` interface to get this functionality. But the `ServicedComponent` class takes care of that for you. COM+ calls the `Construct` method before it calls the `Activate` method.

I have not implemented the `ConstructionEnabled` attribute in the `PooledObject` class, as you need the connection string to be in the class's constructor. Because COM+ constructs the object before any calls to `Activate` or `Construct` occur, you are not able to take advantage of this feature.

Analyzing the Client

The code for your test application is shown in Listing 7-2. Admittedly, this is a rather simplified test, but it helps to demonstrate the benefits of object pooling.

Listing 7-2: Object Pooling Client

```
using System;
using ObjectPoolLib;
static void Main(string[] args)
{

  int i = 0;
  long lStart;
  long lEnd;

  lStart = System.DateTime.Now.Ticks;
  for (i = 0; i < 1000; i++)
```

```
  {
    ObjectPoolLib.PooledObject po = new
ObjectPoolLib.PooledObject();
    po.ExecuteCategoryQuery();
  }

  lEnd = System.DateTime.Now.Ticks - lStart;
  Console.WriteLine("Results for PooledObject: " + lEnd.ToString());

  lStart = System.DateTime.Now.Ticks;
  for (i = 0; i < 1000; i++)
  {
    ObjectPoolLib.NonPooledObject npo = new
      ObjectPoolLib.NonPooledObject();
    npo.ExecuteCategoryQuery();
  }

  lEnd = System.DateTime.Now.Ticks - lStart;
  Console.WriteLine("Results for NonPooledObject: " +
lEnd.ToString());
  Console.WriteLine(Console.ReadLine());
 }
```

This test application creates 10 instances of each of the pooled and nonpooled classes and determines the elapsed time that occurs when the method is called. The elapsed time is determined by computing the difference between the number of ticks before and after the loop. Incidentally, `System.DateTime.Now.Ticks` represents the number of hundred-nanosecond intervals that have occurred from January 1, 2001, at 12:00 a.m.

When I run this on my machine, I get the following output:

```
Results for PooledObject: 157726800
Results for NonPooledObject: 216110752
```

The results you get may differ somewhat depending on your system's configuration. The point here is to show how much faster pooled components can be for this type of component. As you can see from the test, object pooling can provide significant benefits.

Summary

In this chapter, you have delved into the world of object pooling. You have seen how the `ServicedComponent` class and the `ObjectPooling` attribute are used to write a poolable object. No longer do you have to write these classes in C++.

You have gained some criteria to apply to an object when you try to decide whether it should be pooled or not. Remember that the more generic your object is, the more likely it is a candidate for the object pool.

Finally, you have seen how pooled objects compare with nonpooled objects. You have seen a rather dramatic increase in performance for the pooled component. I hope this whets your appetite for pooled components.

Chapter 8

Queued Components

IN THIS CHAPTER

- ◆ Making the case for queued components
- ◆ Introducing Microsoft Message Queue
- ◆ Understanding queued components in COM+
- ◆ Using other COM+ services along with queued components
- ◆ Developing queued components in C#

IT HAS OCCURRED TO me over the years that when I need to contact someone, either by phone or e-mail, I go through a process to determine the best way to reach the person. If I cannot proceed with my day without talking to the person, I phone or page him or her. If, however, I can get by without the person's immediate attention, I usually send an e-mail. For me, at least, the phone provides synchronous communication, but e-mail provides asynchronous communication.

In the world of remote method calls, queued components provide a way for a client to send a message that contains method calls to a remote component. Similarly to the way I use e-mail, you can use queued components to provide asynchronous communication.

In this chapter, you see how queued components stack up against other forms of remote method calls such as Remote Procedure Calls (RPCs) and the Simple Object Access Protocol (SOAP). Also, you encounter some criteria to use when trying to decide between these two method calls.

Because Microsoft Message Queue (MSMQ) is the underlying transport mechanism behind queued components, you receive an introduction to its features and architecture. This is by no means a complete explanation of the features of MSMQ, but you explore the relevant features as they pertain to queued components.

In the last three sections of this chapter, you learn the architecture of queued components and some of the subtle issues that arise when designing these types of components. Some of these design issues come into play when other services of COM+, such as security, must be used. In the final section, you write several queued components. You learn to write a basic queued component by using the .NET Framework and C#. From there, you move forward to more advanced techniques, such as combining queued components with loosely coupled events.

It's fun stuff, so get ready!

Making the Case for Queued Components

For years, developers have been using various technologies to transport their method calls across the network to remote components. Some of these technologies, such as RPC DCOM, which uses RPC under the covers, provide synchronous communication. When a client instantiates a component, the instantiation request is made to some form of proxy component on the client, which then forwards the request to the server hosting the component. At the server end, the request is picked up, and the component is instantiated. From that point on, as each method or property is set on the remote component, the call goes out across the network, and it is picked up on the other end by the component. Each time the client makes a call, it waits for the remote component to respond. The more method calls a client makes, the more network traffic and the slower the application. If you combine a chatty client with a slow network, you are likely to get a frustrated user.

Even newer protocols such as SOAP behave in a similar fashion to RPC. SOAP uses HTTP as its transport mechanism. HTTP is, for all purposes, a request-response type of protocol. A SOAP client sends a method call in the form of an HTTP request to some end point on a Web server. The end point can be almost anything, but often it is an Active Server Page or an ISAPI extension DLL. After the client sends its request to the Web server, it blocks as it waits for the Web server's response.

Both of these types of method invocations – RPC and SOAP – have the same inherent limitations:

- They are unable to guarantee delivery of a method call.
- The client must wait for each method call across the network to return.

If the client makes a method call to a remote component and the server that hosts the component is down, the client has no way to ensure that the call succeeds. In this type of situation, the client has only a couple of options: the client can keep retrying the method call or give up. Either of these options can be rather frustrating for the user.

By saying that RPC and SOAP are synchronous protocols, I mean that method calls are made one after the other. Each time the client calls a method, a round trip to the server is required to send parameters and to receive a return value. While all this is occurring, the client must wait for the call to return. If you have a slow or unreliable network, this can greatly slow down your application.

Products such as IBM's MQ Series and MSMQ are designed to alleviate these problems. These products provide two big benefits: asynchronous messaging and guaranteed delivery. Both of these products ship with COM and the procedural API, which developers use to send and receive messages to and from computers. I am not going to demonstrate the use of these APIs in this chapter, but here is a rundown of the tasks you typically need to perform when writing queued applications:

1. Create a public or private queue (administratively or programmatically).
2. The sender opens the queue, specifying whether to peek at the message, read it, or send it. The share level of the queue is determined at this time.
3. The sender creates the message to be sent on the queue. Properties such as the body of the message and priority are set at this time.
4. Once the message is configured, the sender sends it to the appropriate destination queue.
5. The receiver opens the queue.
6. The receiver either peeks at the queue or reads the message.

Admittedly, this is an oversimplification of the process, but I think you get the idea of how most queued applications work. This is roughly the same scenario that occurs when you use queued components. However, queued components hide most of this from you. As you might guess, the fact that queued components hide a certain amount of complexity comes at the cost of flexibility. Some tasks, such as peeking at messages in the queue, cannot be performed if you are strictly using queued components.

Queued components provide you with the typical features you expect from a message queue, such as guaranteed delivery and asynchronous processing. Also, queued components hide the grungy queue communication work you perform if you are using the MSMQ COM API.

Queued components are particularly well suited to provide several benefits over synchronous method calls:

- Availability and lifetime of the component
- Scheduling of workload
- Reliability of method calls
- Scalability

Because the lifetimes of the client and the component do not need to overlap, clients are able to operate independently of the components they are calling. This has benefits if the server hosting the component is unavailable or if the network between the client and component is unavailable. In the event of server down time, calls from the client can be queued and stored until the hosting server is back up and running. This has benefits also for disconnected clients such as laptops and handheld devices. Applications running on these types of devices can continue to function while disconnected from their networks.

The fact that the client and component lifetimes do not need to overlap enables you to schedule when the component should do its work. As you see later in this chapter, queued components must be configured as a server application. This server application must be running in order for the component to process method calls.

Queued components allow you to specify when the server application (`dllhost.exe`) runs. This schedule can be set to run the application during the hosting server's less busy hours.

When queued-component method calls are made across the network, MSMQ uses transactions to deliver the messages. On the component side, messages are read from the queue in a transactional manner. These transactions are not necessarily COM+ transactions, but they benefit from many of the same features. If a queued component reads a message from the queue and an error occurs, the read rolls back, and the message returns to the queue. All this adds up to a much more reliable delivery mechanism than you get from nonqueued method calls.

The final benefit – scalability – is perhaps the biggest, at least in my mind. First, because the client does not block during each method call, it is able to make many calls in rapid succession and to move on to the next task. The client, and ultimately the user, does not have to wait for method calls to be transported over the network and received by a remote component that may or may not be available. Second, because the server process, `dllhost.exe`, can be scheduled to process messages during off-peak hours, the server hosting the component can have more resources available during peak times. All of this amounts to the application's being able to do more work at a faster rate.

Introduction to Microsoft Message Queue

Understanding how queued components work is hard if you do not understand the basics of MSMQ. It is even harder to diagnose problems when they occur in your applications if you are not at least familiar with the underlying transport mechanism. Take a look at the components that make up an MSMQ network.

Installing MSMQ

Windows 2000 Server provides MSMQ 2.0 as a core component of the operating system. You have the option of installing MSMQ when you install the operating system or anytime thereafter. MSMQ is not installed by default.

MSMQ can be installed in either a Windows 2000 workgroup or a Windows 2000 domain. MSMQ is tightly integrated with Windows 2000 Active Directory. If you wish to gain Active Directory support, install MSMQ on a domain controller. MSMQ extends the Active Directory schema to hold queue configuration and status information.

The workgroup installation option is somewhat more limiting. For instance, only private queues can be used in a workgroup configuration. In addition, routing servers cannot be used with the workgroup configuration. Integrating with Active Directory allows you to use internal certificates to authenticate messages. Because internal certificates come from Active Directory, this option is not available in the workgroup installation. External certificates are the only option for a workgroup installation. External certificates come from an outside certificate authority. Fortunately for queued component developers, you can still use your components in a workgroup installation.

Depending on whether you are installing MSMQ on a client, a domain controller, or a member server, you have a number of options to choose from. For servers, you have the option of installing MSMQ as a routing server or as a regular server that has public and private queues. A routing server's job is to take messages from clients and to move them to their final destination queues. The routing server is not responsible for processing incoming messages unless those messages are for one of its own queues. For performance reasons, Microsoft does not recommend installing a routing server on a domain controller. Routing servers should be installed on member servers.

The client can be an independent or dependent installation. To send messages, dependent clients must be connected to the network. Workstations wired to the local network are good candidates for dependent clients. The only exception to this is domain controllers. MSMQ cannot be installed on a domain controller as a dependent client. Independent clients, on the other hand, do not have to be connected to the network to send messages. As applications running on independent clients send messages, MSMQ stores those messages locally until the client reconnects to the network. Once the client reconnects, messages are sent accordingly. Laptops and handheld devices are good candidates for independent clients. These mobile devices are not always connected to the network when they are being used. Independent-client installations allow users to use their applications as if they were connected to the network. The next time users connect to the networks, messages can be sent and their data can be processed.

Once MSMQ is installed into a domain, it can be administered by using the Computer Management Console. Figure 8-1 shows where you can find MSMQ under the Services and Applications node. This snap-in is enabled for only MSMQ installations in a domain.

Understanding Queues

Queues are similar to a mailbox. Just as you use a mailbox to send and receive mail, applications use queues to send and receive messages. In MSMQ, two categories of queues exist – application queues and system queues. Application queues can be any of the following types of queues:

- Message queues
- Administration queues
- Response queues
- Report queues

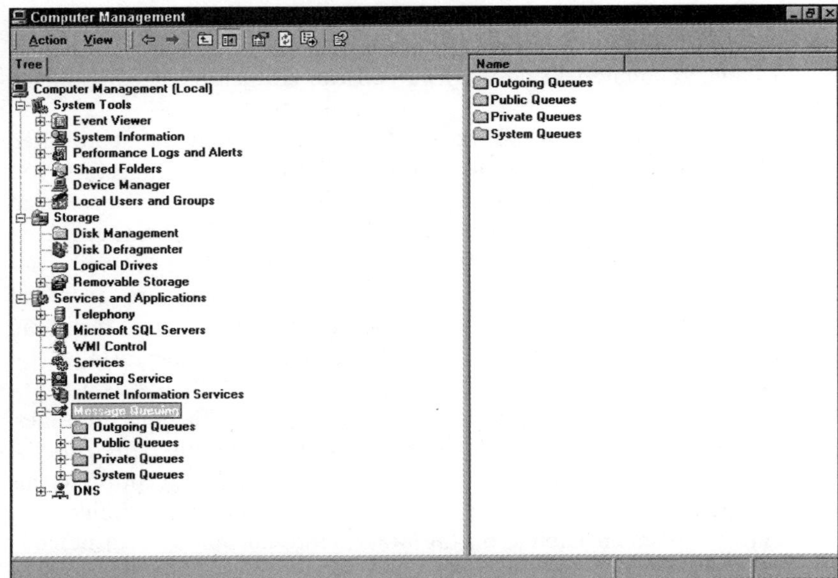

Figure 8-1: MSMQ administration snap-in

COM+ queued components and their clients use messages queues to send and receive method calls. Message queues can be public or private. Public queues are registered in Active Directory, but private queues are available only if you specify the machine name. When you install queued components in a Windows 2000 domain, COM+ creates a public message queue for the component.

When sending applications send messages, they can require a response from MSMQ. The response can be in regard to the message reaching the queue or the message being read from the queue or, if you wish, both actions can generate a response from MSMQ. Response queues are similar to administration queues except that the receiving application generates the response message (back to the sender).

Report queues hold messages that MSMQ generates, as messages move from routing server to routing server. By enabling tracing for a message, an application can specify that it wants to use a report queue.

MSMQ uses system queues internally. System queues make up the dead letter queue and journal queues. The dead letter queue holds messages that cannot be delivered to their destination queues. Each installation has two dead letter queues. One dead letter queue holds transactional messages, and another holds regular messages. You see a little later in this chapter how queued components use transactional dead letter queues.

Each time a public or private queue is created, MSMQ creates an associated journal queue. The purpose of the journal queue is to hold copies of messages until they are read from the queue. Journaling is not turned on by default. Journaling can be enabled for a queue by going into the queue properties by using the MSMQ snap-in in the Computer Management Console. Figure 8-2 shows the General tab for a public queue called `helloworld`. This queue is created after the installation of a COM+ queued component.

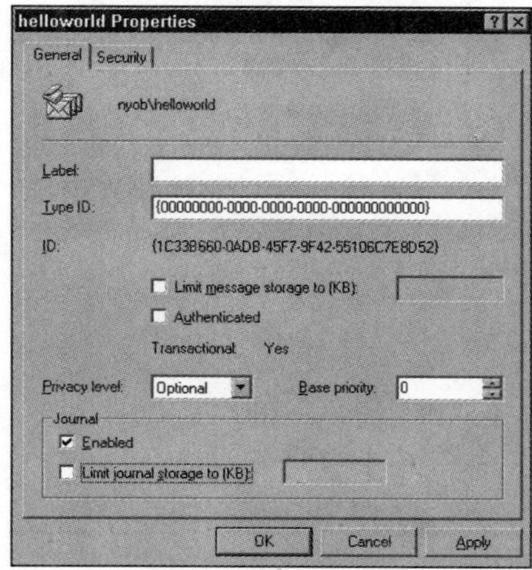

Figure 8-2: Enabling journaling for a queue

MSMQ Messages

Essentially, messages are composed of a message body and its associated properties, which determine the behavior of the messages as they are routed through the network. The body of any message is the actual payload or data. Many properties can be set programmatically by a sending application. Some of the more common properties are the body type, the message priority, the formatter, and the destination queue. The *body type* property describes the data type contained in the body of the message. Message types can be any number of data types such as integers or strings and even other objects such as `DataSets`. The *message priority* gives a higher priority to critical messages as they are routed through the network. By default, messages have priority 0. Messages that have a higher priority number get routed quicker than those that have a lower priority number.

Formatters specify the manner in which the message payload is streamed to the body property. By default, .NET streams the payload as XML. Other formatters are the `ActiveXMessageFormatter` and the `BinaryMessageFormatter`. Both of these formatters stream data in a binary format. The `ActiveXMessageFormatter` allows you to stream basic data types such as integers and strings, as well as classes, enumerations, and anything else that can be converted to a `System.Object` type.

You can set many of the message properties when you use queued components. Although you do not interact directly with the messages sent to queued components, you can set some properties by using the moniker. You encounter monikers later in this chapter.

Developing MSMQ Applications by Using C#

For years, developers have used MSMQ COM components or MSMQ API functions to develop applications that use message queuing. These APIs allow developers to read from queues, write to them, and perform management tasks such as creating them. The .NET Framework provides a similar set of APIs for the C# developer. The `System.Messaging` namespace (`System.Messaging.dll`) contains all the classes, interfaces, and enumerations you need to develop .NET applications that take advantage of of MSMQ's features. This section provides a brief introduction to the `System.Messaging` namespace and commonly used classes to give you a feel for developing messaging applications without using queued components.

The two most commonly used classes in `System.Messaging` are the `MessageQueue` class and the `Message` class. The `MessageQueue` class is used to read, send, and peek at messages that arive at a particular queue. The queue name and path can be specified when the class is instantiated or by using the `path` property. Table 8-1 lists the constructors for the `MessageQueue` class.

TABLE 8-1 MESSAGEQUEUE CONSTRUCTORS

Constructor	Description	Example
`MessageQueue()`	Creates new instance of the `MessageQueue` class which is not bound to a queue	`MessageQueue mq = new MessageQueue();`
`MessageQueue(string path)`	Creates a new instance of the `MessageQueue` class and binds it to the queue specified by path	`MessageQueue mq = new MessageQueue (".\queueName");`
`MessageQueue(string path, bool sharedModeDenyReceive)`	Binds queue specified in path to instanceof the `MessageQueue` class and grants exclusive read access to the first application that reads from the queue	`MessageQueue mq = new MessageQueue (".\queueName, true);`

The `Message` class is used to manipulate the properties of an outgoing or incoming MSMQ message. This class contains the body, or payload, of the message. Typically, you create a new `Message` object, by using one of its three constructors, when you are about to send a message to a queue. The constructors for this class are shown in Table 8-2.

TABLE 8-2 MESSAGE CONSTRUCTORS

Constructor	Description	Example
`Message()`	Creates an empty message class. You must fill in the desired properties.	`Message m = new Message();`
`Message(Object body)`	Creates a new class, setting the payload of the message to the object passed in. Any class that inherits from the object can be passed.	`MyClass mc = new MyClass() Message m = new Message (mc);`
`Message(Object body, IMessageFormatter formatter)`	Sets message body equal to body parameter. The formatter specifies how the body is streamed to the message.	`MyClass mc = new MyClass() Message m = new Message( mc, new XmlMessageFormatter());`

Look at what it takes to send and receive a message from a queue. The code in Listing 8-1 opens a connection to a private queue called `OrderQueue`, sends a `struct` called `Order`, reads the message out of the queue, and prints out the fields of the `Order struct`.

Listing 8-1: Sending and receiving messages from a queue

```
using System;
using System.Messaging;

namespace OrderMessage
{
  public struct Order
  {
    public string CustomerName;
    public string Sku;
```

```
        public int Quantity;
    }

    public class COrderApp
    {
        public static void Main()
        {
            // create a new order
            Order order;
            order.CustomerName = "Acme, Inc.";
            order.Sku = "sku123";
            order.Quantity = 100;

            // open the OrderQueue queue and send the order
            MessageQueue mq = new MessageQueue
                    ("Server1\\private$\\OrderQueue");
            mq.Send(order);

            // specify the type of formatter we want to use
            XmlMessageFormatter xmlf = (XmlMessageFormatter) mq.Formatter;

            // tell the formatter the types we want
            // to stream from this message
            xmlf.TargetTypeNames = new
                    string[]{"OrderMessage.Order,OrderMessaging"};

            // read the message from the queue
            Message m = mq.Receive();
            Order orderIn = (Order)m.Body;
            Console.WriteLine("Customer Name: " + orderIn.CustomerName);
            Console.WriteLine("Sku: " + orderIn.Sku);
            Console.WriteLine("Quantity: " + orderIn.Quantity);
        }
    }
}
```

The `MessageQueue` class is created by using the second constructor in Table 8-1. Notice the path of the queue. The first part of the path, `Server1`, is the name of the machine hosting the queue. The second part of the path specifies the queue as a private queue. The final part of the path is the queue name.

Once the new `MessageQueue` instance has been created, you need only to send the `Order struct` onto the queue. You do not need to define a formatter for this queue, because one has been defined already by default: `XmlMessageFormatter`.

Before you read the message back off the queue, however, you must define the types you want to extract from the body of the message. In your case, transform the body back into an `Order struct` so you can print the order back to the console.

`xmlf.TargetTypeNames` defines the types you want the formatter to stream back to you. The string array assigned to the `TargetTypeNames` property holds the fully qualified type name of your `struct` and the assembly that implements it. A fully qualified type name contains the namespace and the type name.

Once the formatter knows which types you are going to extract from the message body, you are free to read the message from the queue. `Mq.Receive()` reads a message from the queue and returns an instance of a `Message` class. If multiple messages are on the queue, this call retrieves the first message. If no messages are on the queue, this call blocks (waits) until messages arrive or until the receive timeout has expired. Because this method is overloaded, it can be called by passing in a `System.TimeSpan` instance, which defines the maximum amount of time the call waits for messages to arrive on the queue.

I have to admit that this example makes certain atypical assumptions. First, it is generally good practice to check for the existence of the queue before trying to open it and send messages. Second, you do not want to force the client to block by making the client wait for messages for an infinite amount of time. This example is not necessarily intended as a real-world example of messaging. However, it is intended to demonstrate how some of the more common tasks, such as sending and receiving messages and using the `XmlMessageFormatter`, are accomplished with the `System.Messaging` namespace. At the end of this chapter, you see examples of how queued components hide much of this work from you.

Understanding Queued Components in COM+

Queued components provide you with a mechanism for making method calls across the network to remote machines. As you already know, MSMQ provides the transport functionality to make this happen. This section breaks down the pieces of the COM+ queued component architecture, displaying how method calls are packaged into MSMQ messages and how they are unpacked on the component side. Also, this section addresses some of the design considerations you must explore when developing your queued components.

Client and Server Requirements

It can be hard to understand how queued components work if you do not understand what needs to be installed on the client and server. As you have probably guessed already, MSMQ must be installed on the client and server. MSMQ provides the underlying transport mechanism for queued components.

Perhaps the most important requirement, and the one that can easily be overlooked at first, is the fact that the component must be registered on the client as well as on the server. Because you are dealing with COM+ components, it follows that COM+ must be installed also. As you see in a moment, the client does not access the local version of the component. The local version is more of a template that provides information to the client. With the queued component installed locally, the client can consume the queued interfaces of the component. COM+ can use the local copy of the component to determine if an exception class should be used during error conditions.

With queued components, you must deploy your components not only on your Web server or application server but on each of your client machines as well. This is not so bad if you have only one client machine and one server, but chances are you have to deploy to multiple client machines. .NET's deployment model, particularly as it applies to COM+ components, excels at this. In the past, if you deployed queued components to client machines, you had to find a way to deploy components, register them in COM+, and configure the appropriate attributes. COM+ replication can help you with this, but things can get hairy if clients become misconfigured. In this event, an administrator may have to reconfigure the COM+ application. Because `ServicedComponents` contain their COM+ attributes directly in their assemblies, the assembly needs simply to be re-registered.

Recorder, Listener, and Player

Figure 8-3 illustrates the architecture of the queued component system. The components in this system are the client, recorder, listener, player, and, of course, the queued component itself. As you can see in this diagram, both the client side and the server side must have COM+ installed for a client to be able to use a queued component. The recorder, listener, and player are all components of COM+, and COM+ uses them to hide the details of MSMQ programming.

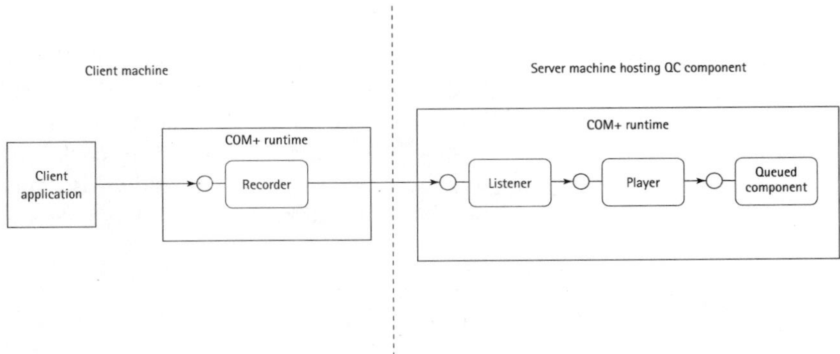

Figure 8-3: Queued-component architecture

When the client creates an instance of a queued component, it receives an instance to a special COM+ component called the *recorder* in return. Once the client has a reference to a recorder, it can call the recorder's methods as if it were the actual queued component. The recorder accepts the method calls as if it were the queued component and bundles them into an MSMQ message. When the client releases the reference to the recorder, the recorder submits the method calls to the queued component as a single MSMQ message. The message goes to the queued component's public input queue to await processing by the listener component. At no time is the client communicating directly with the queued component.

You may be wondering if nondeterministic finalization and Garbage Collection play a role in the release of the recorder object. After all, in most cases, a managed object is not released until the Garbage Collector collects it. Fortunately, for those of us writing queued components, nondeterministic finalization is not a problem. As you see later in this chapter, you explicitly release your references to queued components (for example, the recorder).

At the server, the listener component waits for messages to arrive in the queued component's public input queue. Figure 8-4 shows the public queue for a COM+ application called *queued components*. The name of this queue is the same as that of the COM+ application; in your case, it is *queued components*.

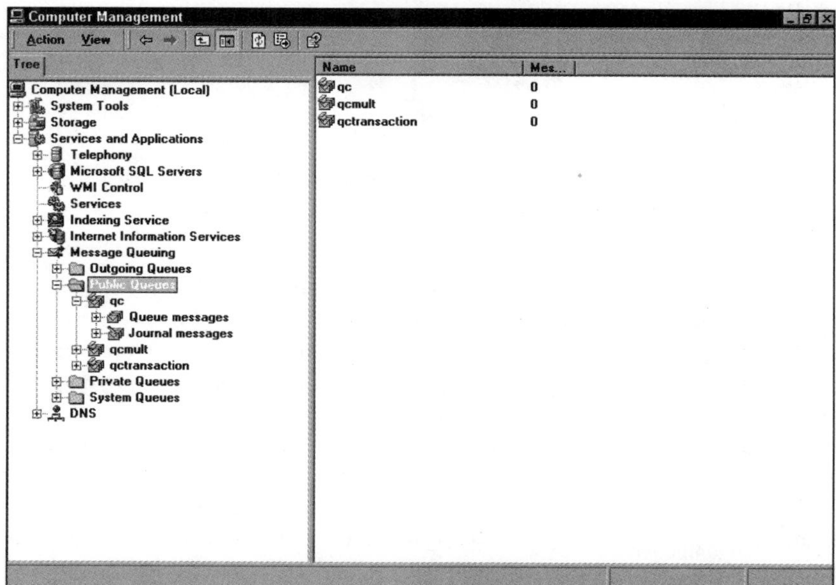

Figure 8-4: Public input queue for queued components application

The listener is responsible for taking messages off the application's queue and instantiating a player object. The listener does not directly instantiate the player component; instead, it instantiates another COM+ component called the `ListenerHelper`. The `ProgId` for this component is queued `components.ListenerHelper`. I mentioned earlier that the recorder, listener, and player are COM+ components. This is true in the sense that they are installed and registered as part of the standard COM+ installation on Windows 2000. However, only the recorder and `ListenerHelper` are truly configured components. Figure 8-5 shows where the `ListenerHelper` and recorder can be found in Component Services Explorer. COM+ comes with a library application called COM+ Utilities, which houses these components.

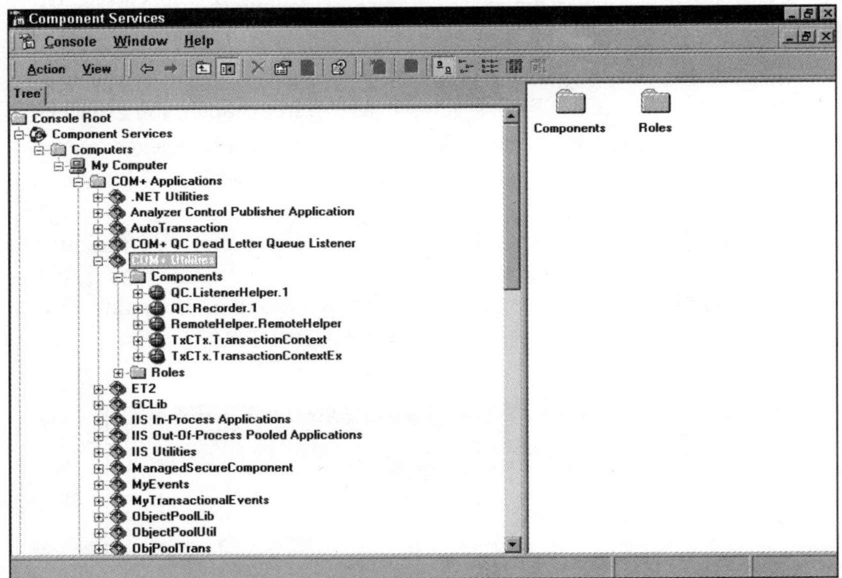

Figure 8-5: ListenerHelper and recorder in COM+ utilities application

The job of the `ListenerHelper` component is to create a player component. Each incoming MSMQ message is assigned a player component. The player component reads the contents of the message (the method calls), creates the actual queued components, and plays back each method call from the client. The player plays back the method calls in the same order in which the client called them.

Now that you know a little more about the queued-components architecture, review these concepts by expanding Figure 8-2.

Figure 8-6 starts with the client creating an instance of the queued component. In return, the client gets a reference to the queued `components.Recorder` configured component. The client proceeds to make method calls on this reference just as if it were actually using the queued component. Once the client releases its reference to the recorder object, COM+ creates an MSMQ message and sends the message to the queued component's input queue. This entire process represents steps 1 through 5.

When the message reaches the component's public input queue, the listener takes the message off the queue and creates an instance of the player component. The listener uses the queued `components.ListenerHelper` component to do this (step 7). Then the listener passes the message to the player component, which in turn plays back the method calls contained in the message. At step 9, the player plays the calls back in the same order in which the Recorder component records them.

Instantiating Queued Components

Until this point in the book, I have been using the C# keyword `new` to create instances of components. This has served you well, as you have wanted to create and directly access instances of your components. The `new` keyword leaves you with a couple of limitations when you wish to use queued components. First, in most cases, the client and the component reside on two different computers. You need a way to tell COM+ not only which component you wish to create but also on what computer you wish to create it. The `new` keyword does not allow you to do this. Second, as I mention in the previous section, what you really want back after instantiating a component is a reference to the recorder, not a reference to the actual component.

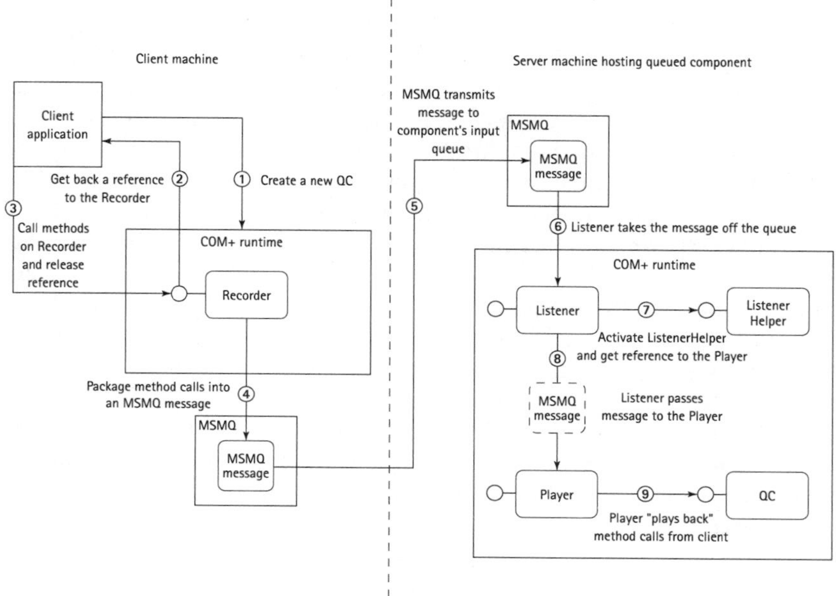

Figure 8-6: Expanded view of the queued components architecture

Monikers are special types of components that allow you to specify which computer hosts the queued components you want to use. Monikers, in essence, are factory components. If you are familiar with COM, you may know about the class factory. Class factories in COM exist to create other COM components. Class factories are written specifically for a component. Because of this, they can have special knowledge of the components they create. Monikers are similar to COM class factories; they exist to create other components. Monikers can get you around specifying a computer name because they can take input parameters during object initialization. I should point out that you do not create monikers directly. Monikers are not created in the way you normally create classes or components by using the `new` keyword. Monikers are created indirectly by passing a string to a method on some class. The string specifies the name of the moniker and, optionally, its parameters. The moniker is created *under the covers* for you. This becomes clearer in the next few paragraphs.

To create a queued component, use a particular moniker component called the queue moniker. The queue moniker knows how to create the recorder component (this solves the second limitation of `new`). One of the parameters you can pass to the queue moniker is the name of the computer hosting the queued component. Also, you can specify several parameters that affect the behavior of the message once it is placed on the queue. I am not going to list all of the parameters the queue moniker can take, but a few of them are: the message priority level; the destination queue name; time to reach the queue; whether or not to generate tracing messages as the message is routed; and the journal level for the queue. I think you get the idea. You can reference the MSDN documentation on queued components for the complete list of queue-moniker parameters.

When a COM developer wishes to use monikers, he or she does not use the normal `CoCreateInstance` (C/C++) or the Visual Basic command `CreateObject`. Instead, monikers have been created with a similar call such as `GetObject` in Visual Basic or `CoGetObject` in C/C++. C# developers have a similar means to instantiate components with monikers. The Framework's `System.Runtime.InteropServices` namespace contains a class called `Marshal` that you use to create monikers. The `Marshal` class contains many methods used to manage the interaction between the Common Language Runtime (CLR) and the unmanaged runtime of Windows, particularly the COM runtime. Many of these methods deal with memory management between the two runtimes. In this chapter, I will focus on two of the `Marshal` class's methods only: `BindToMoniker` and `ReleaseComObject`. Both of these methods are static, which means you do not need to create an instance of the `Marshal` class to use them.

You use the `BindToMoniker` method to create the moniker and, ultimately, the recorder. This method takes one parameter, a string, which represents the name of the moniker and its parameters, if any. Take a look at a few lines of code to make this concept clearer:

```
IQC iqc;
iqc = (IQC) Marshal.BindToMoniker("queue:/new:queued
componentsNamespace.queued components");
iqc.SomeMethod();
```

In the preceding code, the `Marshal.BindToMoniker` creates an instance of a queued component called `QCNamespace.QC`. The string parameter specifies the name of the moniker—`queue`—and the name of the queued component, `QCNamespace.QC`. In this string, I am using two monikers. The second moniker is the `new` moniker specified with `/new:`. These two monikers are used in conjunction to create an instance of the queued components or, more specifically, the COM+ recorder. I leave the explanation of the rest of the code until later in the chapter. The `iqc` variable is your reference to the recorder object, which you treat as a reference to the actual queued component.

So that takes care of creating an instance of the queued component or, more precisely, gaining a reference to the recorder. Previously in this chapter, I stated that I have a way of overcoming the problems Garbage Collection introduces to queued components. The problem stems from the fact that you need to release your reference to the recorder to get COM+ to create the MSMQ message and to send it to the queued component's input queue. If you rely on Garbage Collection to release this reference, you are not certain when your message will be submitted to the component's input queue. Fortunately, the `Marshal.ReleaseComObject` method call allows you to release your reference explicitly. This method takes one parameter: the reference you gain from the `BindToMoniker` call. Remember that because the recorder is an unmanaged, configured component, your access to it goes through COM Interop. When you make a call to `ReleaseComObject`, you are releasing your reference to the runtime callable wrapper, which in turn decrements the recorder's reference count. Once the reference count reaches zero, the recorder is released, and the message is submitted to the queue.

Exception Handling

Although queued components provide a robust environment for distributed applications, problems can still arise. For example, a client may not have sufficient rights to send a message to a component's input queue. In other situations, a component may not be able to process a message that has reached its queue. The second scenario can be particularly nasty because it can lead to a *poison message*. To handle client errors and server-side errors, COM+ provides a way for you to specify an exception-handling class when these problems arise. Before you get into that, examine what happens when clients and servers have trouble processing messages.

SERVER-SIDE ERROR HANDLING

As you know, when a message reaches a component's input queue, the listener server picks up the message and hands it to the player. Even after the message has reached the input queue, problems can arise. For some reason, the message can be unreadable. A more likely scenario might be that the method calls inside the message contain data that the component cannot process.

A poison message occurs when the player attempts to play back the method calls on the component and one or all of the method calls fail. If the component returns a failed `HRESULT` or raises an exception, the player aborts the process and puts the message back on the queue. As the message goes back on the queue, the listener picks it up again and passes it to the player, and the whole process starts again. If there is no mechanism in place to handle the error, the message can loop through the listener and player continuously. Figure 8-7 illustrates this process.

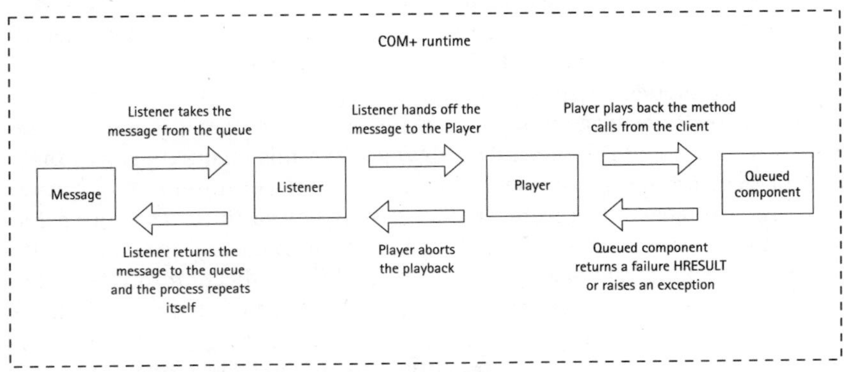

Figure 8-7: Poison messages in queued components

Messages the component cannot process are put on several retry queues. The first time a message fails, it is put on the first retry queue. The first retry queue is `ApplicationName_0`, where `ApplicationName` is the name of the COM+ application hosting the queued component. After one minute, the listener takes the message off the first input queue and tries to process it again. The message is tried three times once it has been taken off the first retry queue. If, after these attempts, the message still cannot be processed, it is placed on the second retry queue: `ApplicationName_1`. Once the message is placed on the second retry queue, the listener waits two minutes before it tries the message again. Assuming the message continues to fail, it is placed on each of the five retry queues. The duration the message sits on each queue becomes longer each time the message falls to another queue. Just as with the first and second retry queues, the message is tried three times on each queue. Table 8-3 lists each of the retry queues, the number of retries for each, and the length of time the message sits on the queue.

TABLE 8-3 QUEUE TIMEOUTS AND RETRY ATTEMPTS

Queue Name	Number of Retries	Time to Wait on Queue (Minutes)
ApplicationName_0	3	1
ApplicationName_2	3	2
ApplicationName_3	3	4
ApplicationName_4	3	8
ApplicationName_5	3	16
ApplicationName_DeadQueue	0	Indeterminate

The last queue in Table 8-3 is the component's final resting queue. A message goes into this queue if it cannot be processed during the other retry attempts. Messages in this queue remain here until they are manually removed with MSMQ Explorer. Once a message is placed in this queue, the listener does not attempt to retrieve it.

The final resting queue and each of the retry queues are private and are created when the COM+ application is marked as queued. If you do not want a message to be retried this many times or to take as long to reach the final resting queue, you have the option of deleting any or all of the retry queues. If you delete all of the queues, a poison message goes directly to the final resting queue. If you delete only a few of the retry queues, the other queues below the ones you delete are moved up in priority. For instance, if you delete the third queue, the fourth queue behaves like the third. In this case, the fourth queue is tried after the second queue fails. Accordingly, messages wait on the fourth queue for eight minutes.

CLIENT-SIDE ERROR HANDLING

For a number of reasons, a client may have problems sending a message to the component's input queue. For example, a client may not have sufficient privileges to submit the message. COM+ handles these types of errors in a similar fashion to the way it handles errors on the component's end. This becomes clearer in the next section.

Unlike the server component, a client does not have retry queues. When a message is determined to be undeliverable, it is moved to the client's Xact dead letter queue. A client has one chance to reuse the message once the message has fallen into the dead letter queue. As a final effort to reclaim the message, COM+ supports the use of a special configured class called an *exception class*.

EXCEPTION CLASSES

Exception classes are special kinds of COM+ components. They are specified through a COM+ attribute called `Queued Exception Class`. Figure 8-8 shows the Advanced tab for a queued component called `QCMarshal.MarshalClass`. In Figure 8-8, I have specified an exception class called `QCMarshal.QC`.

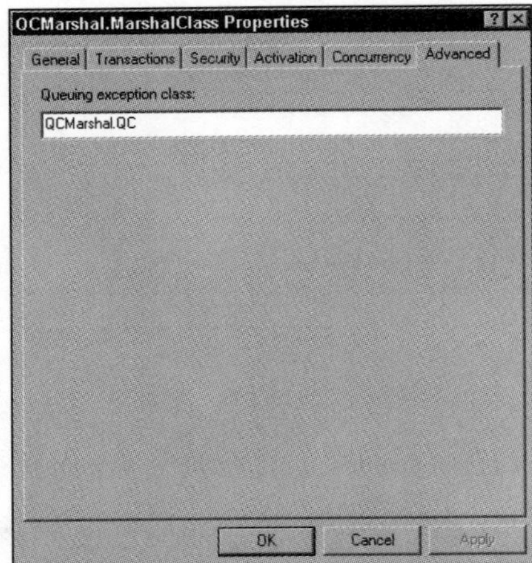

Figure 8-8: Exception class in Component Services Explorer

COM+ uses this exception class in a similar way for both server errors and client errors. This component must implement the `IPlaybackControl` interface. Before COM+ places a message on the component's final resting queue, it looks to see if the component has defined an exception class. If an exception class is present, COM+ calls the `IPlaybackControl.FinalServerRetry` method. This method allows the exception class to try to determine what has gone wrong and to report errors to the developer. For client-side errors, a similar process exists. Before a message goes onto the dead letter queue, COM+ calls the `IPlaybackControl.FinalClientRetry` method. This method is used similarly to the way the `IPlaybackControl.FinalServerRetry` method is used on the server side.

In addition to supporting the `IPlaybackControl` interface, the exception class must implement the queued component's queued interface. After COM+ calls one of the methods on the `IPlaybackControl` interface, it replays method calls on the exception class. At this point, the exception class has one chance to make the transaction happen. If the exception class throws an error, the message is put in the dead letter queue or the final resting queue, depending on which side (server or client) the error has occurred.

Queued Component Design Considerations

Using queued components and components that use loosely coupled events requires specific design considerations. Remember from Chapter 6 that when you design loosely coupled events, you have to keep in mind that method calls go only one way: from the publisher to subscribers. The same is true for queued components. Queued components are perhaps an even more extreme case of one-way processing, as the lifetimes of the client and component do not necessarily overlap. Keeping this central concept in mind helps you understand why queued components must meet the requirements stated in this section.

Before you get into the requirements that components must meet in order to be queued, examine some questions you should ask yourself when trying to decide if you should use queued components.

- Do my clients and components need to talk to each other in real time?
- Do my clients even need a response from the component?
- Must my method calls be guaranteed to make it across the network?
- Can a time lag exist between when the method calls are made and when the component processes them?

These questions are intended to drive your thinking about the differences between synchronous calls and calls made by using MSMQ messages. For instance, in the first question, if your clients do not need access to components in real time, you might consider using queued components. As a general rule, queued components do not respond to their clients about the success or failure of a method call. If your clients are content to make a few method calls and then proceed with other processing, queued components may work for you. The third question deals with guaranteed delivery of MSMQ messages. Because queued components use MSMQ as their transport, method calls can be guaranteed to reach the component. MSMQ provides a more robust delivery mechanism than other techniques such as remote procedure calls.

The final question should drive your thinking regarding batch-processing your method calls. If your clients are comfortable with the fact that the component may not process their method calls in a timely manner, you may be able to use queued components to batch-process your method calls. Think of an order-entry scenario in which users are entering orders all day into an order-entry application. At the end of the day, everyone goes home, and computers are idle. What if those orders can be processed at night – in a type of batch mode – while everyone is gone, instead of being processed as users are entering them? Queued components are an excellent fit for this type of processing. Because the COM+ server application must be running to listen for incoming messages, you can schedule the application to start during off hours. Until that time, messages from the clients sit in the component's input queue.

In addition to the questions mentioned previously, queued components must meet certain requirements before they can be installed as queued components. First and foremost, method calls must not contain output parameters or return values. Remember that return values from a method call in C# are converted to `[out, retval]` parameters in the component's type library. In other words, methods in `ServicedComponent` classes that return values are no good for queued components.

C# supports two keywords, `ref` and `out`, that are illegal in queued components. Both of these keywords affect the behavior of method parameters. The `ref` keyword forces a method parameter to be passed in by reference. Parameters passed in with the `ref` keyword must be initialized before the method is called. During method execution, the method can modify the parameter value, and the new value is returned to the client. The `out` keyword behaves in a similar way, except that the client does not have to initialize parameters before they are passed in. You cannot queue your interfaces if they contain methods that use either of these keywords. In fact, the `Regsvcs` utility does not install your component if it sees methods that have these keywords (assuming you are installing queued components).

C# classes, even those derived from `ServicedComponent`, cannot be passed as parameters to methods. Because the lifetimes of the client and component cannot overlap, a copy of the class must be made as it is sent to the component. Components passed to a queued component's method parameters must be marshaled into an MSMQ message before they can be sent to the component. `ServicedComponent` classes do not support this functionality by default. If you wish to pass your managed components as method parameters, they must derive from a COM interface called `IPersistStream`. This interface enables the recorder to marshal the object into a message and enables the player to unmarshal the component from the incoming message.

Using Other COM+ Services with Queued Components

Other COM+ services such as transactions, security, and loosely coupled events can be used in combination with queued components. Some services, such as loosely coupled events, provide a nice complement to queued components. Other services, such as role-based security, introduce limitations. This section does not address all of the services of COM+ but hits upon the most noteworthy services.

Role-Based Security

COM+ role-based security is supported for queued components even though the lifetimes of the client and component do not overlap. When the recorder packages method calls into an MSMQ message, the client's security context is also included in the message. When the message reaches the component, the player unpacks the client's security context. As the player begins to play back the method calls, the queued component sees the calls as if they were coming directly from the client. Because of this, the queued component can define roles and allow or deny access to its interfaces based on those roles. In addition, calls such as `ContextUtil.IsCallerInRole` are based on the context of the original caller, the client.

Transactions

Transactions are an integral part of queued components. COM+ transactions occur on the client side when the recorder is invoked and on the server side when the ListenerHelper returns the unconfigured player object. For your server-side objects, this means that they are invoked in the `ListenerHelper`'s transaction if they support or require a transaction. If your component runs in the `ListenerHelper`'s transaction and it calls `ContextUtil.SetAbort` or `ContextUtil.DisableCommit()`, the message goes back on the queue and is retried. This can lead to a poison message that ends up on the component's final resting queue if the component consistently aborts the transaction.

The recorder is configured to require a transaction. Clients that run in transactions include the recorder in their transactions when they invoke the queued component through the moniker. If the client aborts the transaction, the message is not delivered to the queued component's input queue. These messages can be taken off the queue during a failed transaction because of MSMQ's support for COM+ transactions. MSMQ provides a resource manager that participates in DTC transactions.

Loosely Coupled Events

Of all the services COM+ offers, loosely coupled events implement the closest development model to queued components. Like queued components, loosely coupled events provide one-way processing of client calls to components.

Queued components can be used to provide asynchronous notification of events. There are a couple of ways queued components can be used with events. Your first option is to make the event class a queued component. In this scenario, publishers use the `Marshal` class and queue moniker to instantiate the queued event class. Method calls are generated and inserted into an MSMQ message as normal. When the messages reach the event class, the recorder plays the methods, and the events fire to subscribers.

Your second option is to queue the interfaces of subscribers. In this option, publishers consume the event class as they normally do but without MSMQ interaction. As events fire, the event system passes method calls to the recorder, and MSMQ delivers messages to subscribers.

Developing Queued Components in C#

This section shows you how to write three implementations of queued components:

- A HelloWorld queued component
- A queued subscribers class in a loosely coupled event
- A queued component implementing an exception class

You will see how .NET supports the development of queued components through attributes from the `System.EnterpriseServices` namespace. Unless I specify otherwise, all of these attributes are in this namespace.

HelloWorld Queued Component

In this example, the client and component are implemented in the same namespace. This may not be your typical implementation, but it serves to demonstrate how the client and component interact. The client in this example is a console application implemented in the `MyApp` class.

Before you get into the code, examine the COM+ attributes and development model for queued components. Figure 8-9 shows the properties dialog for a COM+ application that holds queued components. Two queuing attributes are set at the application level: `Queued` and `Listen`. If the `Queued` attribute is set, the public application queue and the private retry queues are created (at installation). The `Queued` attribute allows the application to receive MSMQ messages. The `Listen` attribute tells COM+ that it should process messages once the application starts.

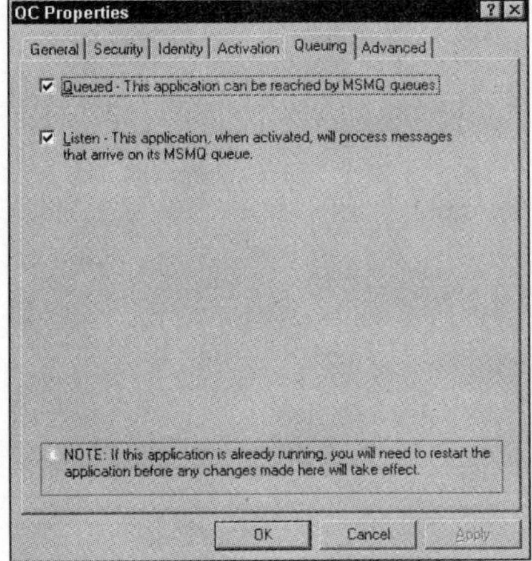

Figure 8-9: Application-level attributes

The next level down from the application is the queued component itself. The only attribute specified on the component is the exception class. In Figure 8-10, the Advanced tab displays an exception class I have configured called `QCNamespace.QCException`. The exception class attribute can be a `ProgID` or `CLSID`.

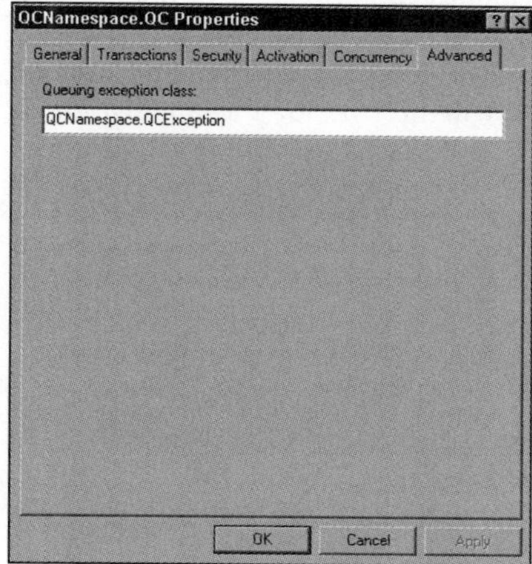

Figure 8-10: Exception class attribute

For the component's interfaces, the final attribute related to queued components is `Queued`. In Figure 8-11, you can see that the `Queued` attribute has been checked on the Queuing tab for the `IQC` interface. When this attribute is enabled, clients can use it to record method calls.

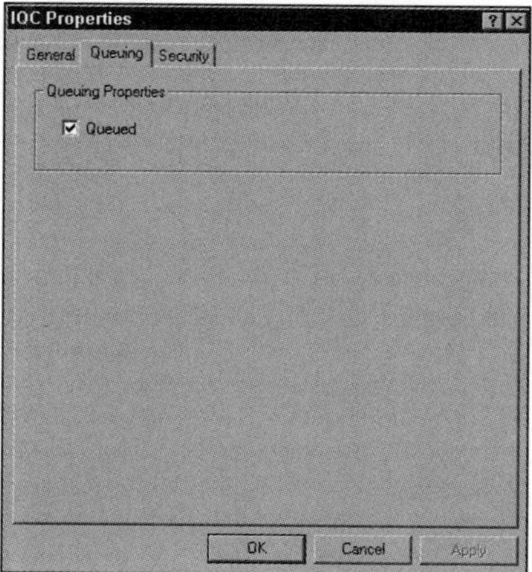

Figure 8-11: Queued attribute for IQC interface

Take a look now at the HelloWorld application. To specify the application-level attributes, use the .NET Framework ApplicationQueuing attribute. The constructor for this attribute sets the attribute's properties to their default values, which means the application is marked as Queued but is not marked to listen for incoming messages.

To enable listening, the QueueListenerEnabled property must be set to true. When the assembly is installed, this property enables the Listen attribute you saw in Figure 8-9.

The ApplicationQueuing attribute has one other property called Enabled. Enabled is a Boolean property that specifies whether or not the application is queued. Using the default constructor sets this property to true and enables queuing for the application. In the code in Listing 8-2, I have set the QueueListenerEnabled and Enabled properties to true.

Listing 8-2: Hello World Queued Component

```
using System.Reflection;
using System.EnterpriseServices;

[assembly: AssemblyKeyFile("QCKey.snk")]
[assembly: ApplicationActivation(ActivationOption.Server)]
[
  assembly:
    ApplicationQueuing(Enabled=true,QueueListenerEnabled=true)
]

namespace HelloWorld
{
  using System;
  using System.EnterpriseServices;
  using System.Runtime.InteropServices;
  using System.Windows.Forms;

  [InterfaceQueuing]
  public interface IQC
  {
    void SayHello(string msg);
  }

  public class QC : ServicedComponent, IQC
  {
    public void SayHello(string msg)
    {
      MessageBox.Show("HelloWorld.QC: " + msg);
    }
```

```
    }

    public class MyApp
    {
      public static void Main()
      {
        IQC iqc;
        iqc = (IQC) Marshal.BindToMoniker("queue:/new:HelloWorld.QC");
        iqc.SayHello("Hello!");
        Marshal.ReleaseComObject(iqc);
      }
    }
}
```

The development of queued components revolves around the interface you define as queued. Interfaces act as the glue between the client and component. Interfaces provide a mechanism that allows the client and component to agree on how they interact with each other. In your example, I have created an interface called `IQC`. This interface has only one method defined: `SayHello`. `SayHello` takes a string parameter. Notice that this method is void; it does not return a value. This is in keeping with the rules for queued components I stated earlier in this chapter. The `InterfaceQueuing` attribute marks this interface as queued when the component is registered. This attribute maps directly to the COM+ attribute you saw in Figure 8-11.

The queued component class is defined below the definition of the `IQC` interface. This class, like all other COM+ classes written in C#, inherits from the `ServicedComponent` class. This class also implements the `IQC` interface. The implementation of the `ICQ.SayHello` method for this class shows the `msg` variable in a message box.

So far, this should be pretty straightforward. This model of interface-based programming should look pretty familiar. In Chapter 6, you write your components in a similar fashion. Things get a little trickier in the console application. I start off by defining an interface variable: `iqc`. This variable holds a reference to the queued component the moniker returns. To invoke the moniker and create the component, use the `Marshal.BindToMoniker` class. The return value for this method is always a `System.Object` class, regardless of the type the moniker is creating. To be able to call methods on this object, cast it to an `IQC` type. The (`IQC`) between the method call and the assignment operator (equal sign) accomplishes this.

Once you have a valid reference to the queued component (specifically, to the recorder) and you have converted the queued component to a type you can use, you can call its methods and release the reference. When you are done with the object, call `Marshal.ReleaseComObject` to release the reference. At this point, the recorder creates the MSMQ message and attempts to place it on the component's input queue.

Loosely Coupled Events and Queued Components

You can extend the preceding HelloWorld example to support loosely coupled events. In the next example, I convert the preceding queued components class into an event class by setting the EventClass attribute. Because the queued components class is now an event class, I can remove the message box function from the SayHello method, as it will not be called anyway.

When these components are installed and registered, the queued component is configured as an event class, and its IQC interface is marked as queued. The QC class still acts as a queued component. After the client calls the SayHello method and releases the object reference, the method calls are packaged into a message and sent to the application. On the server side, the player reads the message and plays back the method calls. At this point, the COM+ event system engages and notifies subscribers (in your case, the QCSubscriber class).

Listing 8-3: Combining Events with a Queued Component

```
using System.Reflection;
using System.EnterpriseServices;

[assembly: AssemblyKeyFile("QCKey.snk")]
[assembly: ApplicationActivation(ActivationOption.Server)]
[
  assembly:
    ApplicationQueuing(Enabled=true,QueueListenerEnabled=true)
]

namespace HelloWorld
{
  using System;
  using System.EnterpriseServices;
  using System.Runtime.InteropServices;
  using System.Windows.Forms;

  [InterfaceQueuing]
  public interface IQC
  {
    void SayHello(string msg);
  }

  [EventClass]
  public class QC : ServicedComponent, IQC
  {
    public void SayHello(string msg)
    { }
```

```
  }

  public class QCSubscriber : ServicedComponent, IQC
  {
    public void SayHello(string msg)
    {
      MessageBox.Show("HelloWorld.QCSubscriber: " + msg);
    }
  }

  public class MyApp
  {
    public static void Main()
    {
      Iqueued components iqc;
      iqc = (IQC) Marshal.BindToMoniker("queue:/new:HelloWorld.QC");
      iqc.SayHello("Hello!");
      Marshal.ReleaseComObject(iqc);
    }
  }
}
```

Exception Classes

In this final example, you extend the queued components class from Listing 8-2 to define an exception class. The `ExceptionClass` attribute defines an exception class `ProgID` or `CLSID` for a queued component. This attribute has one constructor that takes a string representing the exception class's `ProgID` or `CLSID`. If you specify the exception class's `CLSID`, you need to define one by using the `System.Runtime.InteropServices.GuidAttribute` attribute. If you do not define this attribute, one is defined for you when you register the class with COM+.

Listing 8-4: Implementing an Exception Class

```
using System.Reflection;
using System.EnterpriseServices;

[assembly: AssemblyKeyFile("QCKey.snk")]
[assembly: ApplicationActivation(ActivationOption.Server)]
[
  assembly:
    ApplicationQueuing(Enabled=true,QueueListenerEnabled=true)
]
```

```
namespace HelloWorld
{
  using System;
  using System.EnterpriseServices;
  using System.Runtime.InteropServices;
  using System.Windows.Forms;
  using COMSVCSLib;

  [InterfaceQueuing]
  public interface IQC
  {
    void SayHello(string msg);
  }

  [ExceptionClass("HelloWorld.QCException")]
  public class QC : ServicedComponent, IQC
  {
    public void SayHello(string msg)
    {
      MessageBox.Show("HelloWorld.QC: " + msg);
    }
  }
  public class QCExceptionClass :
      ServicedComponent, IPlaybackControl, IQC
  {
    // method from IQC Interface
    public void SayHello(string msg)
    {
      MessageBox.Show("HelloWorld.QCExceptionClass: " & msg);
    }
    // method from IPlaybackControl interface
    public void FinalClientRetry()
    {
      // prepare for the final retry of the message
      MessageBox.Show("HelloWorld.QCExceptionClass:
FinalClientRetry");
    }
    // method from IPlaybackControl interface
    public void FinalServerRetry()
    {
      // prepare for the final retry of the message
      MessageBox.Show("HelloWorld.QCExceptionClass:
FinalServerRetry");
    }
  }
```

```
  public class MyApp
  {
    public static void Main()
    {
      IQC iqc;
      iqc = (IQC) Marshal.BindToMoniker("queue:/new:HelloWorld.QC");
      iqc.SayHello("Hello!");
      Marshal.ReleaseComObject(iqc);
    }
  }
}
```

Remember that exception classes must implement not only the queued interface but also the `IPlaybackControl` interface. `IPlaybackControl` comes from the COM+ services type library (`comsvcs.dll`). To gain access to this interface from the assembly, use the Type Library Importer utility (`tlbimp.exe`). The COM+ services type library carries over as the `COMSVCSLib` namespace. Normally in the `FinalClientRetry` and `FinalServerRetry` methods, you prepare for the queued interface methods to be called. Here, I am just showing a message box on screen that contains the name of the component and the name of the method being called.

Summary

If you retain anything from reading this chapter, I hope you understand how queued components can help you leverage the asynchronous computing benefits of MSMQ. Queued components – when used in the right places – can greatly help you scale your applications. As you go forward and develop .NET applications, ask yourself if your clients need an immediate response from their components. If the answer is no, queued components may be a good solution for you.

Part III

Advanced COM+ Computing

Chapter 9

Remoting

IN THIS CHAPTER

- The .NET Remoting Framework
- Introduction to SOAP
- Remoting ServicedComponents

REMOTING INVOLVES TWO APPLICATIONS talking to each other across a network or some other boundary. Prior to using .NET, developers used remoting architectures such as DCOM. DCOM enabled developers to call other COM components across the network or across a Win32 process boundary. Generally, this worked fine if developers were making calls inside their Intranets. However, as the Internet gained popularity, weaknesses appeared in the DCOM computing model. Often, when an Internet application using DCOM needed to make calls across the Internet, it had to go through firewalls, proxy servers, or routers performing Network Address Translation (NAT). All of this added up to a veritable minefield for DCOM applications.

One of the more recent evolutions in remoting is Simple Object Access Protocol (SOAP). SOAP is a wire protocol that allows you to send and receive method calls across the network. SOAP uses XML to encode method calls and HTTP to transport those calls to their destinations. SOAP solves many of the problems that arise when DCOM is used for Internet applications. Because SOAP uses HTTP, SOAP method calls and normal HTTP requests from a Web browser look virtually the same to a firewall or proxy server.

Nearly seamlessly, the .NET Remoting Framework supports SOAP. In addition, it supports remoting by using other transports and encoders, such as TCP/IP and binary encoders (also called formatters). The beauty of the .NET Remoting Framework is that it allows you to mix and match transport protocols and formatters. You can also develop your own classes to handle the networking and formatting of method calls.

You may be wondering what .NET remoting has to do with COM+. It just so happens that all classes derived from `ServicedComponent` can be plugged into the .NET Remoting Framework. All `ServicedComponent`-derived classes inherit from `System.ContextBoundObject`, which inherits from `System.MarhsalByRefObject`. `ContextBoundObject` and `MarshalByRefObject` ensure that a derived `ServicedComponent` is transported safely across a network or application-domain boundary.

.NET Remoting Framework

The .NET Remoting Framework is a complicated subject. I am sure entire books will be written on the topic. In this chapter, I am not trying to cover everything you can do with the .NET Remoting Framework. You can extend the framework quite a bit by implementing your own channels, `ObjRef`'s, formatters (these terms become clearer later), and so on. This chapter provides an introduction to the pieces of the remoting architecture and framework that apply to most .NET types, such as `ServicedComponents`.

The terms *Marshal, endpoint,* and *well-known object* are used over and over in this chapter. It can be difficult to jump into any topic as complicated as remoting without understanding at least some of the common terms. Before you go on, review what these terms mean in .NET remoting.

Marshaling Defined

When a client creates an instance of a component, it essentially receives a pointer to a memory address where the instance resides. These pointers make sense to the application creating the instance. These pointers, however, cannot be passed outside of their original application domain without a little help. Marshaling addresses this issue by converting references to memory locations that make sense in one application domain into addresses that make sense in another application domain.

However, marshaling involves a little more than just converting memory address *A* to memory address *B*. Marshaling is responsible for transferring a method's call stack from the client to the server. For the purposes of this discussion, think of the *call stack* as the block of memory that defines a method call as it is executing. A call stack consists of the following:

- Parameter types and current values
- Executable code of the method
- Return values
- Any exceptions the method throws

Marshaling takes a method call and transforms it into some format that can be sent across the wire (or application boundary) so the receiving application can pick up the message and re-create the object reference and the method call. The framework performs marshaling in the other direction: from the server back to the client. Often, methods contain out parameters, ref parameters, or return values that need to be marshaled back to the client.

Endpoint Defined

Endpoints are common in any remoting discussion. If you are familiar with HTTP URLs, you should comprehend end points quite easily. In HTTP, a URL looks something like this:

```
http://www.hungryminds.com/mandtbooks/index.html
```

A URL defines an endpoint of sorts to a Web server. Here, the `http://` identifies the protocol being used. For a Web request, the protocol is, naturally, HTTP. Immediately following the protocol definition is the name of Web server. In the preceding URL, the Web server is `www.hungryminds.com`. Following the name of the Web server is the folder and page being requested. In this example, we are requesting `index.html` in the `mandtbooks` folder. The folder and the name of the page tell the Web server at what path the requested resource can be found. Together, the protocol, Web server name, and path define an endpoint.

In the .NET Remoting Framework, endpoints are defined in a similar manner. A client that wishes to invoke a method of a remote component must define an endpoint. As with an HTTP URL, the client must specify an endpoint by providing the protocol, server name, and name of the resource. For example, if you have a Web service on a server called `www.someserver.com` that you want to access from a client application, you can define the endpoint as such:

```
http://www.someserver.com/myappfolder/mywebservice.aspx
```

This should look very familiar. Again, define the protocol, Web server, and path to the resource you are trying to consume. In this example, the Web server hosts the remote component you are trying to access. Once the client connects to the Web server, the `mywebservice.aspx` page instantiates the component and makes the requested method call.

However, to access remote components, the .NET Framework allows you to use other protocols, such as TCP. As you can see in the "Channels" section of this chapter, remote components can be hosted in Windows services. Any Windows service that hosts .NET components for the purpose of remoting must listen on some TCP/IP port for incoming requests. In this scenario, the client must specify the port number when it provides the endpoint to the remoting framework. For example, if you have a client that wishes to connect to a remote component on a Windows service listening to port 9000, the endpoint might look something like this:

```
tcp://www.someserver.com:9000/RemoteComponentName
```

In this example, I specify the protocol as TCP. The server name is still `www.someserver.com`, but this time I have added the port number, 9000. When the client instantiates an instance of the remote component, the remoting framework is intelligent enough to know that you are requesting a component called `RemoteComponentName`.

Well-known Objects

Well-known objects have been registered with the remoting runtime. These are objects in which type information in the form of metadata is available. These objects are considered to be well known because both the client and server are aware of their existence and how they are to be processed. You see in the next section that remotable objects fall into two broad categories: client activated and server activated. Both of these types of objects are considered well known. In fact, all of the COM+ components you write in this chapter are considered well known.

In the preceding discussion regarding endpoints, I give you a TCP example of an endpoint. The last section of the endpoint defines the name of the remote object. This is the name of the well-known object that the hosting application on the server registers.

Marshaling by Reference Versus Marshaling by Value

One of the first things you should think about when designing a remote class is whether you want the client to get its own local copy of the class or whether you want the class to stay on its original server and have clients access the component remotely. The framework considers classes that follow the former scenario to be `MarshalByVal` (marshal by value) types. When a client accesses these kinds of classes, the framework makes a copy of the running instance of the class and transports it across the network to the client. Classes that fall into the latter scenario are called `MarshalByRef` (marshal by reference). `ServicedComponent`-derived classes fall into this category.

MARSHALING BY VALUE

`MarshalByVal` classes are copied in their entirety whenever they are referenced. By nature, class references can be made to `MarshalByVal` types (or to any other type) in any of the following ways:

- Instantiating a new instance of the class
- Passing a class as a parameter to a method call
- Returning an instance of a class as a method's return value
- Accessing a property or field of another class

Classes marshaled by value must implement the `System.Runtime.Serialization.ISerialiable` interface or be decorated with the `System.Serializable` attribute. The `ISerializable` interface and the `Serializable` attribute are used during the marshaling process to convert the in-memory representation of the class into a format that can be transmitted across the network. `ISerializable` gives you greater control over how the class is serialized. This interface defines one method: `GetObjectData (SerializationInfo,`

StreamingContext). The first parameter of this method, System.Runtime. Serialization.SerializationInfo, is a class that allows you to define the types and their values that will be serialized. The second parameter, System.Runtime. Serialization.StreamingContext, is a structure that allows you to define source or destination contexts of the class. The context can be specified as originating from another application domain or from a different computer, among other places. It is important to note that MarshalByVal classes need not implement these two options directly. It is sufficient to inherit, either directly or indirectly, from an ancestor class that implements ISerializable or is attributed with the Serializable attribute.

Decorating a class with the System.Serializable attribute is a little less involved than implementing the ISerializable interface. If you choose to go this route, you gain simplicity and ease of implementation, but you lose a certain amount of flexibility. In other words, you pretty much get what the runtime hands you. In a class that has been marked with this attribute, all fields are marshaled into the destination-application domain, with one exception. The System. NonSerializable attribute is used for fields (of a class marked with Serializable) not to be serialized. As the runtime serializes a class, it skips fields marked with NonSerializable.

MARSHALING BY REFERENCE

MarshalByRef classes stay in the application domain in which they are created. As clients instantiate new instances or reference existing ones, MarshalByRef objects stay put.

For the remoting runtime to marshal a class by reference, the class must inherit from System.MarshalByRefObject or from a derived class such as System. ContextBoundObject. As you know by now, all classes that wish to utilize COM+ services derive from the ServicedComponent class. The ServicedComponent class inherits from the ContextBoundObject class, which inherits from MarshalByRefObject. This means that all ServicedComponent-derived classes can be marshaled by reference. Figure 9-1 depicts the class hierarchy for a ServicedComponent-derived class.

The MarshalByRefObject and ContextBoundObject classes are defined as abstract-base classes. Abstract-base classes such as these cannot be instantiated directly. They are intended to be used solely as base classes for other components. For classes such as ServicedComponent that inherit directly from base classes, the child must implement all methods the class defines. Incidentally, because ContextBoundObject is an abstract class, it does not have to implement the methods of MarshalByRefObject.

DECIDING BETWEEN MARSHALBYVAL AND MARSHALBYREF

If you are implementing ServicedComponent-derived classes, choosing between MarshalByRef and MarshalByVal is moot. Because ServicedComponent inherits from ContextBoundObject, you know that all of your COM+ components are marshaled by reference. But how do you decide which to use if other parts of your application need to be remoted without the help of `ServicedComponent`? Let me give you some criteria to help make that decision.

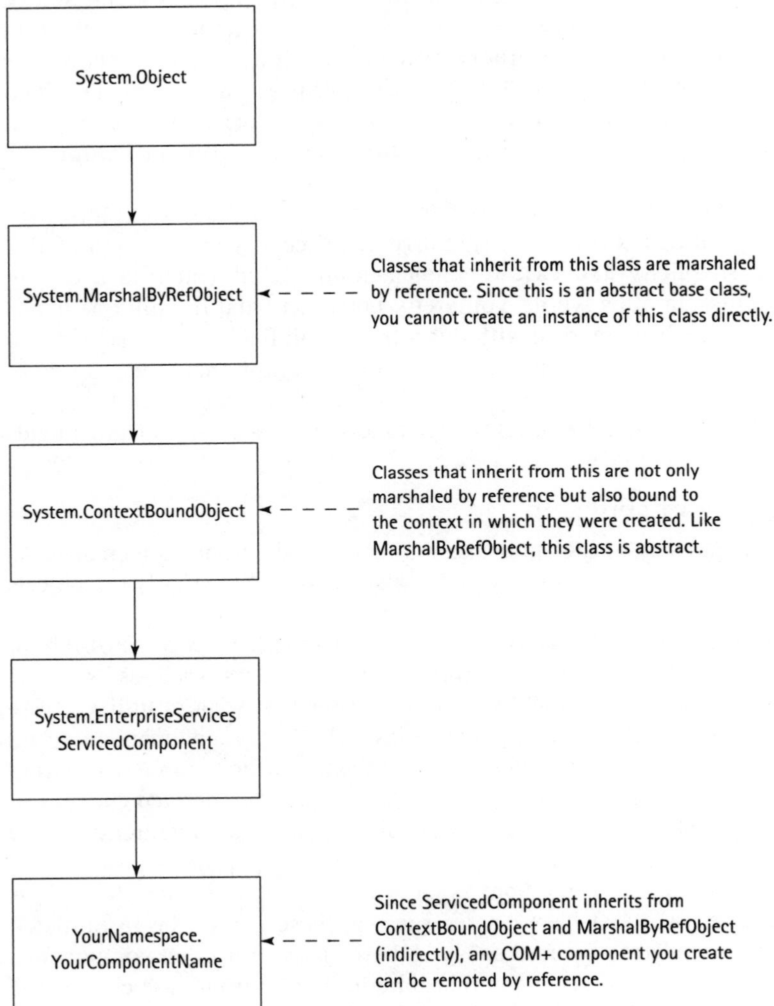

Figure 9-1: Class hierarchy for ServicedComponent

Objects whose complete state can be moved across the network with a minimal performance impact are often good candidates for being marshaled by value. As an object becomes larger, the performance impact from making a copy of it and transferring it across the network can become prohibitive.

Usually, objects that maintain state specific to a particular machine cannot be marshaled by value; thus, marshaling by reference becomes your only option.

Consider a class that wraps access to a file on a particular machine. Unless the entire file itself can be copied to each client, it is not feasible to marshal this class by value.

Many applications that extensively use COM+ services such as object pooling and transactions are deployed on a server farm that has multiple servers. Usually, these servers are much more powerful than your typical client machine. Often, they are configured to perform a specific task. Marshaling these components by reference makes sense in this situation, as you want the component to do its work on the server farm.

CONTEXT-BOUND OBJECTS

Before I go on, I want to explain what a `ContextBoundObject` derived class is and why `ServicedComponent` inherits from this class. A context in .NET remoting is very similar to a context in COM+ (discussed in Chapter 4). Contexts can be viewed from two angles. One way to think of a context is as a property bag for a class. The property bag might contain properties that tell the remoting runtime that access to this class must be serialized or that this class is performing transactional work. A context can also be thought of as a subdivision of an application domain. Remember that an application domain in .NET is a logical process. A Win32 process can have multiple application domains running inside of it. Following that, an application domain can have multiple contexts within itself. Figure 9-2 shows the breakdown of Win32 processes, application domains, and contexts for a remoting application.

Each application domain has at least one context. This is called the *default context.* When a class such as `ServicedComponent` is instantiated inside an application domain, a new context may be created. When types from one context access types in another context, calls are made through a proxy object, unknown to the type originating the call.

`ServicedComponent` derives from `ContextBoundObject` because all COM+ components, and thus all `ServicedComponent`-derived classes, are created either in their own contexts or in the context of their creators. The remoting runtime must be able to bind a `ServicedComponent`-derived class to its context to ensure that none of the access rules such as access serialization are violated.

Activating a Remote Object

To call methods on any kind of class, you must create an instance of the class. When it comes to instantiation, remotable components fall into two categories: client-activated objects and server-activated objects. In both cases, clients continue to use some form of object creation API, such as `new`. *Client-activated objects* are created when the client creates a new instance of the object using the C# keyword `new`. *Server-activated objects,* on the other hand, are activated when the client calls a method.

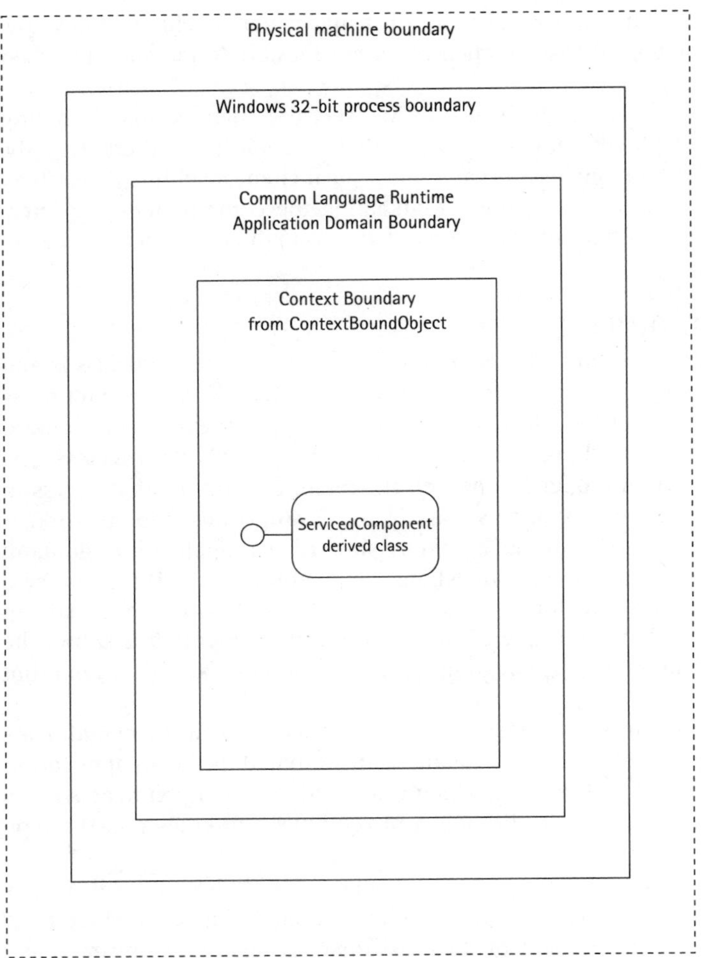

Figure 9-2: Contexts, application domains, and Win32 processes

CLIENT-ACTIVATED OBJECTS

In client-activated objects, the client controls when the object is created. When the client makes an API call to create an instance of the component, the remoting architecture creates the remote component and returns a reference to the client. Each instantiation the client makes creates a new component on the server.

Remember that the client controls when a client-activated object is created. The server, on the other end of the remoting architecture, does not differentiate between a client-activated object and a server-activated object. The client decides when the component is instantiated by using specific APIs.

Client-activated objects, unlike server-activated objects, allow you to create instances of remote objects by using *parameterized constructors*. Using the `new` keyword is probably the most straightforward way to use parameterized constructors. Another way to use parameterized constructors is with the `Activator.CreateInstance` method. The `Activator` class comes from the `System` namespace. `CreateInstance` is an overloaded method that can be used to pass in an `object []` array. The array contains the parameters for the object's constructor.

SERVER-ACTIVATED OBJECTS

Server-activated objects fall into two categories: `Singleton` and `SingleCall`. Instead of the client, the remoting runtime running on a server creates the instances. Both of these types of objects are created when the client calls a method on the object. The first time the client calls a method, an object-creation request appears in the network transmission. The .NET Remoting Framework does not support the creation of server-activated objects by using parameterized constructors.

`SingleCall` objects are very similar to JIT components in COM+. The remoting runtime instantiates an instance of a `SingleCall` object each time the client calls a method (Figure 9-3). Remember that if a component is marked to enable Just In Time Activation (JITA), COM+ automatically creates an instance of the component just before a method call occurs; in addition, COM+ destroys the instance after the call returns. `SingleCall` objects work in the same way. A new instance of the remote object services each method call coming from the client. The `Singleton` object is alive only for the duration of a method call.

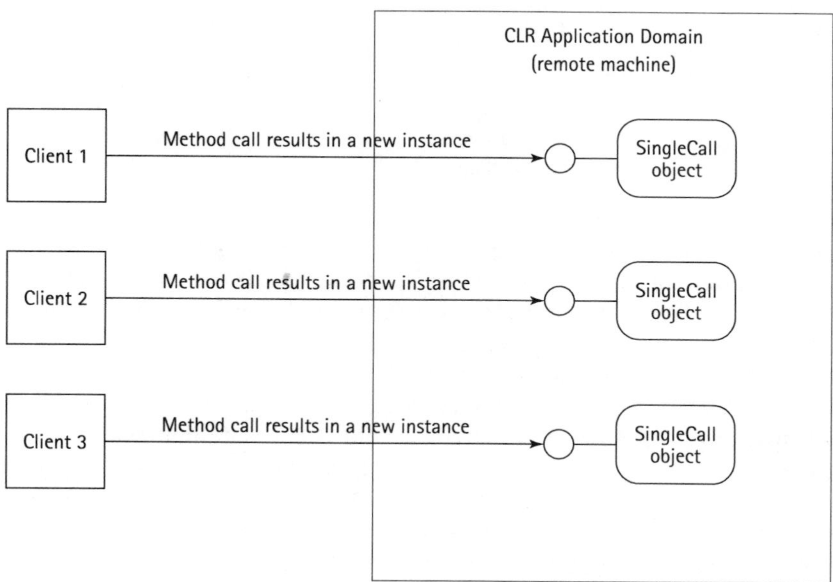

Figure 9-3: SingleCall object with multiple clients

`Singleton` objects are created when the client makes a method call. The first client to make a method call takes whatever hit is associated with the creation of the object. Subsequent calls from the client, or calls from other clients, are serviced from the original instance of the object (Figure 9-4). In other words, `Singleton` objects service all client requests from one instance. A lease determines the lifetime of a `Singleton` object when the object is instantiated. The lease has a default expiration associated with it. Once the remoting runtime has determined that the lease has expired, the runtime deactivates the object. Once this happens, the object becomes eligible for Garbage Collection.

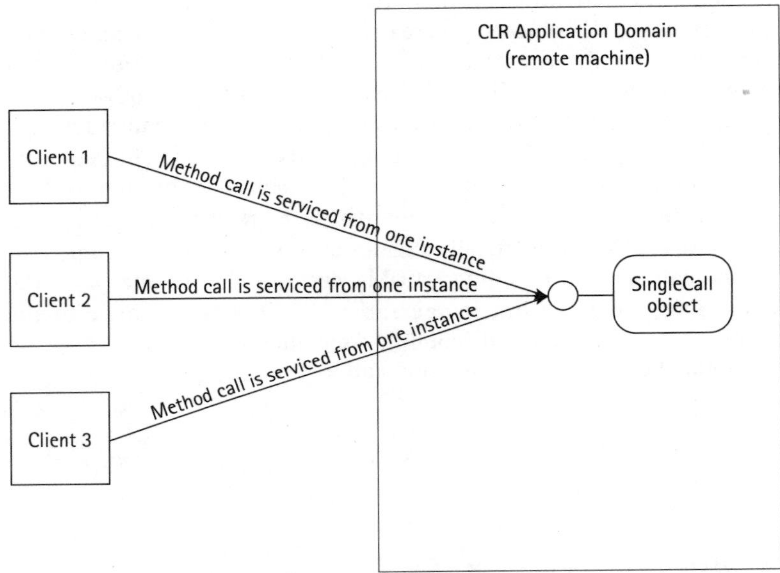

Figure 9-4: Singleton object with multiple clients

It is important to understand state issues when dealing with both types of server-activated objects. Both of these types of objects are stateless. If you understand how JIT components in COM+ become stateless, you are well on your way to understanding how `SingleCall` objects are stateless. The concept is the same for both development models. Because a `SingleCall` object is destroyed after each method call, there is no way for the object to hold any state — at least not any client state. Technically speaking, a `Singleton` object can hold client state, but this is a bad idea for a couple of reasons. First of all, if one of these types of objects holds client state, at some point it might contain state from multiple clients. If the object were to update a database by using properties previously set by a number of clients, the database might become corrupted. Another reason to avoid holding state in a `Singleton` object is that the object's lease can expire at any time without the client's knowledge. If this happens, no exception can be raised for the client to detect. The original object is disconnected from the remoting runtime. A new instance of the object is created when the next method call is made. The state the original object holds is lost when the object is destroyed.

If you need to maintain state in your remote objects, client activation is your best route. Because a new instance services each client, these types of objects can safely hold state. Keep in mind, however, that many of the rules related to non-deterministic finalization apply here. If the object holds expensive resources, it should implement some sort of close method or dispose method. If the network goes down before the client can call one of these methods, the resource may be released only when the remote object becomes unreachable (by going out of scope) and Garbage Collection occurs. The object does not go out of scope until the lease has expired and the remoting runtime has released the object.

Proxies

When the client instantiates an instance of a remote component, it is able to call methods on the component as if it were running within its own application domain. Once you figure out how to instantiate a component in the manner you like, you are free to use the instance as if it were any other type within your application. Proxies fool the client into thinking it is dealing with an actual instance of the remote object. In reality, the proxy is forwarding method calls to the remoting framework, which, in turn, connects to the remote machine and delivers the method call to the remote component. The remoting framework implements two proxies that work together to provide this functionality: the transparent proxy and the real proxy.

THE TRANSPARENT PROXY

The *transparent proxy* intercepts calls from the client and forwards them to the real proxy object. When the client creates an instance of a remote object, regardless of the object's activation type (server activated or client activated), the remoting run-time returns a transparent proxy. As the client calls methods, the transparent proxy verifies that the methods (and their parameters) are consistent with the type being used. In other words, if the client instantiates a class called `CFoo` and calls one of `CFoo`'s methods, such as `CFoo.DoSomething`, the transparent proxy intercepts the call to `DoSomething` and explores several questions:

- Does `CFoo` have a `DoSomething` method?
- Are the method parameters the correct type?
- Is this a public method?
- Does `CFoo` live in another application domain?

The transparent proxy uses the client's local copy of the remote object's assembly to verify the method call. Take a look at Figure 9-5 to clear this up.

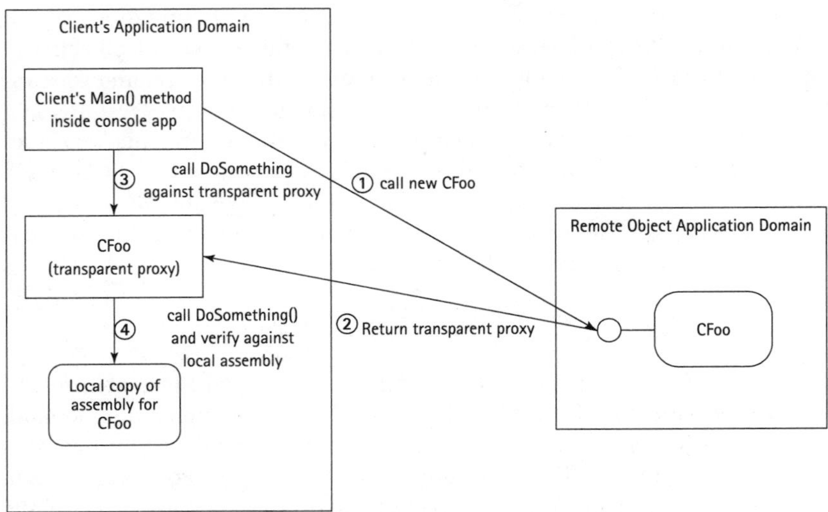

Figure 9-5: The transparent proxy intercepts method calls.

In Figure 9-5, you see a console application creating a new instance of the `CFoo` class. Assume that this is a client-activated object and that `CFoo` inherits from `MarshalByRefObject`. When the client's call to new `CFoo` (step 1) returns, the client gets an instance of the transparent proxy, although it thinks the proxy is `CFoo`. When the call to `DoSomething` is made, the transparent proxy intercepts the call and verifies it against the type information in the client's local assembly. This assembly contains the definition for `CFoo`. Assuming the parameters for `DoSomething` are correct, the transparent proxy forwards the call to the next step in the remoting process: the real proxy.

The transparent proxy is responsible for transforming a client's method call into a message that can be handed off to the real proxy. The message contains all of the method's parameters and their values. The transparent proxy takes a snapshot of the method call at runtime and converts it to a message-class object. The message object must implement the `System.Runtime.Remoting.Messaging.IMessage` interface. I discuss messages later in this chapter. For now, understand that the transparent proxy is responsible for constructing the message and forwarding it to the real proxy.

The transparent proxy is an internal class the remoting framework implements. You never create an instance of the transparent proxy yourself. However, sometimes it is useful to know if you are dealing with a remote proxy or an actual instance. `RemotingServices.IsTransparentProxy` is a static method you can use to determine if the instance of a class is a transparent proxy or a real object instance. This method takes a `System.Object` parameter. In the preceding example, if the variable holding your instance of `CFoo` were called `foo`, this call would be `RemotingServices.IsTransparentProxy (foo)`.

THE REAL PROXY AND OBJECT REFERENCES

The *real proxy* is responsible for communication between the transparent proxy and the rest of the remoting runtime. I mentioned previously that the transparent proxy forwards method calls in the form of an `IMessage` interface to the real proxy. The real proxy takes the message and forwards it the appropriate channel. I discuss channels in the next section. For now, think of a channel as the piece of the remoting framework that knows how to send and receive data from the wire.

The transparent proxy forwards a message to the real proxy through the real proxy's `Invoke` method. The `Invoke` method takes one parameter, an object that implements the `IMessage` interface. The real proxy class is defined in the `System.Runtime.Remoting.Proxies` namespace. The real proxy class is yet another abstract class that a client cannot instantiate directly. Just as the transparent proxy is implemented for you, so is the real proxy. However, unlike the transparent proxy, the real proxy can be extended if it needs to be.

The real proxy handles communication coming from the remote object. When a remote object is instantiated, the real proxy forwards the activation request to the remote object and waits for a response. If the remote object is to be marshaled by reference, the response that comes back is in the form of an object reference, called an `ObjRef`. The `ObjRef` is a class that contains the following information about the remote object:

- The remote object's strong name
- The remote object's class hierarchy
- The remote object's supported interfaces
- The remote object's URI
- The remote object's list of channels registered on the server

The real proxy uses the information in `ObjRef` to create an instance of a transparent proxy. To understand how all of this works, take a look at Figure 9-6 to see what happens when a client (through client activation) instantiates an instance of a remote `MarshalByRef` object.

In Figure 9-6, the client's activation request goes out to the remote object's application domain when the client creates a new `CFoo` instance by using the `new` keyword. Once the remote object is created, the remoting runtime returns a reference to it in the form of an `ObjRef`. In stage 2, the remoting runtime on the client sees that a response has come back from the server and creates an instance of `System.Runtime.Remoting.Proxies.RealProxy`. The real proxy reads the information about the remote object from `ObjRef` and creates an instance of the transparent proxy (stage 3). Once stage 3 is complete, the client is free to make method calls on the remote object.

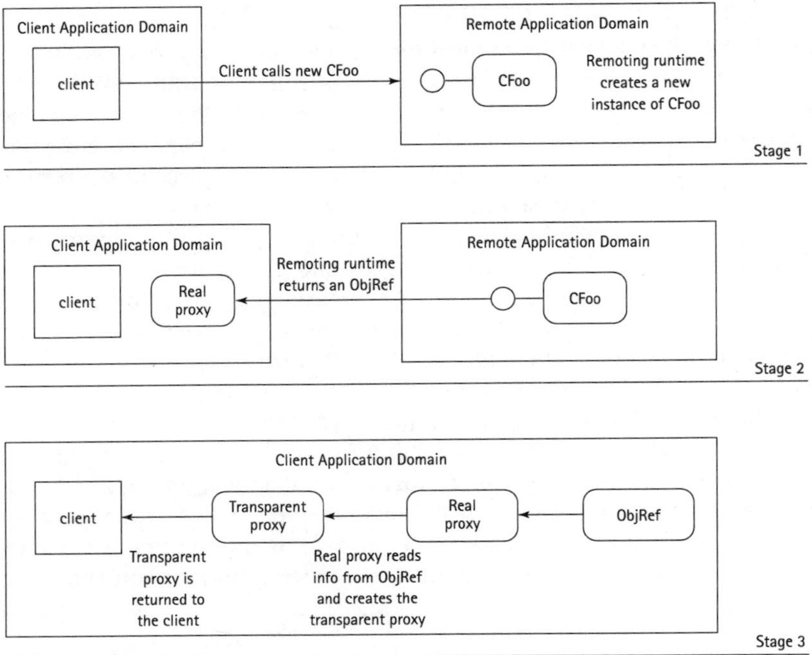

Figure 9-6: Client activation of marshal by reference object

Channels

Channels are the part of the remoting framework that takes a message and sends it across the network to the destination machine. They know how to communicate by using various network protocols: HTTP, TCP/IP, SMTP (used for e-mail), and even MSMQ. The only two protocols the .NET Framework supports out of the gate are HTTP and TCP/IP. To use the preceding protocols, or any other, for that matter, you have to implement your own channel. All of the types needed to work with channels are in the following namespaces:

- `System.Runtime.Remoting.Channels`
- `System.Runtime.Remoting.Channels.Tcp`
- `System.Runtime.Remoting.Channels.Http`

The Channels namespace contains classes needed to register channels and interfaces needed to implement custom channels. A channel is registered for an entire application domain. If a client or object wishes to communicate remotely, at least one channel must be registered in the application domain. Multiple channels can be registered with multiple application domains in a process.

Two channels cannot be registered to listen on the same TCP/IP port. To understand this limitation, take a step back and consider the TCP/IP protocol. Note that when I mention TCP/IP here, I am not talking about the TCP channel but the networking protocol itself. TCP/IP defines a remote application as an IP address plus a port. TCP/IP maps a port to a Win32 process. The IP address specifies the machine. Together, the IP address and the port number define an endpoint in TCP/IP. One of the rules of TCP/IP is that no two processes can be listening for traffic on the same port. When I say that no two channels in .NET can be registered on the same port, I do so because it is a requirement in TCP/IP.

Channels fall into three categories:

- Client-side channels
- Server-side channels
- Channels that are both client side and server side

Client-side channels implement the `IChannelSender` interface from the `Channels` namespace. Client-side channels can send only messages going from the client to the server. Server-side channels listen for incoming messages from the client. Server-side channels must implement the `Channels.IChannelReceiver` interface. Channels that wish to send and receive message must implement both interfaces.

I mentioned previously that the remoting framework supports two channels for the HTTP and TCP/IP protocols. As you can guess, the HTTP channel uses a Web server to host remote objects. Both client and server HTTP channels use types from the `System.Net` namespace to communicate to and from the Web server. If you choose the HTTP channel, the remoting framework encodes messages in XML by default. The XML takes the form of SOAP messages. The TCP channel encodes messages into a special binary format before it transfers the message over the wire. Server-side TCP channels are commonly hosted in Windows services. Of the two channels, TCP offers better performance for applications. Messages that go through the TCP channel do not have to go through the Web server before they can be processed, and they do not have to be read in by an XML parser. The HTTP channel, however, does offer greater interoperability with the Internet. Because HTTP uses well-known ports such as port 80, it is more firewall friendly than the TCP channel. In addition, HTTP can be proxied easily if clients are accessing the Internet through proxy servers.

Remote Object Lifetime

In the good ol' days of COM, an internal reference count determined object lifetimes. As clients passed around references to components, the reference count increased. As clients released their references, the component's reference count decreased. When the last client released its hold on a component, the reference count went to zero, and the component deleted itself from memory. Problems arose when COM components were remoted across the network. If a client was disconnected from the network before it could release its reference to the component, the reference count could not reach zero, and the component could not delete itself. The .NET remoting infrastructure takes a slightly different approach to object lifetime. When a client instantiates an instance of a marshal by reference class, a lease is created for that class. The lease determines the lifetime of the remote class. If the lease expires and the remoting runtime cannot renew the lease, the class is dereferenced and becomes eligible for Garbage Collection.

Leases are types that implement the `ILease` interface. `ILease` comes from the `System.Runtime.Remoting.Lifetime` namespace. This interface contains properties that define a number of aspects of the lease:

- The time remaining in the lease
- The current state of the lease
- The initial lifetime of the lease
- The timeout for trying to connect to a sponsor
- The amount of time for which the lease is renewed when called

Essentially, the time remaining in the lease is the time that the remote object has left to live before it is disconnected from the remoting runtime and marked for Garbage Collection. A lease can be in any of the following states:

- Active
- Expired
- Initialized but not activated
- Not initialized
- Currently renewing

The fourth property of the preceding list (Not initialized) is the initial length of time for which the lease is valid. Once this period has expired, the remote object is released, assuming the lease has not been renewed. If this property is set to null, the lease does not time out. In this case, the remote object attached to the lease is not freed until the application domain is torn down. A sponsor is a class that can renew the lease. The sponsorship timeout value of the lease determines how long the remoting runtime waits while it tries to connect to one of the specified sponsors. If the lease is about to expire and a sponsor cannot be reached to renew the lease within the time the sponsorship timeout specifies, the lease expires, and the remote object is released.

The final property of the preceding list (Currently renewing) is the amount of time by which the lease increases when the lease is renewed. Leases can be renewed in a number of ways:

- The client specifically calls the lease's Renew method.
- The remoting runtime contacts a sponsor to renew the lease.
- A client calls a method on the remote object.

For the lease to be renewed when a client calls a method, the lease's RenewOnCallTime property must be set.

The ILease interface defines methods that can be used for the following:

- Registering a sponsor for the lease
- Renewing the lease
- Removing a sponsor from the lease

A sponsor is registered with the Register method. This is an overloaded method that takes an ISponsor interface as one of its parameters. The ISponsor interface can also be found in the System.Runtime.Remoting.Lifetime namespace. The overloaded Register method takes a TimeSpan instance in addition to an ISponsor interface implementer. The TimeSpan maps to the RenewOnCallTime property.

The lease is renewed through the ILease.Renew method. This method takes a TimeSpan instance used to increase the lifetime of the lease. The TimeSpan passed to this method is added to the CurrentLeaseTime property to increase the lease's lifetime.

The runtime holds a list of sponsors for any particular lease. When a sponsor is to be removed from the lease, the UnRegister method is called. UnRegister takes an instance of ISponsor to unregister the sponsor. This instance is one of the classes used in a call to Register.

Implementers of the MarshalByRefObject class initialize leases. MarshalByRefObject contains two methods — GetLifeTimeService and InitializeLifetimeService — used to initialize and return classes that implement the ILease interface. GetLifetimeService returns an instance of type object. A caller of this method is expecting a type that implements the ILease interface. Any MarhalByRefObject implementer should ensure that an object this method returns implements the ILease interface. The IntializeLifetimeService method initializes a new lease and returns it to the caller. By implementing this method, implementers of MarshalByRefObject can initialize the lease properties such as the sponsorship timeout and the initial lifetime.

Introduction to SOAP

Certainly, you have heard a lot of noise about SOAP, specifically noise related to Web services. SOAP is an acronym for Simple Object Access Protocol. SOAP is a specification. It establishes a format that remote method calls can take when they are transferred across the network. SOAP uses XML to describe the data involved with a method call. The SOAP 1.1 specification, fully supported in .NET remoting, allows any transport protocol to be used to carry SOAP messages across the wire. The most common transport protocol used with SOAP is HTTP, but others can be used as well:

- Simple Mail Transfer Protocol (SMTP)
- File Transfer Protocol (FTP)
- Message Queuing (MSMQ or IBM MQ Series)
- Remote Procedure Call (RPC)

This is by no means an extensive list of protocols that can be used in conjunction with SOAP, but I hope the list gives you an idea of how extensible SOAP can be. For the purposes of this discussion, focus on using HTTP with SOAP, as this is the most common implementation.

HTTP Header

To make a method call using SOAP and HTTP, the client must know how to formulate a proper HTTP request header. Take a look at an HTTP header you might see in a typical SOAP request:

```
POST /MyApp/MyPage.aspx HTTP 1.1
Host: www.myserver.com
Content: text/xml
Content-Length: 100
{crlf}
<< post data here >>
```

The first line of the request header specifies three pieces of information:

- The HTTP request method
- The path to the requested resource
- The version of HTTP being used

The request method can be any valid HTTP request method. The two most common are `Get` and `Post`. When you open your browser and type a URL or click a link on a Web page, you are using the `Get` method. Often, but not always, when you fill in a form on the Web and submit it, you are using the `Post` method. The `Post` method is favored when dealing with SOAP for a couple of reasons. First, the `Post` method allows you to send more data than a `Get` method allows you to send. Second, when you pass information with a `Get` request, that information must be appended to the end of the path via a question mark. This can become rather cumbersome if you are trying to send a lot of information with the request. The second line of the request represents the Web server for which the request is intended. Usually, this is the fully qualified domain name, but it can be a NetBios name or TCP/IP address. The third and fourth lines of the request represent the type and length of the content, respectively. For SOAP requests, the content type is `text/xml`, meaning that the following data is XML. The `Content-Length` tells the Web server how many bytes of data it can expect in the request. Here, I set the content length to 100 bytes. The carriage return, line feed combination (`{crlf}`) after the content length signifies the end of the HTTP header and the beginning of the request payload. In my example, the line that reads `<< post data here >>` is intended to represent the request payload. For SOAP requests, this represents the SOAP message. I talk about the SOAP message in the next section.

SOAP Message

A SOAP message is an XML document that consists of two parts: the SOAP header and the SOAP body. The header and body of the message are put inside the top-level XML element known as the SOAP envelope. Conceptually, a SOAP message looks like Figure 9-7.

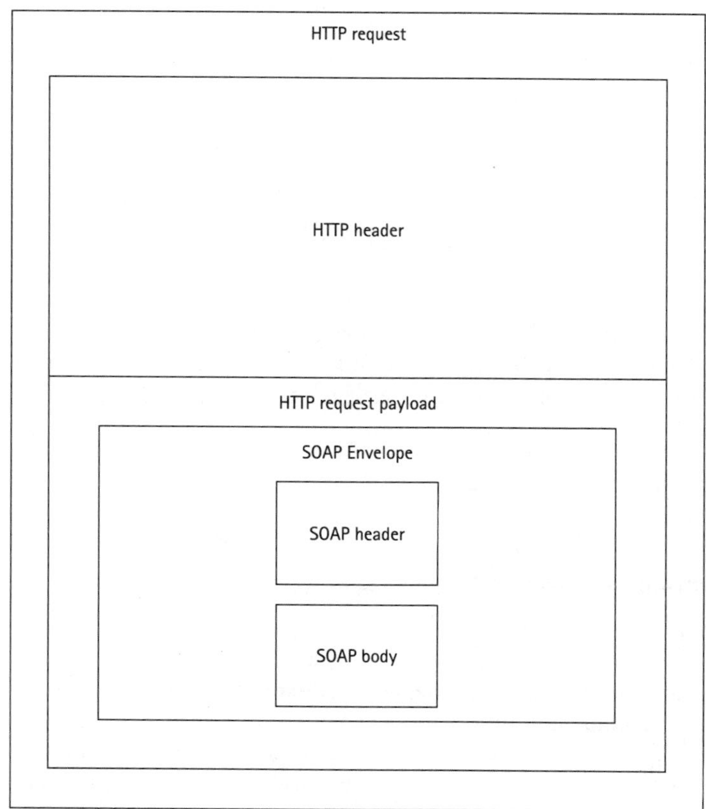

Figure 9-7: SOAP message logical structure

Usually, the SOAP envelope element looks something like this:

```
<SOAP-ENV:Envelope
xmlns:SOAP-ENV="http://schemas.xmlsoap.org/soap/envelope/"
SOAP-ENV:encodingStyle="http://schemas.xmlsoap.org/soap/encoding/"
/>
```

The first line of this code listing specifies the element name. The SOAP envelope element is named, logically enough, `Envelope`. The `Envelope` element must be present in every message. The `SOAP-ENV` part is a namespace alias. The `SOAP-ENV` alias is used to provide an easier handle to the namespace defined in the second line. `xmlns` is an XML attribute used to specify a schema. For the SOAP envelope, the schema is defined at the URL: `http://schemas.xmlsoap.org/soap/envelope/`. The envelope schema contains information that defines the header and body elements, as well as other attributes that affect the processing of the message. I describe other attributes in a moment. The last line of the code listing specifies a schema to be used for the encoding of the method call. The encoding schema defines the data types that can be used with SOAP. Some of the data types are the following:

- Doubles
- Strings
- Boolean values
- Floats
- Arrays
- Dates

The SOAP header is an optional element. If the header is present, the SOAP specification says that the header must be the first child of the `Envelope` element. A SOAP header can be used for a number of purposes, each related to customizing the SOAP message:

- Custom authentication
- Transaction processing
- Associating this message with other messages
- Routing the message

Implementing a custom authentication scheme is probably the first thing people think of when they look at implementing SOAP headers. In this scenario, a receiving application can read the header information and authenticate the client before processing the rest of the message. The rest of the scenarios mentioned previously work in a similar fashion. The purpose of the header is to allow the remoting framework to extend the message in whatever way it sees fit.

I want to back up for a moment and talk about the attributes from the SOAP-ENV namespace I mentioned previously. This namespace defines two global attributes that affect the header: actor and mustUnderstand. The actor attribute defines a recipient (in the form of a URI) for which a particular header element is intended. A SOAP message may not go directly from the sender to the ultimate receiver of the message; somewhere along the way, other applications may need to read the message and perform some processing on it before sending it on. The actor attribute indicates what header elements are intended for what receivers. Once a receiver reads a header element, it must either remote the element or replace it with another intended for the next recipient.

The second attribute defined in the SOAP-ENV namespace is mustUnderstand. This attribute is boolean (set it to 0 or 1). If it is set to 1, the receiver of the message must either process the header element or completely reject the SOAP message and return an error to the sender. This tag ensures that the processor of the message at least attempts to process the element and does not just skip it. To get a feel for how these attributes are applied to a SOAP header, I have given you a sample header in Listing 9-1. For readability, I have not included the top-level Envelope element.

Listing 9-1: Example of a SOAP Header

```
<SOAP-ENV:Header>
  <auth:CustomAuthentication
    xmlns:auth="http://www.myserver.com/schemas/auth/"
    SOAP-ENV:mustUnderstand="1"
    SOAP-ENV:actor="http://myserver.com/myOtherApp/somepage.asmx">
      MyAuthenticationMethod
  </auth:CustomAuthentication>
</SOAP-ENV:Header>
```

Following the header is the mandatory Body element. The Body element can include any of three types of child elements:

- Method call
- Method response
- Error response (fault)

A method call contains the name of the method, the name of the parameters, and their values. The current version of the SOAP specification supports only one method call per message.

Suppose a client makes a call that looks like the following on a method named PlaceOrder:

```
// method signature: PlaceOrder(string Sku, int CustomerNumber, int
Qty)
int OrderNumber = someobj.PlaceOrder("sku123", 1009, 3)
```

In this method call, the client is placing an order for customer 1009 and for 3 units for product number sku123. The body of the SOAP message for this call looks like Listing 9-2.

Listing 9-2: Example of a SOAP Body

```
<SOAP-ENV:Body
  <order:PlaceOrder
    xmlns:order="http://myserver.com/schemas/orders">
      <sku>sku123</sku>
      <customernumber>1009</customernumber>
      <qty>3</qty>
  </order:PlaceOrder>
</SOAP-ENV:Body>
```

In Listing 9-2, the method parameter names and their values are converted to elements beneath the method name element: `PlaceOrder`. When the server successfully processes this request, it sends the response back in the form of a method-response message. Method-response messages return method-return values and out parameters to the sender. In the example, the `PlaceOrder` method returns an integer but no out parameters. The resulting SOAP message looks something like this:

```
<SOAP-ENV:Body
  <order:PlaceOrderResponse
    xmlns:order="http://myserver.com/schemas/orders">
      <PlaceOrderResult>988</PlaceOrderResult>
  </order:PlaceOrder>
</SOAP-ENV:Body>
```

The naming convention for a method call response is to add the word `Response` to the end of the method name. A similar convention is used with the return value. Instead of `Response`, `Result` is used to name the element that contains the return value of the method call. If you have out parameters in the method call, they show up as sibling elements to the result.

A fault message is the last child element that can be found in a body section. A fault message is sent as the result of some sort of error that has occurred on the receiver side of the transmission or as the result of some status information that needs to be displayed. A SOAP fault element defines four subelements that make up the fault message:

- `faultcode`
- `faultstring`
- `faultfactor`
- `detail`

The `faultcode` is an error code conceptually similar to the response code in the HTTP protocol. The client or other software should use the `faultcode` to determine the reason for the error programmatically.

The `faultstring` is similar to the error messages you may have seen from HTTP from time to time. This element provides a human-readable error message for the user or developer to view.

The `faultfactor` identifies the source of the error. This takes the form of a URI. If the header element of the request message has specified an `actor` and the `actor` has produced the error, the `faultfactor` points to the URI of the `actor`.

The `detail` element contains information specific to the processing of the body of the message. If this element is not present, the receiver of the fault message can assume that the body of the original request has not been processed. The following is an example of a fault message:

```
<SOAP-ENV:body>
  <SOAP-ENV:fault>
    <faultcode>SOAP-ENV:VersionMismatch</faultcode>
    <faultstring>invalid namespace for SOAP Envelope</faultcode>
  </SOAP-ENV:fault>
</SOAP-ENV:body>
```

Remoting ServicedComponents

I mention previously that `ServicedComponent`-derived classes are automatically remotable by virtue of being indirect children of the `MarshalByRefObject` class. This means that any `ServicedComponent`-derived class can be marshaled by reference across the network. In this section, you develop three kinds of `ServicedComponent` classes:

- A `SingleCall` component using SOAP and the HTTP channel
- A `SingleCall` component using the TCP channel
- A client-activated `ServicedComponent`

SingleCall Component Using SOAP and HTTP

Start with a SingleCall ServicedComponent called CFoo. The code for this component is shown in Listing 9-3.

Listing 9-3: SingleCall Component Using SOAP

```
Namespace RemoteComponent
{
  using System.EnterpriseServices;
  public class CFoo : ServicedComponent
  {
    public int PlaceOrder(string Sku, int CustomerNumber, int Qty)
    {
      // do some database work here to add the order
      // return the order number
      return OrderNumber;
    }
  }
}
```

As you can see, nothing is special about the CFoo class. The resulting assembly name for this namespace is RemoteComponent. Things get interesting when this component needs to be hosted. For this example, I use the Web server to host the component. Because I am using the Web server, I also choose the HTTP channel and the SOAP formatter. To host this component, a virtual directory must be created. Virtual directories can be created by using the Internet Services Manager snap-in. Assume that a virtual directory has been created on a server called www.myserver.com. The name of the virtual directory is RemoteComponent. There must be a directory called bin under the RemoteComponent directory. When a client tries to access this component on the Web server, the remoting runtime looks in the bin directory to find the assembly dll file. The last thing needed is the web.config file. This configuration file is used by many applications such as ASP.NET pages. For this example, the web.config file tells the remoting runtime what type of server activation (SingleCall or Singleton) you want to use for this component. The web.config file that I use for this example is shown in Listing 9-4.

Listing 9-4: Using web.config for Remoting

```
<configuration>
  <system.runtime.remoting>
    <application>
      <service>
        <wellknown mode="SingleCall" type="RemoteComponent.CFoo,
        RemoteComponent"
```

```
        objectUri="/RemoteComponent/RemoteComponent.soap"/>
      </service>
    </application>
  </system.runtime.remoting>
</configuration>
```

The real information conveyed here is in the `wellknown` element and its attributes. The `mode` attribute specifies the server-activation mode (in this example, `SingleCall`). The `type` attribute specifies the fully qualified type name (namespace + class name) and the name of the assembly. Both the assembly name and the namespace of the component are called `RemoteComponent`. The final attribute is the `objectUri`. The `RemoteComponent.soap` file at the end of the URI does not exist. When the Web server sees a request for a file with a `.soap` extension, it invokes a handler. The handler for a `.soap` extension forwards the request to the remoting runtime.

This is pretty much all it takes to host a component in Internet Information Services. Notice that I do not specify a channel or a formatter. Because I am hosting the component in the Web server, the HTTP channel and the SOAP formatter are assumed by the remoting runtime. The code in Listing 9-5 is for the client of the `RemoteComponent` class.

Listing 9-5: RemoteComponent Class Client

```
using System;
using System.Runtime.Remoting;
using System.Runtime.Remoting.Channels;
using System.Runtime.Remoting.Channels.Http;
using RemoteComponent;

Public class ClientApp
{
  public static void Main()
  {
    HttpChannel http = new HttpChannel();
    ChannelServices.RegisterChannel(http);
    Type trc = typeof(RemoteComponent);
    RemoteComponent rc =
      Activator.GetObject(trc,
"http://www.myserver.com/RemoteComponent/RemoteComponent.soap");
    int OrderNumber = Rc.PlaceOrder("sku123", 1009, 3);
    Console.WriteLine(OrderNumber.ToString());
  }
}
```

Essentially, the client goes through a three-step process:

1. Create and register an HttpChannel.
2. Create a new instance of the RemoteComponent.
3. Use the RemoteComponent by calling the PlaceOrder method.

The Activator class is a static class from the System namespace. It can be used to create objects that are either inside or outside of the current application domain. The GetObject method defines the type of remote component created and the component's endpoint. The typeof() statement is a C# keyword that returns an object of type System.Type. With the type information specified in the local copy of the RemoteComponent assembly and the endpoint, the remoting runtime is able to find and consume the remote component. Notice that the endpoint the client specifies is the same path as that specified in the web.config file on the server. The remoting runtime uses the path information on the client and server to match the request to the RemoteComponent component. Because this is a server-activated component, the component is not instantiated until the PlaceOrder method is called.

In Listing 9-5, the client specifies the endpoint and channel information in code. You can include this information in a configuration file. In Listing 9-6, I have taken this information out of the client's code and placed it in a configuration file called ClientApp.config.

Listing 9-6: ClientApp.config Configuration File

```
// filename: ClientApp.config
<configuration>
  <system.runtime.remoting>
    <application>
      <client url="http://www.myserver.com/RemoteComponent">
        <wellknown
          type="RemoteComponent.CFoo, RemoteComponent"
  url="http://www.myserver.com/RemoteComponent/RemoteComponent.soap"
          />
      <channels>
        <channel type="HttpChannel, System.Runtime.Remoting"/>
      </channels>
    </application>
  </system.runtime.remoting>
</configuration>
```

In this configuration file, I have created a well-known type: RemoteComponent.CFoo. When the client starts, it instructs the remoting framework to load the configuration file and to register CFoo as a well-known type on the client. Because I have specified the HTTP channel, the remoting runtime forwards requests to http://www.myserver.com/RemoteComponent/RemoteComponent.soap over this channel. The new client code, shown in Listing 9-7, is greatly simplified.

Listing 9-7: Using ClientApp.config in the Client

```
using System;
using System.Runtime.Remoting;
using RemoteComponent;

Public class ClientApp
{
  public static void Main()
  {
     RemotingConfiguration.Configure("ClientApp.Config");
     CFoo foo = new CFoo();
     int OrderNumber = foo.PlaceOrder("sku123", 1009, 3);
     Console.WriteLine(OrderNumber..ToString());
  }
}
```

The RemotingConfiguration class is used to configure the remoting framework on behalf of the client. Once the configuration file is loaded, you are free to use the remote class as if it were local.

SingleCall Component Using Binary Formatter and TCP

Using the TCP channel on the client and server is not much more difficult than using the HTTP channel. If you use the TCP channel, however, you must find a host other than the Web server to host the component. For this example, I use a console application to host the component. Usually, you want to host the component in a Windows service so that someone does not need to be logged on to the server console, but for this example a console application adequately demonstrates the TCP channel. You can use a configuration file on the component end to configure the remoting framework. The configuration file for this process looks similar to the web.config file I use earlier and is registered in a similar manner similar to the way the client registers ClientApp.config file. Because I have already covered how to use the web.config file, I do not repeat these steps in the next example. Instead, I register a well-known type through code. The code for the console application that hosts the component is shown in Listing 9-8.

Listing 9-8: Console Application for RemoteComponent

```
Using System;
Using System.Runtime.Remoting;
Using RemoteComponent;
public class ComponentApp
{
  public static void Main()
  {
    TcpChannel tcp = new TcpChannel(8000);
    Type t = typeof(RemoteComponent.CFoo);
    string uri = "tcp://www.myserver.com/RemoteComponent/";
    RemotingConfiguration.RegisterWellKnownServiceType(
      t,
      uri,
      WellKnownObjectMode.SingleCall);
    Console.WriteLine("Listening for Requests on port 8000 ...");
    Console.ReadLine();
  }
}
```

The port I have chosen for this example is 8000. The remoting framework listens for requests coming in on this port. The call to `RegisterWellKnownServiceType` registers the `RemoteComponent` as a `SingleCall` object. I place the last two lines in the `Main` method so the application does not exit as soon as I register `CFoo`. If the console application is not running, it cannot listen for requests.

If I continue with the previous client, `ClientApp`, I do not have to change any of its code. To use the correct endpoint, channel, and port, I need to change only the configuration file, as shown in Listing 9-9.

Listing 9-9: Using the TCP Channel from ClientApp.config

```
// filename: ClientApp.config
<configuration>
  <system.runtime.remoting>
    <application>
      <client url="http://www.myserver.com/RemoteComponent">
        <wellknown
          type="RemoteComponent.CFoo, RemoteComponent"
          url="tcp://www.myserver.com:8000/RemoteComponent/"
          />
      <channels>
        <channel type="TcpChannel, System.Runtime.Remoting"/>
      </channels>
    </application>
```

```
  </system.runtime.remoting>
</configuration>
```

The modifications to the configuration file change the URL of the component to use the TCP protocol on port 8000 and the channel listing to a `TcpChannel` instead of an `HttpChannel`. The fact that I do not break the original client code is one of the benefits of using a configuration file to configure the remoting framework.

Notice that neither of these examples specifies a formatter. It is possible to mix and match formatters and channels by using the remoting framework. When I specify a channel such as `HttpChannel`, the remoting framework associates a default formatter. The default formatter for the `HttpChannel` is SOAP; the default formatter for the `TcpChannel` is the `Binary` formatter.

Client-Activated ServicedComponent

The `CFoo` class can be activated upon a client's request. This is accomplished either through a call to `new` or by using the `Activator.CreateInstance` method. For this example, I choose the `Activator.CreateInstance` method. The server-side code can remain untouched. You can host the component in any number of hosts such as the Web server, a console application, or a Windows service. For this example, assume you are hosting the component by using the Web server. The code for the client is shown in Listing 9-10.

Listing 9-10: Client-Activated ServicedComponent Class

```
using System;
using System.Runtime.Remoting;
using System.Runtime.Channels;
using System.Runtime.Channels.Http;
using RemoteComponent;

Public class ClientApp
{
  public static void Main()
  {
     RemotingConfiguration.Configure("ClientApp.Config");
     CFoo foo = (CFoo) Activator.CreateInstance(Typeof(CFoo));
     int OrderNumber = foo.PlaceOrder("sku123", 1009, 3);
     Console.WriteLine(OrderNumber.ToString());
  }
}
```

In Listing 9-10, the client loads the configuration file and calls one of the overloaded `CreateInstance` methods. When this method is executed, the creation request goes to the remote component. The remote component's constructor is called, and an ObjRef is passed to the client. When the remoting runtime on the client receives the ObjRef, it creates the RealProxy, which, in turn, creates the transparent proxy. Once the RealProxy creates the transparent proxy, it returns the transparent proxy reference to the client.

CreateInstance has eight overloaded methods in all. Some of these overloads allow you to create instances of the component without having to make a reference to the assembly. In this case, the method returns an instance of a System.Runtime.Remoting.ObjectHandle class. This class can be used for passing a reference to the RemoteComponent to application domains other than the client's application domain. Yet another overload of this method allows you to specify arguments to a remote component's constructor. For instance, if the RemoteComponent class has a constructor other than the default, you can pass a System.Object array to one of the overloads. Each element in the array represents an argument to the component's constructor.

Summary

The .NET Remoting Framework is a vast topic. A single chapter is really not enough to cover all the ground. In this chapter, I have tried to give you an overview of the basic components of the framework as well as related technologies such as SOAP.

As a COM+ developer using the .NET Framework, you have a number of options for remoting your components. Because ServicedComponent-derived classes can be made visible from COM clients, you have the option of using DCOM. As you see in the Chapter 8, you have the option of using queued components to transport method calls via MSMQ. As you see in this chapter, the .NET Remoting Framework offers a third option for remoting your components. The .NET Remoting Framework is much more extensible than either of the previous options. Less experienced developers can get up and running faster by using the framework's default functionality, although more experienced developers can get down to the metal and write their own formatters and channels.

Chapter 10

The Future of COM+ and .NET

IN THIS CHAPTER

- New features of COM+ 1.5
- New features of IIS 6.0
- New features of MSMQ

So far in this book, I have covered every major feature of COM+ in Windows 2000. I thought it might be fun for you to get a sneak peak at the new features of COM+ in the next version of Windows 2000 Server, called Windows 2002 Server. At the time of this writing, the next version of COM+ on Windows 2002 server is code-named COM+ 1.5, although this name is likely to change before it goes out to the public. In addition to covering the new features of COM+ 1.5, I give you the low-down on the new features of IIS 6.0 and MSMQ. As you'll see in this chapter, many of these features center on improving the robustness of your Web applications. Before I go on, I should point out to you that the information in this chapter comes from the beta 2 version of Windows 2002. Some of the features described in this chapter may not make it into the final version of the product. Conversely, some features not mentioned in this chapter may appear in the product's final release.

New Features of COM+ 1.5

As MTS and COM+ have matured, we have seen features added to the services provided for serviced components. COM+ 1.5 continues this trend. Many of its new features provide a more reliable environment for applications. Some of its features help you version and deploy your applications. Even as this chapter is being written, Microsoft has included nine new features in beta 2 alone:

- COM+ applications as Windows NT Services
- Application partitions
- Application process dump
- Component aliasing

- Configurable isolation levels
- Low-memory activation gates
- Process recycling
- Public and private components
- Application pooling

COM+ Applications as Services

Windows 2000 offers such operating-system services as IIS, the COM+ Event System, and the Computer Browser services. Even the COM+ System package in Windows 2002 has been configured to run as a service. Services can be configured to start automatically (when Windows starts) or to start manually.

COM+ 1.5 offers a new activation option that allows a COM+ application to become a Windows service application. Figure 10-1 shows the new options for this feature in a COM+ application.

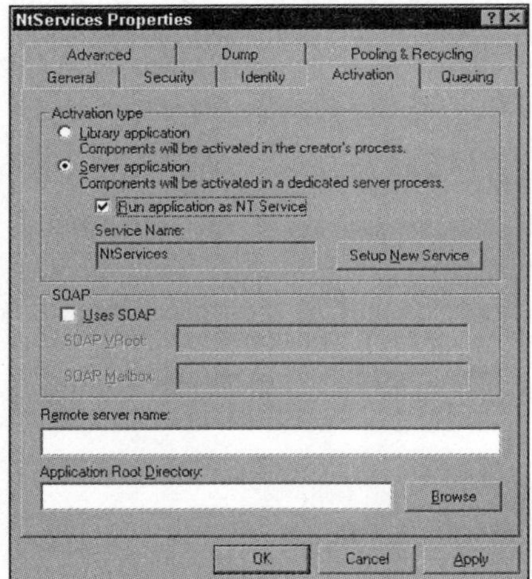

Figure 10-1: New service activation options

An application must be configured as a server application before it can be run as a service. In Figure 10-1, I have checked the Run Application as NT Service option to enable this application to run as a service. Once this change has been applied, I can configure the service just as I configure other services in Windows.

When you click the Setup New Service button, you get the Service Setup dialog box, shown in Figure 10-2. Here you can configure any of the usual service options:

- Service name
- Startup type (manual or automatic)
- Error handling
- User account to run the service as
- Any dependencies on other services

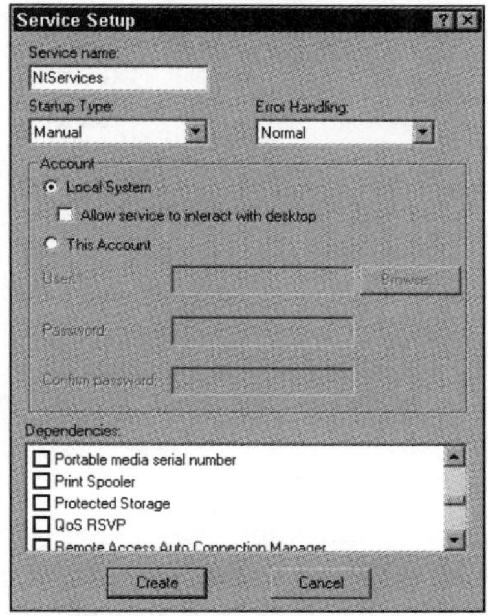

Figure 10-2: The Service Setup dialog box

The service name is simply the name that shows up in the Services MMC snap-in. If the service's startup type is set to automatic, the service starts when the operating system starts. If the manual option is checked, on the other hand, an administrator must go into the Services snap-in and start the service. The Error Handling option is used to specify a level of severity should the service not start up. Various actions can be taken to remedy the situation, based upon a level of severity. The user account that the service runs under can also be configured in this step. Just as with any other service, you can choose to run the service as the local system account or as another local-user account or domain-user account. At the bottom of the dialog box shown in Figure 10-2, you have the option of specifying other services on which the application depends. For instance, if your application is accessed through IIS, you can specify that IIS is a dependency.

Once the application has been configured to run as a service, you are able to see it in the Services snap-in. Figure 10-3 shows the NtServices application listed in the Services snap-in. Although you cannot see the full description, this field is carried over from the description field in the application.

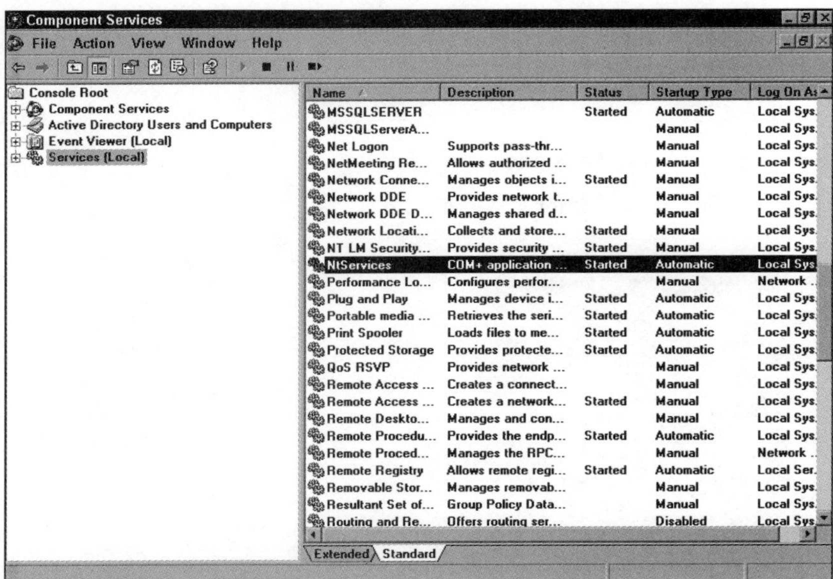

Figure 10-3: NtServices application as a Windows service

So when might this feature be useful? Your application may benefit from this feature in a couple of scenarios. At some point, you may want an application to run under the identity of the local system account. Although this may not always be wise for security reasons, it may be something you need for other reasons. You may want the application to start when the operating system starts. It's wise to reboot your servers when users are not trying to use them. This feature allows you to start the application before user requests start coming in. This way, the first user to request a component out of the application won't be subject to the performance hit of starting a server package. Along this line, you may want server applications that contain pooled components to be configured as services. If the application starts as a service, the component pool is populated (to the minimum value, of course) and is ready for use. Again, the first user does not take a performance hit when the server application starts and populates the component pool.

Application Partitions

Application partitions allow multiple versions of an application (server or library) to be installed on one computer. Installing various versions of an application on a computer allows you to configure various aspects of the package, such as security settings and roles. If the application being partitioned is a server application, it can be configured to run under various user accounts. Figure 10-4 shows the logical relationship between an application and two application partitions. In this figure, Application *A* is configured in Partitions *A* and *B*.

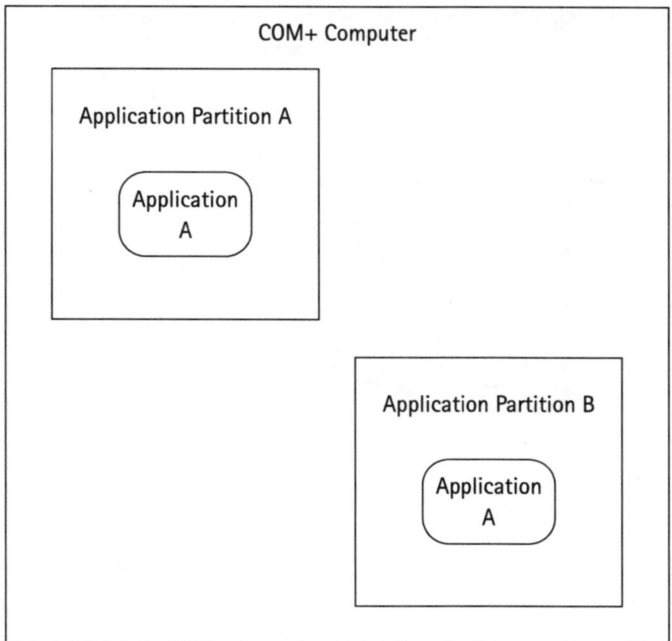

Figure 10-4: One application in two partitions

You should understand that the application is essentially copied from one partition to another. The components that reside inside the application do not change. It is not necessary for you to change your components in any way when you create an application partition. Depending on the client's security credentials, COM+ will service a component request from any one of the permitted application partitions.

You set up an application partition by first creating a partition inside the COM+ Application Partitions folder. The first step in creating a new partition is to give the partition a name. In Figure 10-5, I call my new partition SalesAccounting. During this step, a Partition ID is automatically assigned to the partition. The Partition ID is a GUID like those assigned to any application, interface, or component. In addition to the Partition ID, a partition has four attributes similar in function to those in an application. The partition attributes are the following:

- Partition name
- Partition ID
- Description
- Disable Deletion
- Disable Changes

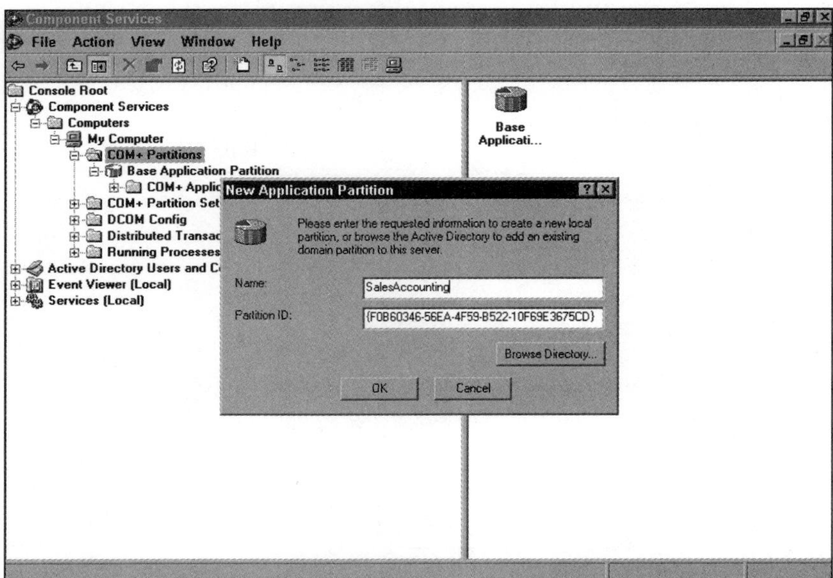

Figure 10-5: Creating a new application partition

Once the application partition is created, it is listed in the COM+ Partitions folder. In Figure 10-6, you can see the new SalesAccounting partition listed in the COM+ Partitions folder.

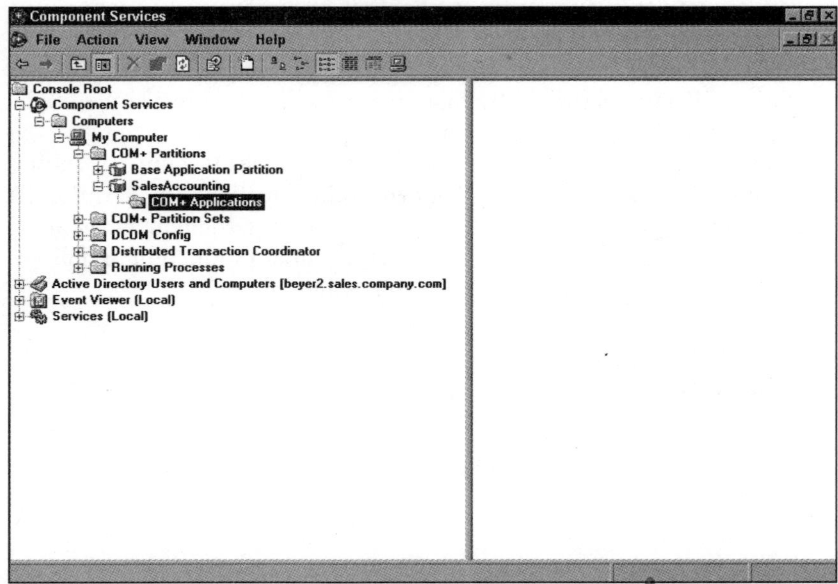

Figure 10-6: The new SalesAccounting partition

Applications can be created inside partitions just as any normal application is created. Once an application has been created in a partition, it can be copied to another partition. Different application partitions can be mapped to different users. Users can be either local machine users or domain users.

You may have noticed in Figure 10-6 the Base Application partition. This acts as a default partition for applications not assigned to a particular partition.

Partitions themselves can be organized into partition sets. *Partition sets* can be created for local machine users or domain users. A partition set created on a domain controller can be made available to domain users and groups. In an Active Directory domain, users are mapped into *Organizational Units (OUs)*. You can define access to a partition set by using OUs. When a domain user requests an application that is part of a partition set, the user's OU is mapped to a partition set. If the user's OU cannot be mapped to a partition set, the user has access to applications in the Base Application partition only. A user's domain identity also helps COM+ determine the partition where an application is located. Incidentally, the Base Application partition is part of every partition set by default.

Application Process Dump

A COM+ application can be configured to dump an image of its process upon application failure. An administrator can manually dump a running application. The dump is a snapshot of an application's memory space at runtime. This information can be used later to diagnose problems such as memory exceptions associated with the application. Figure 10-7 shows the Dump tab in an application's property dialog box. By default, COM+ dumps an application's memory state to the `%systemroot%\system32\com\dmp` folder. The number of dump images can be configured in the Dump tab.

An application can be dumped at runtime. Here an administrator can take a nonintrusive snapshot of a running application. A developer can view the dump at a later point by using a tool such as the Windows debugger in the Platform SDK.

Component Aliasing

Component aliasing allows you to install multiple instances of a component in an application or in multiple applications. When a component is aliased, it is given a new ProgID and a new CLSID. An administrator or developer can optionally specify the new ProgID and CLSID, but the Component Services snap-in provides default values. Figure 10-8 shows the Alias Component dialog box. Using this dialog box, you can specify the application in which the component is aliased.

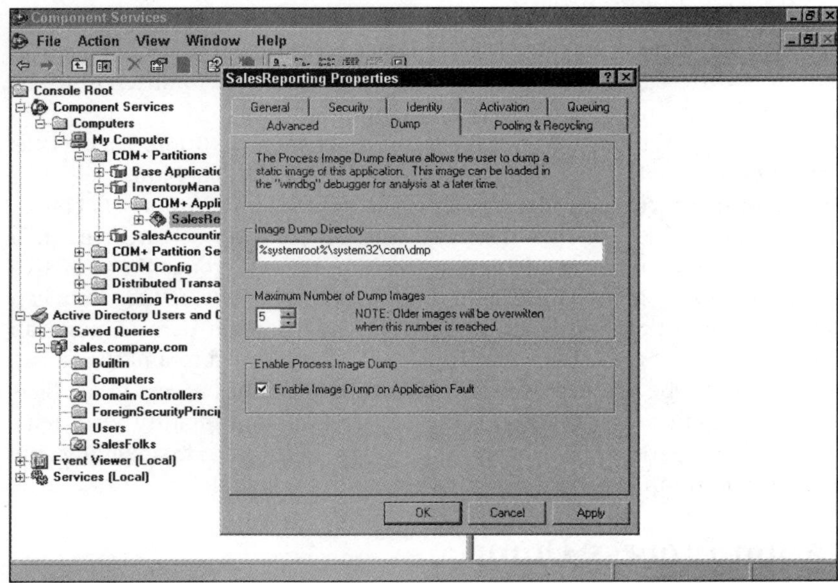

Figure 10-7: Application Dump tab

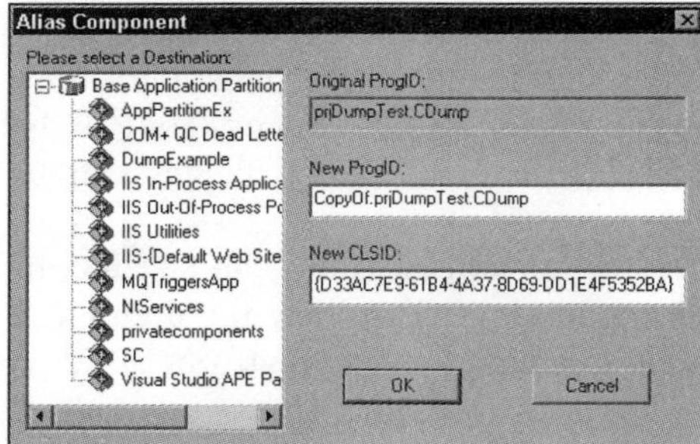

Figure 10-8: Alias Component dialog box

With component aliasing, a developer can alias a component in order to specify multiple constructor strings, perhaps for use with different databases. Any component property (for example, transaction support, activation characteristics, and the level of concurrency) can be changed for an aliased component.

Configurable Isolation Levels

In Chapter 4, I talk about isolation levels in terms of COM+ transactions. The isolation level determines the level of locking of resources during a transaction. The higher the isolation level, the more restrictive the locking scheme. The highest isolation level is Serialized. This is the only isolation level supported in COM+ on Windows 2000.

The next version of COM+, on the other hand, allows the isolation level to be configured to any of the following values:

- Any
- Read uncommitted
- Read committed
- Repeatable read
- Serialized

Choosing an isolation level lower than Serialized improves the performance and throughput of applications. Be aware that choosing an isolation level other than Serialized, however, may allow other readers of your data to see it in an inconsistent state. A component must have a transaction attribute of Supported or higher before the isolation level can be set.

Low-Memory Activation Gates

The purpose of the *low-memory activation gate* feature is to prevent components from being created during low-memory conditions. When components are created under low-memory conditions, problems can occur later in the application. If the application has a memory leak, the leak can exhaust all available memory. When this occurs, the application becomes unresponsive and must be shut down.

COM+ prevents low-memory activation for components by checking an application's virtual-memory usage against a threshold value. If the available virtual memory falls below the threshold value, COM+ fails the client's creation request. COM+ predetermines the threshold value for all applications. The client cannot change the value of the threshold.

Process Recycling

I have experienced countless applications that have become unresponsive. When an application becomes unresponsive, the only thing you can do is go into the Component Services Explorer and shut it down. An application can become unresponsive for a number of reasons. Unless you are collecting runtime information from the application as this is happening, it can be impossible to determine the problem.

Running your applications in a managed environment such as .NET can reduce some of these problems. But face it; if someone writes bad code – managed or not – his or her application is going to fail, and someone is going to have to shut down the application periodically.

Microsoft understands that the need to shut down an application from time to time is a reality. Process recycling can be used to shut down an application that has become unresponsive. An administrator or developer can use a number of criteria to determine when an application should be shut down:

- Lifetime limit
- Memory limit
- Expiration timeout
- Call limit
- Activation limit

The *lifetime limit* specifies a timeout (in minutes) for an application. When an application starts, COM+ starts the timeout. As soon as the application has run for the allotted time specified by the lifetime timeout, COM+ shuts it down. The next client instantiation request starts the application, and the process restarts.

Applications whose memory usage exceeds the memory-limit criteria are also shutdown. The application is shut down if its memory usage exceeds the limit for more than one minute. The *memory limit* can be set to any value between 0 and 1,048,576 kb.

COM+ uses the *expiration timeout* value to determine when a process that has been recycled should be shut down. The expiration timeout value differs from the lifetime limit in that the former applies to a recycled process whereas the latter applies to a process that has not been recycled yet.

The *call limit* determines the number of calls an application services before being shutdown. Calls can be instantiation requests for a component, or they can be method calls.

The *activation limit* specifies the number of component creations the application can serve before being shut down. Components that use JITA may need a higher limit than components that service multiple method calls with the same component instance.

To accommodate this new feature, Microsoft has added a tab in the Application Properties dialog box. Figure 10-9 displays the new Pooling & Recycling tab in Component Services Explorer. In the Application Recycling section, the recycling criteria are set to their default values.

Application Pooling

You may in Figure 10-9 another section called Application Pooling. This feature allows multiple Windows processes to act as one application. When an application starts, COM+ creates as many instances of the `dllhost.exe` process as the pool size defines. As client requests come in, they are equally distributed across these instances of `dllhost.exe`. Figure 10-10 demonstrates how requests from three clients are serviced from four instances of `dllhost.exe` – together acting as a single application. In this illustration, any instance of `dllhost.exe` can service any client request.

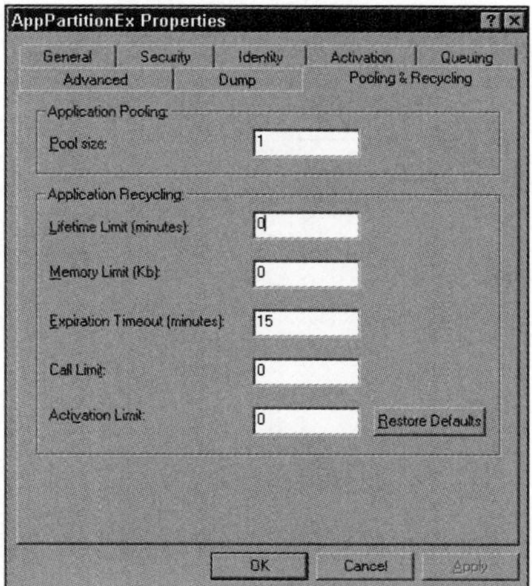

Figure 10-9: Pooling & Recycling tab in Component Services

New Features of IIS 6.0

It seems that every application today uses a Web server in one way or another. Many COM+ applications use IIS to make components available to users on the Internet or on a company Intranet. The features of IIS and COM+ are closely related. In fact, some of the features in IIS come directly from COM+. Because such tight integration exists between IIS and COM+, it is particularly relevant to cover the new features of IIS 6.0.

IIS 6.0 offers many enhancements that administrators and developers can leverage. Often, features targeted toward administrators are of interest to developers as well. Although I do not cover all of the new features of IIS, I do cover those that developers are most interested in. The features discussed here can help you increase the performance, scalability, and reliability of your applications.

- New server architecture
- Application pools and Web gardens
- Server modes
- Worker-process management
- ASP template cache tuning
- XML support for the metabase

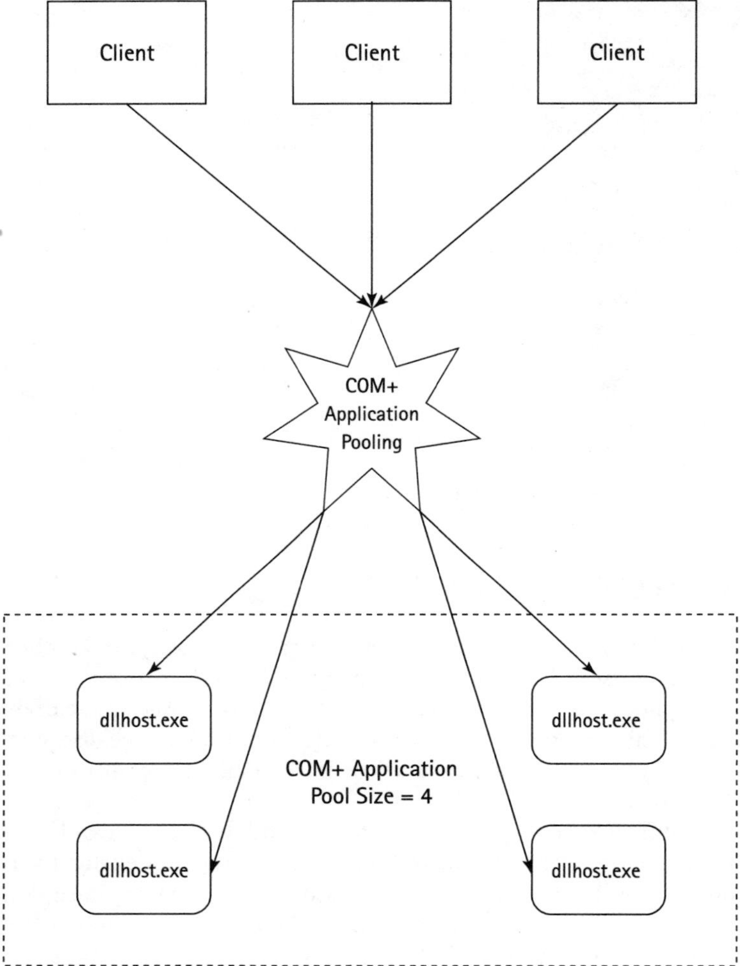

Figure 10-10: Application pooling

New Server Architecture

In IIS 5 (Windows 2000 version), the core functionality of the Web server resides in a service called W3SVC. In IIS 6.0, the architecture of the W3SVC service has been modified. The new Web-server architecture consists of four new or modified components:

- New kernel mode driver: `http.sys`
- Web Administration Service (WAS)

- XML metabase
- Worker processes for applications

Figure 10-11 illustrates the order in which these components are used to service a request. When a request comes in for a URI, `http.sys` sees the request and passes it up to the *Web Administration Service (WAS)*. WAS uses data from its XML metabase to apply rules or settings to the request. WAS then passes the request to the Web application. The Web application can be run from a separate worker process.

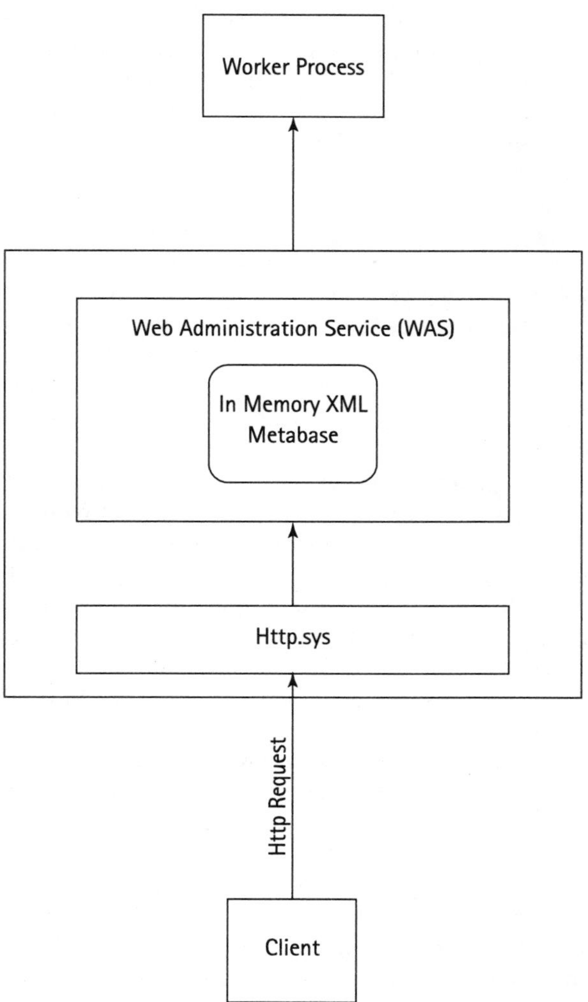

Figure 10-11: IIS 6.0 W3SVC architecture

One of the more exciting (at least to me) enhancements to IIS is the use of a kernel mode driver called `http.sys`. This file sits directly on top of the TCP/IP stack, which means it can handle requests much faster than older versions of IIS. `http.sys` has several responsibilities.

- Taking HTTP requests off the wire and passing them through the Web server
- Throttling bandwidths of HTTP requests
- Logging texts

`http.sys` implements a response-caching mechanism. When a request for a particular URI comes in, `http.sys` checks its own internal cache to see if it has already sent a response for that URI. If the requested URI is found in the cache, `http.sys` services the request from cache without forwarding the request to the Web application. This results in a much faster response time, as IIS does not have to switch from kernel mode to user mode to process the request. This enhancement even allows output from Active Server Pages to be cached in this manner. Figure 10-12 shows two clients requesting the same resource (`http://myserver.com/someApp/default.asp`). Assume for the purposes of this discussion that Client A's request finishes before Client B's request reaches the Web server. When Client B's request comes in, `http.sys` already has output from `default.asp` in its cache. Client B's request is serviced from cache. If Clients C, D, and F exist, each requesting the same `default.asp` page, their requests are serviced from cache as well. This allows the cost of Client A's request to be spread among all clients, resulting in greater scalability.

`http.sys` implements a request-queuing mechanism as well. Requests are queued if IIS cannot process older requests before new ones come in. As requests pile up, `http.sys` queues them into application-specific pools. IIS returns an HTTP error to the user once a request queue fills for an application. In Figure 10-13, requests from Clients A, B, C, and D fill the request queue for an application called `someApp`. Because Client D fills the queue, Client E's request cannot be serviced. As a result, Client F receives an error.

Web Administration Service (WAS) is the other major component of the W3SVC service. Like `http.sys`, WAS runs in kernel mode, which means it can process requests faster than if it were running in user mode. WAS is responsible for configuring both `http.sys` and application-worker processes. WAS gets its information from the IIS metabase. Previous versions of IIS stored the metabase in a binary file. The metabase contains most of the configuration information for the Web server and its applications. For instance, the metabase contains information such as whether or not an application should be run out of process and how many worker threads to use to process client requests. In IIS 6.0, the metabase is stored in an XML file that can be edited with Notepad or any other text editor.

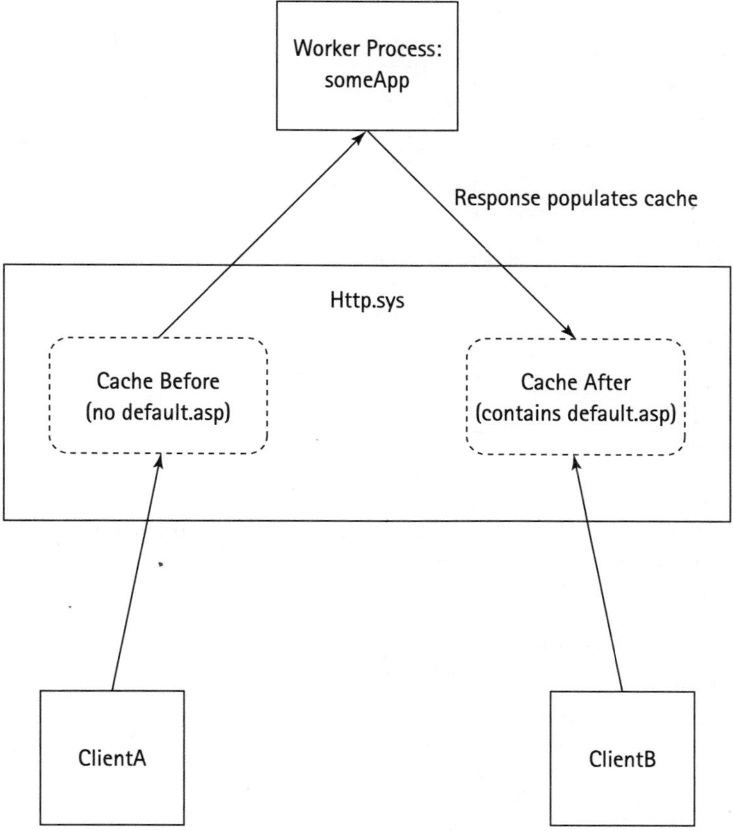

Figure 10-12: http.sys response cache

The worker process appears at the top of Figure 10-11. Worker processes are the workhorses of the Web server. They run the ASP or ISAPI applications. In the previous examples, the `someApp` application can be configured to run inside a worker process. The code for `default.asp` or any other page is executed inside this process. Because IIS separates Web applications from the core server process, it is able to provide a much more stable environment than if it were running user code in its own processes. Although this model provides better stability, it decreases performance because of the process switch that must occur between the Web server and the worker process.

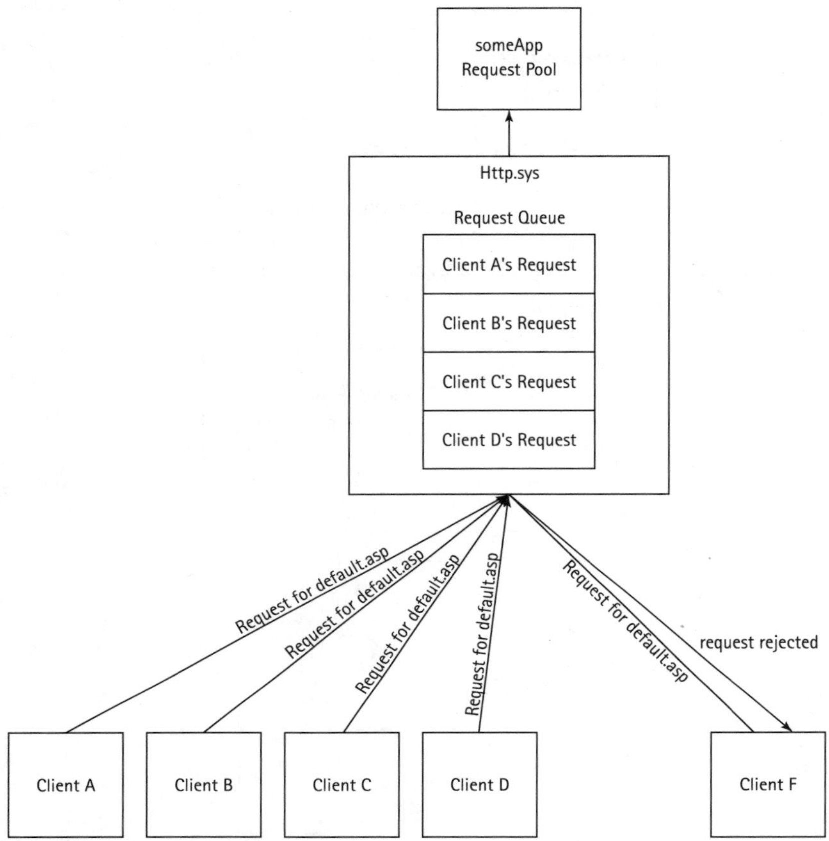

Figure 10-13: http.sys request queue

Application Pools and Web Gardens

In IIS 4 on Windows NT, Web applications can run either in process (with the Web server) or out of process in an instance of `mtx.exe`. IIS 5 on Windows 2000 extends that concept by allowing applications to be pooled in an instance of `dllhost.exe`. In IIS 5, only one pool exists. Applications can run in process, out of process, or in the sole application pool. The advent of IIS 6 provides for multiple application pools. Figure 10-14 shows how multiple applications can be run within an application pool. An application pool can run one or more applications.

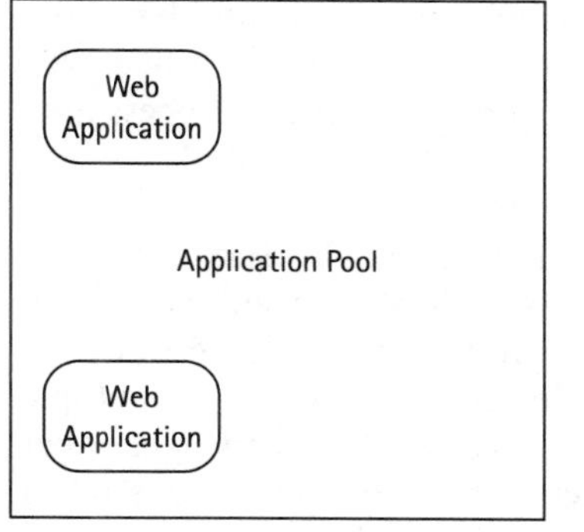

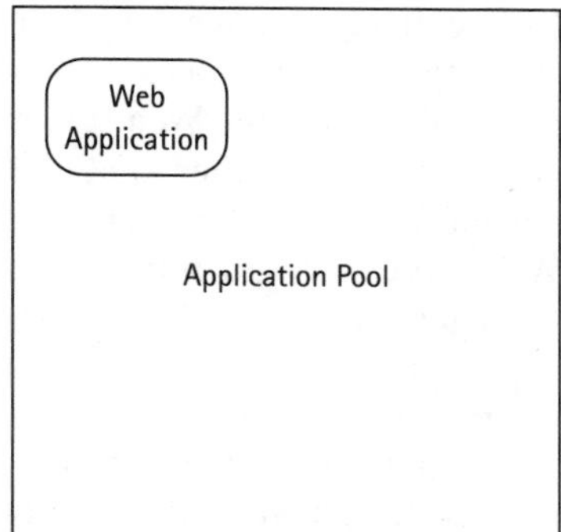

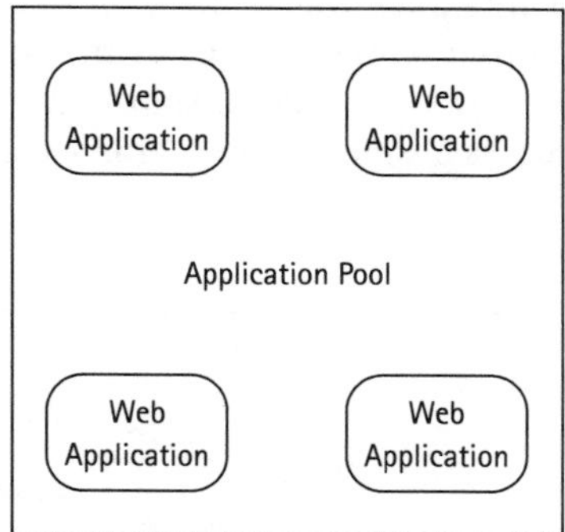

Figure 10-14: Application pools and Web applications

Application pooling is a compromise between stability, performance, and scalability. One of the best ways to help a Web server become stable is to run Web applications out of process. If something in a Web application goes terribly wrong, only the process running the application needs to be shut down – not the entire Web server. As with any compromise, however, the approach has its drawbacks. When a request is made to an out-of-process Web application, that request must cross process boundaries. This can be an expensive endeavor. On some occasions, the Web server must start a worker process to handle a request. This can be even more expensive in terms of performance. Running too many applications out of process can also degrade scalability. As more worker processes start, the operating system must commit resources (CPU time and memory) to handle each process. Pooling provides a middle ground by enabling applications to run out of process while still reducing the number of worker processes needed to handle requests. Because one worker process can service requests for multiple applications, the Web server does not need to create as many processes as it does if each application runs in its own process.

Some of my colleagues have said that pooling simply moves the problem from the Web server to another process. The argument goes as follows: If a bad Web application can take down the Web server, it can take down the pool's process and, in turn, take down all the other applications in the pool. This is certainly a compelling argument. However, this argument misses two important points about pooling. First, Web servers do not serve up just applications. They also serve up static pages. Static pages rarely take down a Web server. As such, static pages can safely be served in process. Given the choice, I think most administrators would rather be able to serve static pages than none at all. Second, in IIS 6.0, there can be multiple pools. One bad application does not have to take down the Web server or other application pools. If applications are pooled correctly, the only applications taken down when a pool goes down are those dependent on the failing application. IIS 6.0 extends the concept of pooling even further by introducing a feature called Web gardens. A *Web garden* is an application pool that multiple worker processes service. Web gardens provide fault tolerance for application pools. If an application causes a worker process to halt, other worker processes in the garden can pick up the extra requests. Figure 10-15 shows the relationship between worker processes and Web gardens. A worker process inside a Web garden can service any client request.

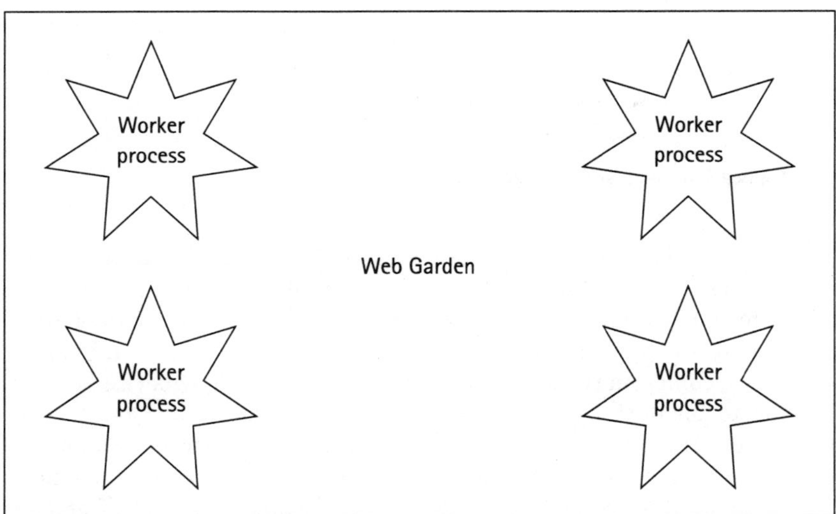

Figure 10-15: Worker processes and Web gardens

IIS 6.0 offers an additional feature that applies to application pools. This feature is known as *Rapid Fail Protection*. When worker processes in a pool fail repeatedly, IIS disables the application. Once an application has failed and IIS has disabled it, `http.sys` returns an error message. The error is an HTTP 503 error response which tells the client that the requested service is unavailable. The feature is useful because it prevents a failing application from consuming too many resources.

Server Modes

IIS 6.0 can be configured to run in two modes: standard and dedicated application. *Standard mode* is intended to be used for Web servers that must provide backward compatibility for applications that have been migrated from IIS 5. Some applications, such as ISAPI (Internet Server API) filters, which read raw data coming in from the client, must be run on a standard mode IIS 6.0 server.

In *dedicated-application mode*, all applications run out of process. Each application and site runs in an application pool. Because isolation can be achieved through the use of pools, IIS 6.0 can provide better scalability than earlier versions of IIS while still providing stability.

Worker-Process Management

You should be getting the picture now that worker processes are one of the most important components of IIS 6.0. IIS 6.0 offers a number of features aimed at improving the stability of worker processes. Some of the more significant features are the following:

- Worker-process recycling
- Worker-process identity
- Health monitoring
- Idle timeout
- On-demand start
- Processor affinity

Worker-process recycling behaves the same as process recycling in COM+. IIS worker processes can be configured to restart based on a number of criteria:

- Elapsed time
- Number of requests served
- Predetermined schedule
- Response to a ping
- Virtual memory usage (think COM+ memory gate)

When IIS determines that a worker process must be recycled, it allows the failing process to finish serving the requests on which it is currently working. No new requests are submitted to the worker process at this time. While IIS is waiting for the worker process to finish processing requests, it starts a new worker process to replace the old one. Once the old worker process is finished processing, it is destroyed. In some situations, the worker process may not be able to finish processing its requests. In this situation, IIS waits a configurable amount of time before it destroys the process. Shutting down the worker process and starting a new process is referred to as *restarting*.

Web applications can be configured to run under a specific user identity, just as COM+ applications can. In previous versions of IIS, a Web application either ran as the local system account (or whatever account IIS was running as) or a default user account (IUSR_MachineName or IWAM_MachineName). This feature can be used to provide more or less access for an application, depending on your needs.

The *ping* mentioned previously is a service of WAS. It enables WAS to provide health-monitoring capabilities to worker processes. WAS keeps an open communication channel to each worker process on the server. Periodically, WAS checks to see if the communication channel is open. If WAS determines that the worker process has dropped the channel, it assumes that the worker process can no longer service requests. When this happens, the worker process restarts.

Worker processes not doing any work consume server resources needlessly. A worker process can be configured to shut down after a configurable period of inactivity. This is a feature known as the *idle timeout*. Incidentally, this is also a feature that COM+ (on Windows 2000) supports for applications.

The *on-demand start feature* of IIS 6.0 allows worker processes to start when the first request comes in from a client. The alternative is for each worker process to start when the Web server or operating system starts. This can an inefficient use of resources if extra worker processes are sitting around waiting to time out. The first client to request a resource from a worker process takes a significant performance hit. The initial hit is due to the worker process starting up. The cost of this hit can be justified, as it can be spread across multiple client requests.

Worker processes can be configured to run on a specific processor and on that processor only. This is known as *processor affinity*. Processors have an internal cache to store data. An application can get a performance boost if the CPU it is running on can get its data from this cache rather than going to memory or disk. Binding a worker process to a CPU increases the chances that the CPU will use data from the cache rather than from memory.

ASP Template Cache Tuning

The *ASP template caching feature* pertains to traditional ASP, not ASP.NET pages. When a request for an Active Server Page is made, the ASP engine must be invoked to compile the page, run the code, and produce the output. All of this can be a rather expensive endeavor, especially if you are dealing with an ASP that has lots of code. The ASP template caching feature saves the compiled output of an ASP to disk. As with on-demand start, the first client to request a page takes an initial performance hit while the page is compiled. However, as long as the page does not change, IIS services subsequent requests from the precompiled page.

XML Support for the Metabase

Usually, when a developer gets excited and starts talking about new features of a product, the last thing he or she talks about is something such as the metabase. The metabase is really more the realm of an administrator. However, a developer who understands what the metabase can do for applications is much better off than one who lets metabase issues slide.

The *metabase* contains most of the configuration information for the Web server and its applications. In earlier versions of IIS, the metabase was stored in a binary file that could be read only with a tool such as MetaEdit (Platform SDK) or by writing an application that used the IIS administration library. To make life a little easier, IIS 6.0 stores its metabase in an XML file. XML, as you probably know, can be saved as a simple text file that can be read with any text editor, such as Notepad.

Several new features have popped up in IIS 6.0 to support the XML version of the metabase:

- Editing the metabase while IIS is running
- Metabase history
- Backing up the metabase
- Server-independent metabase backups

As noted previously, the WAS uses the metabase to configure `http.sys` and Web applications. It does this by reading the most current copy of the metabase and creating an in-memory representation of it. If an administrator edits the metabase while IIS is running, a feature of the operating system notifies IIS that the file has changed. When this happens, WAS re-reads the metabase and applies the new changes. The benefit of this feature is that the Web server does not need to restart in order for changes to be applied. This can help reduce the Web server's down time.

Each time an administrator modifies the metabase file, IIS increases the version number of the file and copies the old version to a history folder. Each file in the history folder is also marked with a version number so that the administrator can go back to a previous version of the metabase if needed. This feature provides a safeguard to accidental corruption or misconfiguration of the metabase.

Three methods exist for backing up a metabase in IIS 6.0:

- Secure backup
- Insecure backup
- Legacy backup

A *secure backup* can be secured with a password. The password is needed to restore the metabase, should the need arise. An *insecure backup* does not require a password. At the time of this writing, a *legacy backup* can be done only programmatically. Backups can also be made server independent. A server-independent metabase can be useful for restoring IIS configuration information to a newly installed operating system. An administrator can restore the backup metabase, rather than configure all the settings by hand.

New Features of MSMQ

In Chapter 8, you see how MSMQ provides the underlying transport mechanism for queued components. The version of MSMQ you deal with in that chapter is 2.0. Windows 2002 will ship with a new version of MSMQ – 3.0. This version has a number of enhancements of interest to developers and administrators:

- LDAP support
- Distribution lists
- Queue aliases
- Message triggers

The *LDAP support* in MSMQ 3.0 allows an MSMQ client to query a domain controller for MSMQ-related information. In MSMQ 2.0, MSMQ had to be installed on a domain controller to support integration with Active Directory. In an Active Directory installation, a MSMQ client talked to the MSMQ server installation on the domain controller to query for public queues and the like. By using LDAP, an MSMQ 3.0 client can query a domain controller for public queues without having to go through an MSMQ server on the domain controller.

Distribution lists allow a message to be sent to a list of message queues or other distribution lists. A distribution list in this sense is not like a distribution list for e-mail. A distribution list in this sense can contain only public queues, aliases, and other distribution lists.

A *queue alias* is a pointer inside Active Directory to another public or private queue. In Chapter 8, I state that public queues are published or advertised in Active Directory, but private queues are not. Private queues are accessible only if you know the queue name and the name of the machine that owns the queue. The new queue alias feature of MSMQ allows a private queue to be advertised inside Active Directory and included in distribution lists.

The *message triggers* feature enables a developer or administrator to associate an action with a set of criteria for an incoming message. The action can be launching another application or even creating a component and calling a method. Together, the action and the message criteria form a rule. If a trigger is associated with a queue, every message that comes in on the queue causes the trigger to fire. The action is taken only if a message meets the trigger's criteria. Previously, triggers were available only as add-ons in the Platform SDK.

Summary

If this chapter has whetted your appetite for Windows 2002, you are not alone. I want many of the features, such as process recycling and pinging. You may have noticed that many of the features in IIS and COM+ are quite similar, as IIS gets many of it features from COM+. These two technologies have been interlinked for several versions now.

Chances are that some of these features will not make it into the final release of the product. Other features, such as support for the .NET Common Language Runtime, not covered in this chapter, may be added before the final release.

Appendix A

What's on the CD-ROM?

THIS APPENDIX PROVIDES YOU with information on the contents of the CD-ROM that accompanies this book.

The CD-ROM contains all of the source code from the book as well as a demonstration application called OfficeMart. OfficeMart demonstrates several COM+ technologies covered in the book. An electronic, searchable version of the book that can be viewed with Adobe Acrobat Reader is also included on the CD-ROM.

System Requirements

Make sure that your computer meets the minimum system requirements listed in this section. If your computer doesn't match up to most of these requirements, you may have a problem using the contents of the CD.

For Windows 2000, Windows XP Beta 2, or Windows NT 4.0:

- PC with a Pentium II processor running at 450 MHz or faster (600 MHz recommended)
- At least 96MB of RAM for Windows 2000 Professional (128MB recommended), 192MB for Windows 2000 Server (256MB recommended)
- 500MB Disk Space on system drive, 2.5GB on installation drive
- Operating System: Windows 2000, Windows XP Beta 2, or Windows NT 4.0
- Video: 800 × 600, 256 colors (high-color 16-bit recommended)
- Mouse: Microsoft Mouse or compatible pointing device
- A CD-ROM drive – double-speed (2x) or faster

In addition to the requirements listed above, you will need 1MB of additional hard disk space to install the code examples from the chapters and appendices as well as the OfficeMart application from the CR-ROM.

Using the CD with Microsoft Windows

To install the items from the CD to your hard drive, follow these steps:

1. Insert the CD into your computer's CD-ROM drive.
2. Open Windows Explorer (explorer.exe).
3. Copy the `OfficeMartWeb` folder to your Web server's root folder.
4. Right click on the `OfficeMartWeb` folder. If the "Read-Only" check box in the attributes section is checked then uncheck it.
5. When you click the OK button, you will be asked if you want to apply the changes to the `OfficeMartWeb` folder only or if you want apply the changes to the `OfficeMartWeb` folder and all subfolders and files. Choose the "Apply changes to this folder, subfolders and files" option.
6. In Windows Explorer, navigate to `OfficeMartWeb\bin` and run `RegOfficeMart.bat`.

What's on the CD

The CD-ROM contains source code examples, applications, and an electronic version of the book. Following is a summary of the contents of the CD-ROM arranged by category.

Source code

Every program in any listing in the book is on the CD in the folder named `BookExamples`.

OfficeMart Demo Application

The OfficeMart demo application demonstrates the use of several COM+ technologies:

- Queued Components
- Distributed Transactions
- Loosely Coupled Events
- Just In Time Activation
- Component Construction
- Object Pooling

Other technologies used by OfficeMart (not included on the CD-ROM):

- Microsoft SQL Server 2000
- Active Server Pages .NET

OfficeMart is an imaginary office supply company with a business-to-consumer site on the Internet. This application allows customers on the Internet to order office supplies. Customers navigate to the order entry ASP .NET page and enter their customer IDs, the SKU number of the product they wish to purchase, and the quantity. This application focuses strictly on how COM+ services can be used in interesting ways in order to solve the problem of taking the customers'order, applying some business logic, and then either processing or rejecting the order. In order to focus on the COM+ technology, I have eliminated the typical things you would find in a B2C Web site:

- Authorization and Authentication Mechanism
- Product Catalog

OFFICEMART ARCHITECTURE

The architecture of the OfficeMart application has been kept simple so that you and I can focus on the COM+ technologies used by the application. Aside from a few Active Server Pages .NET pages, the OfficeMart architecture consists of two pieces: the Microsoft SQL Server database, and the COM+ Library. Both of the pieces of the OfficeMart architecture are explained below.

- **Database:** There are two databases in the OfficeMart application: Inventory, and OfficeMart. The Inventory database contains a single table called Products. This table holds the product data for every product sold on the Web site. The OfficeMart database holds the customer information and the orders information. For readability, no user-defined stored procedures have been added to the database. All SQL code is in-line with the application so you can tell more readily what is going on.
- **COM+ Library:** The `OfficeMartLib` project contains the `OfficeMartLib` namespace, which holds all of the COM+ components used in the application.
  - **`Orders` class:** This class contains one method that allows the ASP .NET page to submit an order. `Orders` is a Queued Component. The idea is that the `Orders` class would run on an application server separate from the Web server hosting the Web site. The Queued Component architecture allows orders to be submitted asynchronously. This provides better scalability as mentioned in Chapter 8.

- `Customers` **and** `Products` **classes:** The `Customers` and `Products` classes contain methods to update the customer's credit and adjust the product inventory levels (respectively) during the purchase process. These are transactional components that operate inside of the `Orders` class's transaction.
- `VerifyCustomer` **and** `VerifyProduct` **classes:** These classes verify that the customer exists, the product has enough available quantity, and so on. These are not `ServicedComponent` classes. It may be tempting to move their logic into their respective `ServicedComponent` classes. The logic contained in these classes is not transactional in nature. If the `Verify` classes were consolidated with their respective customers and `Products` classes, no transactional work would incur the overhead of the distributed transactions. Not only would object creation time be longer, database locks would also be heavier.
- `InventoryConn` **and** `OfficeMartConn` **classes:** These classes are pooled components that manage a connection to one of the two application databases. These classes are used by the `Verify` classes in order to improve performance. I am making the assumption that I can open a database connection within 100 ms.
- `OrderEvt`**,** `CustomerSubscriber`**, and** `AdminSubscriber`**:** `OrderEvt` is a COM+ event class. An event (think method) is raised when an order fails, and when one is successfully submitted into the database. The `CustomerSubscriber` uses this event to notify the customer (via e-mail) upon the success or failure of the orders. The `AdminSubscriber` logs a successful order as an informational message in the event log. An unsuccessful order is logged as an error message in the event log. I implemented an event class here to provide an easy way for additional functionality to be plugged in to the application. As different departments throughout the company decide that they want to be notified about orders, all a developer has to do is implement another subscriber. For example, a subscriber could be written to notify the Accounting department when a customer without sufficient credit attempts to purchase items.

Electronic version of C# COM+ Programming

The complete (and searchable) text of this book is on the CD-ROM in Adobe's Portable Document Format (PDF), readable with the Adobe Acrobat Reader (also included). For more information on Adobe Acrobat Reader, go to `www.adobe.com`.

Troubleshooting

If you have difficulty installing or using the CD-ROM programs, try the following solutions:

- **Check location of `OfficeMartLib.dll`.** The `OfficeMartLib.dll` assembly must be located in `OfficeMartWeb\bin`. The assembly must also be installed in the Global Assembly Cache.
- **Verify that all services are running.** The following services must be running in order for the OfficeMart application to work correctly: World Wide Web Publishing Service (IIS), SMTP Service, COM+ Event System, Distributed Transaction Coordinator (DTC) Service, and SQL Server.
- **Verify that the SQL Scripts ran correctly.** If the SQL scripts ran properly, you should see a Products table in the Inventory database. The OfficeMart database should contain a Orders and Customers table.

If you still have trouble with the CD, please call the Hungry Minds Customer Service phone number: (800) 762-2974. Outside the United States, call (317) 572-3993. Hungry Minds will provide technical support only for installation and other general quality control items; for technical support on the applications themselves, consult the program's vendor or author.

Appendix B

The COM+ Shared Property Manager

IN CHAPTER 4, I talk about resource dispensers. I describe resource dispensers as components responsible for maintaining a pool of volatile resources, such as a pool of database connections or threads. That discussion focuses primarily on a resource dispenser's role in a transaction. The COM+ Shared Property Manager (SPM) is another type of resource dispenser. Instead of managing database connections, the SPM manages memory. Managed memory can be used to store state among components. The SPM provides protected access memory for multiple components.

Until this point, you have manipulated most COM+ services through attribute-based programming. The COM+ SPM is one of the few services that do not use attributes. The object model is strictly API-based. By *API-based*, I mean you utilize services through `System.EnterpriseServices` classes and their methods.

Before you get into the SPM API, take a look at what life is like without it by examining some of the pitfalls that can occur when two or more threads access the same shared memory.

Sharing Memory among Threads

In C# applications, memory can be shared among threads by using the `static` modifier. The examples in this section access global variables that have been declared with the `static` modifier. To understand the code in this section, you should have a solid understanding of the `static` modifier. In case you don't, I give you an introduction to it next.

Static Modifier

The purpose of the `static` modifier is to provide a means of global access to a shared region of memory. The `static` modifier can be applied to any of the following constructs:

- Methods
- Properties

- Operators
- Fields
- Constructors

Static types are not tied to any instance of a class, struct, or other type. A good example of this is the `ContextUtil` class. The properties and methods of this class are static. Have you ever seen me create an instance of the `ContextUtil` class? No. Static types need to be accessed through their class or struct name only. In the case of the `ContextUtil` class, you can get the context ID by calling the static `ContextUtil.ContextId` property.

Figure B-1 shows the relationships among static types and the threads that access them. Any thread within the application can access any type that has been declared `static`.

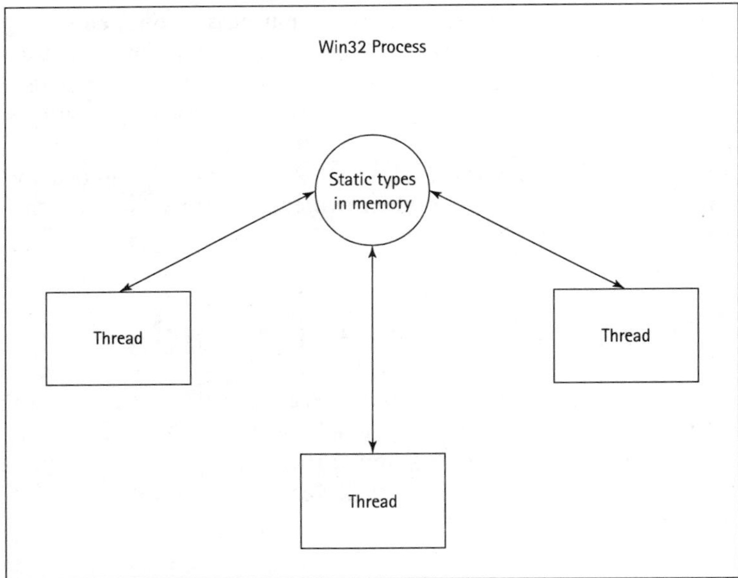

Figure B-1: Relationships among threads and static types

Memory Conflicts and the static Modifier

The `static` modifier is a useful construct that can be perfectly safe to use – assuming you know the pitfalls. In general, the problem with shared memory is that it is not protected from simultaneous access from multiple threads. This is the whole point of the SPM in COM+. To understand the value of the COM+ SPM, look at an example application that uses static fields of a class to share memory. After I cover the SPM API, I come back to this example and fix its problem by using COM+ shared properties.

The code in Listing B-1 uses the `Thread` class from the `System.Threading` namespace. This class has one constructor that takes a `ThreadStart` delegate as an input. The `ThreadStart` delegate is a pointer to a method with no parameters and a void return type. Delegates are creatable types themselves. In the `Thread` constructor, I create a new instance of the `ThreadStart` delegate, passing in a method name. The method I pass to the `ThreadStart` constructor is executed when the `Thread.Start` method starts the thread. Once I have created the two threads (`t1` and `t2`), I am free to start them by calling the `Thread.Start` method. It is possible that the thread executing the `Main` method may exit before the two new threads finish their work. In fact, in this code example, it is quite likely. To prevent this, I call `Thread.Join` on each of the threads. This method forces the caller to block until the thread has finished its work.

Listing B-1: Problems with accessing shared memory with multiple threads

```
using System;
using System.Threading;

namespace StaticProperties
{
  public class CApp
  {
    public static void Main()
    {
      // create two new thread classes
      Thread t1 = new Thread(new ThreadStart(Start1));
      Thread t2 = new Thread(new ThreadStart(Start2));

      // start each thread
      t1.Start();
      t2.Start();

      // wait for each thread to finish
      t1.Join();
      t2.Join();

      // print the value of iCount
      Console.WriteLine(CStatic.iCount.ToString());
    }

    public static void Start1()
    {
```

Continued

Listing B-1 *(Continued)*

```
      CStatic.iCount = 2;
      int iSomeValue = 4;
      // force the thread to sleep so the second thread can
      // interrupt its work and change the value of iCount
      Thread.Sleep(500);

      int iResult = iSomeValue / CStatic.iCount;
    }

    public static void Start2()
    {
      CStatic.iCount = 0;
    }
  }

  public class CStatic
  {
    public static int iCount;
  }
}
```

The two threads — `t1` and `t2` — try to access the same static integer value: `iCount`. The integer is a member of a class called `CStatic`. The first thread (`t1`) attempts to divide `iSomeValue` by `iCount`. The second thread changes the value of `iCount` to zero before the first thread can make its computation. The call to `Thread.Sleep` forces the first thread to sleep for half a second. When the first thread goes to sleep, it provides a chance for the second thread to execute and change the value of `iCount` to zero.

In the `Main` method, once I start each of the threads, I must call `Thread.Join` for each of them. This forces the thread executing the `Main` method to wait until both of the other threads have finished their work.

The last line in the `Main` method is never executed. When the first thread goes to sleep, the second thread changes `iCount` to zero. When the first thread resumes its execution, it tries to divide `iSomeValue` by zero. This raises an `System.DivideByZeroException`.

I admit that this is a rather contrived example. Indeed, it is written to fail. In practice, these types of problems are not always obvious when you first release an application to a group of users. It may take days or weeks before you see this type of problem occur. However, when it does occur, it may take much longer to resolve. If the first thread is able to lock the `iCount` field somehow when it starts and to release the lock when it finishes, the second thread is not able to change `iCount` to zero. Fortunately, the COM+ SPM provides you with such a locking mechanism. But before you can solve this problem, you must learn to use the SPM.

Shared Property Manager API

COM+ organizes shared properties into groups. These groups provide a namespace that organizes the properties for a process. In addition, groups help reduce the number of possible naming conflicts among properties. For instance, a group cannot have two properties by the same name, but two different groups can each have a property by the same name.

The API for the SPM in .NET consists of three classes and two enumerations (described later). These classes are defined in the `System.EnterpriseServices` namespace.

- `SharedPropertyGroupManager class`
- `SharedPropertyGroup` class
- `SharedPropertyClass`

Figure B-2 illustrates the hierarchy of these classes and their relationships to one another.

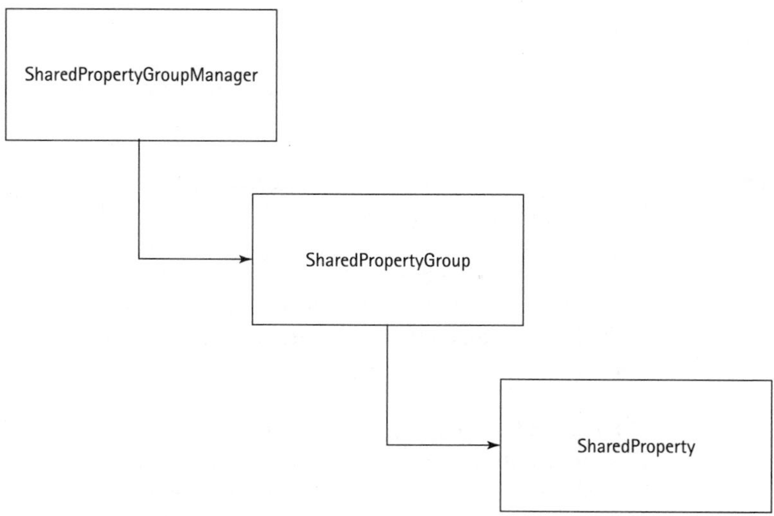

Figure B-2: Hierarchy of the SPM API

SharedPropertyGroupManager Class

Groups are created and accessed by using a class called `SharedPropertyGroupManager`. When it comes to shared properties, this is the only class you instantiate directly. The constructor for this class takes no parameters. If you instantiate an instance of this class, it probably looks something like the code in Listing B-2.

Listing B-2: Instantiating the SharedPropertyGroupManager class

```
using System.EnterpriseServices;
public class SomeComponent : ServicedComponent
{
  public void DoSomething()
  {
    SharedPropertyGroupManager gm =
      new SharedPropertyGroupManager();

    // do something with the Group Manager ...
  }
}
```

Chances are that most of the time you use this class to create a property group. To do this, you use the `CreatePropertyGroupMethod`. This method creates a property group that can be used to create properties. This method's signature looks like the following:

```
SharedPropertyGroup CreatePropertyGroup (
  string name,
  ref PropertyLockMode dwIsoMode,
  ref PropertyReleaseMode dwRelMode,
  out bool fExists
);
```

The first parameter to this method is a string representing the name of the group. If two components must share the properties in this group, they must use the name of the group passed in this parameter.

The second parameter is the `PropertyLockMode`. `PropertyLockMode` is an enumeration in the `System.EnterpriseServices` namespace. This parameter determines how properties are locked in memory when they are accessed. The only two options are `PropertyLockMode.Method` and `PropertyLockMode.SetGet`. When you choose `PropertyLockMode.Method` mode, all properties in this group are locked until the method (of the component) manipulating them returns. The `SetGet` method, on the other hand, causes only an individual property to be locked when the property is set or read. Locking properties at the method level is useful if you need to perform consistent reads or writes across a number of properties within the group. While you are reading or writing to one property in a group, another thread cannot change another of the group's properties. This comes at the cost of higher overhead. If the read and write operations of your properties are not interdependent, you should choose the `SetGet` lock mode.

The `PropertyReleaseMode` is another enumeration from `System.EnterpriseServices`. The release mode determines when the properties for this group are released from memory. When you set the release mode to `PropertyReleaseMode.Process`, the memory this group occupies is freed only when the hosting process terminates. Setting the release mode to `PropertyReleaseMode.Standard` frees the memory when the last client releases a reference to the group. You may have noticed that both the `PropertyLockMode` parameter and this parameter are declared by using the C# `ref` keyword. The reason for this becomes clear in a moment.

The final parameter in this method is a boolean flag telling the caller whether or not the group exists. Because this parameter is marked with the `out` keyword, it does not need to be set before the method is called. I should make clear that this method is used not only to create a property group but also to get a reference to one that exists. This is the reason for the `fExists` parameter. It is also the reason that the property lock mode and property release mode parameters are passed by reference (C# `ref` keyword). If a group with the same name exists, the `fExists` parameter is set to true. The property lock mode and property release mode parameters are set to the values used when the group is created. If the group exists, any values passed in to these parameters are ignored. Generally speaking, if you are not sure that the group you want to use exists, you should use this method.

Using this method can be a little tricky if you are not familiar with enumerations. The key to working with enumerations is to think of them as just another data type. If I extend the preceding `SomeComponent` class to make a call to `CreatePropertyGroup`, it looks like the code in Listing B-3.

Listing B-3: Creating a property group

```
using System.EnterpriseServices;
public class SomeComponent : ServicedComponent
{
  public void DoSomething()
  {
    bool bGroupExists;
    // declare the property lock mode
    PropertyLockMode lm = PropertyLockMode.SetGet;

    // declare the property release mode enum
    PropertyReleaseMode rm = PropertyReleaseMode.Process;

    SharedPropertyGroupManager gm =
      new SharedPropertyGroupManager();
    SharedPropertyGroup pg;
    pg = gm.CreatePropertyGroup(
        "myGroup",
        ref lm,
        ref rm,
        out bGroupExists;
    );
    // use pg to create properties ...
  }
}
```

In Listing B-3, I define the property lock mode as SetGet and the release mode as process. When this call returns, bGroupExists is false, as the group does not already exist. The return value for this group is an instance of a SharedPropertyGroup.

If you know that the group you are trying to access exists, you can use the SharedPropertyGroupManager.Group method. This method's signature is the following:

```
Public SharedPropertyGroup Group (string name);
```

As you can see, this is much less involved than the CreatePropertyGroup method. This method takes the name of the group as its sole parameter and returns the group in the form of a SharedPropertyGroup class. Listing B-3 can be modified to use this method; see Listing B-4.

Listing B-4: Using the Group method

```
using System.EnterpriseServices;
public class SomeComponent : ServicedComponent
{
  public void DoSomething()
  {
    SharedPropertyGroupManager gm =
      new SharedPropertyGroupManager();
    SharedPropertyGroup pg;
    pg = gm.Group("myGroup");

    // use pg to create properties ...
  }
}
```

Instead of passing in the property lock and release modes and trying to figure out if the property exists, I pass in the name of the group to which I want access. This method can simplify your code and make it more readable if you know that the property group exists.

SharedPropertyGroup Class

In Listings B-3 and B-4, you see how the methods of the SharedPropertyGroupManager class create and grant access to property groups. These groups are returned as instances of the SharedPropertyGroup class. Unlike the SharedPropertyGroupManager class, you do not directly create instances of the SharedPropertyGroup class.

The purpose of the SharedPropertyGroup class is to create properties. It implements a number of methods that can be used to create properties by name or by position relative to other properties in the group. Start with the most common method:

```
public SharedProperty CreateProperty (
  string name,
  out bool fExists
);
```

The format of this method should look somewhat familiar. It takes a string representing the name of the property as input and returns a `bool` as an output parameter. Just as with the `CreatePropertyGroup` method, this boolean flag indicates whether or not the property has existed. Because this is an `out` parameter, any value of `fExists` set before the method call is ignored. The return value of this method is a `SharedProperty` class. As you see in the next section, the `SharedProperty` class represents a single property from a shared property group.

In Listing B-5, I have extended the `SomeComponent.DoSomething` method to include the creation of a `SharedProperty` by using the `SharedPropertyGroup.CreateProperty` method.

Listing B-5: Creating a SharedProperty

```
using System.EnterpriseServices;
public class SomeComponent : ServicedComponent
{
  public void DoSomething()
  {
    bool bGroupExists;
    bool bPropertyExists;

    // declare the property lock mode
    PropertyLockMode lm = PropertyLockMode.SetGet;

    // declare the property release mode enum
    PropertyReleaseMode rm = PropertyReleaseMode.Process;

    SharedPropertyGroupManager gm =
      new SharedPropertyGroupManager();
    SharedPropertyGroup pg;
    pg = gm.CreatePropertyGroup(
        "myGroup",
        ref lm,
        ref rm,
        out bGroupExists;
    );
    SharedProperty sp = pg.CreateProperty(
                            "myProp",
                            bPropertyExists);
  }
}
```

The SharedPropertyGroup class can create groups by position. The method used to do this is the following:

```
Public SharedProperty CreatePropertyByPosition(
  int position,
  out bool fExists
);
```

In this method, the position number replaces the property name. The position can be any valid integer value, including positive and negative numbers. I should point out that a property created with one method cannot be accessed by another method. For example, if you create a property by using the CreateProperty method, you cannot later access it by using the CreatePropertyByPosition number.

Each of these property-creation methods has a corresponding property-retrieval method. If a property is created by using CreateProperty, it can be accessed later by using only either CreateProperty again or by using the Property method. The Property method takes a string as an input parameter and returns a SharedProperty. The Property method is useful only if the property has already been created.

The PropertyByPosition method can be used when properties are created with the CreatePropertyByPosition method. Unlike the Property method, the PropertyByPostion method takes an integer as an input parameter instead of a string representing the property name. Assuming a property exists, the PropertyByPosition number can be used as shown in Listing B-6.

Listing B-6: Catching exceptions from the Shared Property Manager

```
using System.EnterpriseServices;
public class SomeComponent : ServicedComponent
{
  public void DoSomething()
  {
    bool bGroupExists;
    bool bPropertyExists;

    // declare the property lock mode
    PropertyLockMode lm = PropertyLockMode.SetGet;

    // declare the property release mode enum
    PropertyReleaseMode rm = PropertyReleaseMode.Process;

    SharedPropertyGroupManager gm =
      new SharedPropertyGroupManager();
    SharedPropertyGroup pg;
    pg = gm.CreatePropertyGroup(
        "myGroup",
```

```
            ref lm,
            ref rm,
            out bGroupExists;
        );
        SharedProperty sp = pg.CreatePropertyByPosition(
                                 5,
                                 bPropertyExists);
    }

    public string DoSomethingElse()
    {
        SharedPropertyGroupManager gm = new
          SharedPropertyGroupManager();
        SharedPropertyGroup pg = null;
        SharedProperty sp;

        try {
          pg = gm.Group("myGroup");
        }
        catch (ArgumentException ae) {
          Console.WriteLine(ae.Message);
        }

        try {
          sp = pg.PropertyByPosition(5);
        }
        catch (ArgumentException ae) {
          Console.WriteLine(ae.Message);
        }
        catch (NullReferenceException nre) {
          Console.WriteLine(nre.Message);
        }

        return "";
  }
}
```

In Listing B-6, I have added a method to the component: `DoSomethingElse`. In this method, I assume that the property group and the property have been created. I do not, however, completely trust that the group and property have been created. If a client calls the `DoSomething` method before calling the `DoSomethingElse` method, `DoSomethingElse` should not trap any errors. Of course, another component within the process can create the group and property also. In case this does not happen, I have added some error handling around my method calls. In the first try-catch block, I attempt to catch a `System.ArgumentException`. If an invalid group name is passed in to the SharedPropertyGroupManager.Group method, this exception is raised. In the second try-catch block, I attempt to access the property in position 5. Notice that I use a position number of 0 or 1. Properties created by position number do not need to be created in sequence as you might think. You may number them in any order you wish. If I try to access the property in position 5 and it does not exist, a System.ArgumentException is raised. This exception is raised only if I obtain a reference to the group named myGroup. In my code example, a System.NullReferenceException is raised if myGroup does not exist when I call the Group method. In all likelihood, you want to do a little more than just print out the error to the screen, but this serves instructional purposes.

SharedProperty Class

The work I have done so far in this appendix has led us to access to the shared property itself. The shared property is accessed through a class called (surprise) SharedProperty. Shared properties are stored in the form of an object instance. object is a C# keyword that represents the System.Object class. This makes the shared property rather versatile in terms of what types it can hold, as you learn in a moment.

To access the System.Object instance in the SharedProperty class, use the Value property. The Value property can be read from or written to. The Shared Property Manager locks both read access and write access to this property. The code in Listing B-7 shows how to use the SharedProperty class to read a string value from the property. Once again, I have extended the DoSomething method from the earlier component.

Listing B-7: Using the SharedProperty class

```
using System.EnterpriseServices;
public class SomeComponent : ServicedComponent
{
  public void DoSomething()
  {
    bool bGroupExists;
    bool bPropertyExists;

    // declare the property lock mode
    PropertyLockMode lm = PropertyLockMode.SetGet;

    // declare the property release mode enum
    PropertyReleaseMode rm = PropertyReleaseMode.Process;

    SharedPropertyGroupManager gm =
      new SharedPropertyGroupManager();
    SharedPropertyGroup pg;
    pg = gm.CreatePropertyGroup(
```

```
        "myGroup",
        ref lm,
        ref rm,
        out bGroupExists;
    );
    SharedProperty sp = pg.CreateProperty(
                            "myProp",
                            bPropertyExists);

    if (bPropertyExists)
    {
      Console.WriteLine((string)sp.Value);
    }
    else {
      sp.Value = "some interesting string";
    }
  }
}
```

Once I get access to the `SharedProperty`, I am free to assign values to it or read values from it. In my example, if the property exists, I write its value to the console. If the `DoSomething` method has created the property, I assign a string to the value. An interesting thing happens here. Notice that if the property exists, I must convert the `object` type to a `string` type. This is known as boxing. To refresh your memory, here is a brief review of boxing.

Boxing converts a value type such as an integer or string to a reference type such as an object. Unboxing is the opposite of boxing; *unboxing* converts a reference type such as an object to a value type. In Listing B-7, if the property exists, I unbox the value to a string and print the string to the console. If the property does not exist, I simply give it a string value. Although it may not be obvious by looking at the code, the string, some interesting string, is boxed into the `Value` property. This is called an implicit boxing conversion. The C# compiler is smart enough to know that I want the string converted into an object type. If I really want to be clear to other readers of my code, I can do something similar to the code that follows.

```
else {
  sp.Value = (object)"some interesting string";
}
```

Here I explicitly convert the string to an object type. Although this is not technically necessary to convert the string to an object, it can help less experienced developers understand what is going on.

Reference types such as classes can also be stored as shared properties. When a reference type is read from or written to, either an explicit or implicit reference conversion occurs. In an explicit reference conversion, the desired reference type must be coded into the application. An implicit reference conversion, on the other hand, does not require the declaration of a desired type. Usually, this is because the C# compiler can determine the type you are trying to reference. To clear this concept up, I have modified the `DoSomething` method. This method adds an instance of a class called `CName` as a shared property.

Listing B-8: Storing a class instance in the Shared Property Manager

```
using System.EnterpriseServices;
public class SomeComponent : ServicedComponent
{
  public void DoSomething()
  {
    bool bGroupExists;
    bool bPropertyExists;

    // declare the property lock mode
    PropertyLockMode lm = PropertyLockMode.SetGet;

    // declare the property release mode enum
    PropertyReleaseMode rm = PropertyReleaseMode.Process;

    SharedPropertyGroupManager gm =
      new SharedPropertyGroupManager();
    SharedPropertyGroup pg;
    pg = gm.CreatePropertyGroup(
        "myGroup",
        ref lm,
        ref rm,
        out bGroupExists;
    );
    SharedProperty sp = pg.CreateProperty(
                            "myProp",
                            bPropertyExists);

    // create a new instance of CName and add it as a property
    CName name = new CName("David", "Roth", "Lee");

    // this is an implicit reference conversion
    sp.Value = name;

    // this is an explicit reference conversion
    name = (CName) sp.Value
  }
```

```
// this is the class we will instantiate and add to the SPM
public class CName
{
  public string FirstName;
  public string LastName;
  public string MiddleName;
  public CName(string sFirst, string sLast, string sMiddle)
  {
    FirstName = sFirst;
    LastName = sLast;
    MiddleName = sMiddle;
  }
```

Once I create an instance of the `CName` class, I assign it to the `Value` property of the `SharedProperty`. When this assignment is made, the C# compiler performs an implicit reference conversion from a `CName` reference type to an object reference type. In the next line of code, I convert the object type (`sp.Value`) to a `CName` type. This is an explicit reference conversion.

Solving the Static Problem

Now that I have covered the Shared Property Manager API, we can solve the shared-memory problem from earlier in the appendix. At the end of the first section, I come to the conclusion that if I can lock the `iCount` static field so that another thread cannot modify it before the first thread is finished, I do not get a `DivideByZeroException`. To solve this problem, I put the `iCount` variable in a protected shared property by using the Shared Property Manager API. The code for this example is shown in Listing B-9.

Listing B-9: Fixing shared memory problems

```
using System;
using System.Reflection;
using System.EnterpriseServices;
using System.Threading;

[assembly: AssemblyKeyFile("C:\\crypto\\key.snk")]

namespace SharedProperties
{

  public class SC : ServicedComponent
  {
```

Continued

Listing B-9 *(Continued)*

```
public void Start1()
{
  PropertyReleaseMode rm = PropertyReleaseMode.Process;
  PropertyLockMode lm = PropertyLockMode.Method;
  bool bPropertyExists;
  bool bGroupExists;

  SharedPropertyGroupManager gm =
        new SharedPropertyGroupManager();
  SharedPropertyGroup pg = gm.CreatePropertyGroup(
        "CounterGroup",
        ref lm,
        ref rm,
        out bGroupExists);
  SharedProperty prop = pg.CreateProperty(
        "Counter",
        out bPropertyExists);

  prop.Value = 2;
  int iSomeValue = 4;

  Thread.Sleep(500);

  int iResult = iSomeValue / (int) prop.Value;
}

public void Start2()
{
  PropertyReleaseMode rm = PropertyReleaseMode.Process;
  PropertyLockMode lm = PropertyLockMode.Method;
  bool bPropertyExists;
  bool bGroupExists;

  SharedPropertyGroupManager gm =
        new SharedPropertyGroupManager();
  SharedPropertyGroup pg = gm.CreatePropertyGroup(
        "CounterGroup",
        ref lm,
        ref rm,
        out bGroupExists);
  SharedProperty prop = pg.CreateProperty(
        "Counter",
        out bPropertyExists);
```

```
        prop.Value = 0;
      }
    }
    public class CApp
    {
      public static void Main()
      {
        Thread t1 = new Thread(new ThreadStart(Start1));
        Thread t2 = new Thread(new ThreadStart(Start2));

        t1.Start();
        t2.Start();

        t1.Join();
        t2.Join();

        Console.WriteLine("Done");
      }

      public static void Start1()
      {
        SC sc = new SC();
        sc.Start1();
      }

      public static void Start2()
      {
        SC sc = new SC();
        sc.Start2();
      }
    }
}
```

The `Main` method should look very familiar. Once again, I create two threads, start them, and wait for each to finish. This time, instead of doing the math inside the thread methods, I let the component do all the work. Each thread creates an instance of the `SC` component. The first thread calls `SC.Start1`. `SC.Start1` contains the same code as the previous example, except for the fact that I get the count from a shared property called `Counter` instead of from a static variable. Because I want the `Counter` property to be locked during the entire duration of the `SC.Start1` method call, I set the `PropertyLockMode` to `Method`. If I set it to `SetGet`, it is locked only while either thread is reading from or writing to it. This means that the second thread is still able to change the property if I set the `PropertyReleaseMode` to `SetGet`.

The second thread calls the `SC.Start2()` method. In `SC.Start2`, it is tempting to avoid creating the group and property all over again. It is quicker to code if I just assume that the group and property are created and if I use the `SharedPropertyGroupManager.Group` and `SharedPropertyGroup.Property` methods to get the group and `Counter` property. The problem with this approach comes from the fact that, as a developer, I do not know when the operating system is going to schedule a thread. The first thread, for example, can be switched out after it creates the group and before it creates the property. This is bad if the second thread is scheduled and tries to access a property that is not there.

When this application is run, thread one and thread two start and call their respective methods on the `SC` class. Just as before, thread one goes to sleep, which gives thread two a chance to change the `Counter` property. Because `SC.Start1` has not finished yet, the Shared Property Manager still locks the `Counter` property. As a result, the second thread cannot change the counter to zero. The second thread blocks while it is waiting for the `Counter` property lock to be released. When the second thread blocks, the first thread is scheduled again. This provides a chance for the `SC.Start1` method to finish and release the lock on the `Counter` property. When COM+ releases the lock, the second thread can change the property value to zero and exit. When this code is run, I no longer get a `DivideByZeroException`. My problem has been solved!

Now you can see some of the problems that shared memory can cause for multithreaded applications. The Shared Property Manager provides you with a convenient way to protect your components' shared memory. Armed with the lessons learned from this appendix, you can now write more robust applications.

Appendix C

Introduction to C#

C# IS THE MOST RECENT addition to the Visual Studio family. The syntax of this language shares many similarities with C++ and even Java. C# is an excellent choice for .NET programming in general and for COM+ programming specifically, as C# is designed to work seamlessly with the .NET Framework. In addition, C# provides the object-oriented language features that lend themselves so well to component-based programming.

If you are just learning about .NET and are not quite familiar with C#, this appendix is an excellent place to start. You learn the features of the C# language in this appendix. Also, you learn some of the common tasks a developer performs in any programming language.

Namespaces

Every component written in this book is contained within a namespace. Namespaces are not strictly necessary for doing COM+ component development, but they do provide a number of benefits. First, a namespace provides a way to organize code. Types of a similar nature or function can be grouped in a single namespace. Other developers who may need to use your classes find them easier to understand if they are grouped in one or more namespaces. Second, namespaces provide a means to resolve naming conflicts among types in your code. To understand this second point, take a look at the following code example.

```
Namespace NsOne
{
  class CFoo
  {
  }
}
Namespace NsTwo
{
  class CFoo
  {
  }
}
```

The preceding code contains two classes, both named CFoo. Usually, two classes of the same name cannot exist within the same assembly. A namespace allows you to define two CFoo classes within the same assembly. When you reference the first CFoo class, you must also use the namespace name. For instance, to create a new instance of the first CFoo class, write something like NsOne.CFoo = new NsOne.CFoo(). Usually, when you write .NET applications, you do not have to use the name of the namespace when referencing types. Because you have a naming conflict in the preceding example, however, you must use the namespace name to reference the first instance of CFoo.

Notice that dot notation is used here to reference CFoo. In C#, almost everything is referenced using a period. Namespaces are no different. In fact, namespace names can also contain a period. You see this quite frequently in the .NET Framework. For instance, the NsOne namespace in the code example above can be changed to MyApplication.NsOne and can still be a legal namespace.

Namespaces can also contain other namespaces. For instance, you can put the two preceding namespaces in a singe namespace called MyApplication.

```
Namespace MyApplication
{
  Namespace NsOne
  {
    class CFoo
    {
    }
  }
  Namespace NsTwo
  {
    class CFoo
    {
    }
  }
}
```

A client can still access the NsOne.CFoo class by adding the MyApplication namespace as MyApplication.NsOne.CFoo.

Somehow, you have to be able to tell the C# compiler what namespaces you are going to use in your application. The C# keyword using serves this purpose. This keyword lets the C# compiler know where to look to resolve types when you reference them in your code. A client who wishes to use one of the CFoo preceding classes may have a using statement at the top of his or her code, as follows. For those of you who have developed applications in C or C++, the using keyword is similar to the #include compiler directive that includes header files in your C or C++ application.

```
Using MyApplication.NsOne;
```

Some namespace names in the .NET Framework can be rather long. If you get into the habit of using the namespace name to reference types, this can become rather tedious for long namespace names. Fortunately, C# allows you to alias a namespace name. An alias is a short name for a namespace. Once it is defined, an alias can be used to reference types just as a full namespace name can. If you decide that the `MyApplication.NsOne` namespace is too long to write out each time you need one of its types, you can do something like this:

```
Using NS1 = MyApplication.NsOne;
```

Now, whenever the client needs to reference a type in the namespace, it simply uses the `NS1` namespace:

```
Using NS1 = MyApplication.NsOne;
NS1.CFoo  = NS1.CFoo();
```

Flow-Control Statements

C# has a number of statements you can use in code to control the flow of your application's execution. In this section, you learn some basic statements such as `if-else` statements and switches. In addition, you learn the jump statements that allow you to jump to different places in your code. You may notice a strong resemblance in these statements to Java and C++. This resemblance is part of the reason why C# is often compared to those two languages.

if-else Statements

I once heard a programmer say that he could program in any language that had an `if` statement. If you have coded in more than one language, or if you have even seen code from different languages, you probably have noticed that most `if-else` statements are quite similar. C# is not much different in this respect. In C#, the condition to be tested is in parentheses. The action carried out if the condition is true is in braces. The followed code illustrates a simple `if` statement in C#.

```
If (iVar == 10)
{
  // do something here
}
```

As with most languages, C# supports an `else` statement. If the condition in the `if` statement evaluates to false, the code in the `else` statement is executed.

```
If (iVar == 10)
{
  // do something here
}
else
{
  // do something else
}
```

It may be necessary to specify an additional condition in case the first condition evaluates to false. C# supports the `else if` statement for this purpose.

```
If (iVar == 10)
{
  // do something here
}
else if (iVar == 20)
{
  // do something else
}
else
{
  // iVar does not equal 10 or 20
}
```

`if` statements can also be nested, as in the following example.

```
If (iVar == 10)
{
  if (name == "fred")
  {
    // do something here
  }
}
```

switch Statements

`switch` statements allow you to evaluate an expression against multiple constants. A `switch` statement provides a clean alternative to multiple `if-else` statements. A typical `switch` statement looks like the following.

```
switch(iVar)
{
  case 1:
    Console.WriteLine("one");
```

```
    break;
  case 2:
    Console.WriteLine("two");
    break;
  case 10:
    Console.WriteLine("ten");
    break;
}
```

The statement that precedes tests the iVar variable against the possible values of 1, 2, and 10. In this statement, iVar is the expression. Each case statement contains a constant that is tested against the expression. Notice that at the end of each case statement, you must add a break statement. case statements in C# must end with some kind of jump statement such as break or goto. Most of the time, the break statement is used. C# does not support fall-through case statements like C++ does. Instead, once C# finds a case statement that matches the expression, it executes the case statement and exits the switch statement.

Strings and integral types are the only data types supported in a case statement. Integral types can be any of the following types from the System namespace.

- Int16
- Int32
- Int64

When the preceding statement is executed, the value of iVar is compared to each of the constants in the case statements. If one of the constants equals iVar, that case statement is executed. Once the case statement has executed, control passes outside of the switch statement. If none of the parameters matches, a default statement can be executed.

```
switch(iVar)
{
  case 1:
    Console.WriteLine("one");
    break;
  case 2:
    Console.WriteLine("two");
    break;
  case 10:
    Console.WriteLine("ten");
    break;
  case default:
    Console.WriteLine("Could not find a match!");
    Break;
}
```

In this example, if iVar does not equal any of the values in the case statements, the default statement is executed.

Jump Statements

Jump statements allow you to move to various places in your code. You have already seen one of C#'s jump statements: break. break can be used in loops or switch statements.

```
for (int j = 0; j < 10; j++)
{
  if (j == 7)
    break;
  EvtLog.WriteEntry(j.ToString());
}
Console.WriteLine("finished");
```

When j equals 7, the loop exits and the Console.WriteLine executes. In this case, j is never incremented past 7.

The continue statement can also be used within loops. continue works similarly to break, except that a loop does not exit if it encounters a continue statement. Modify the for loop to use a continue statement instead.

```
for (int j = 0; j < 10; j++)
{
  if (j == 7)
    continue;
  EvtLog.WriteEntry(j.ToString());
}
```

Here, when j equals 7, control is passed back to the top of the loop. The EvtLog.WriteEntry method does not execute during this time. When j is incremented past 7, the EvtLog.WriteEntry method continues to execute.

The goto statement has received a lot of negative attention over the years. Like many things, if it is overused, it can lead to sloppy code. Typically, goto is used to jump to a label inside your code, as in the following example.

```
if (SomeValue == true)
{
  goto MyLabel;
}
// some other program code
MyLabel:
// this code will execute
```

goto can also be used to jump to case statements inside a switch statement, as follows.

```
switch(iVar)

{
  case 1:
    Console.WriteLine("one");
    break;
  case 2:
    Console.WriteLine("two");
    break;
  case 3:
    goto case 2;
  case 10:
    Console.WriteLine("ten");
    break;
  case default:
    Console.WriteLine("Could not find a match!");
    break;
}
```

If iVar evaluates to 3, the goto statement passes control to the second case statement. Even though the second case statement does not evaluate to true, it still executes, as you have passed control to it by using the goto statement.

The return statement is used inside method calls to return control to the caller. For methods that return values, the return statement is used to return those values. Void methods do not necessarily have to use the return statement.

```
int GetId()
{
  int i;
  return i;
}
```

Exception Handling

Many classes in the .NET Framework throw exceptions at one time or another. C# supports an exception-handling mechanism for these situations. Exception handling in C# is executed by using try-catch blocks. The basic idea is to put code that may cause an exception inside of a try block. The catch statement catches errors that using code inside the catch block may throw.

```
try
{
  DatabaseObject.Open();
}
catch (DBException dbe)
{
  // log the error or report something to the user
}
```

If the preceding database connection cannot be opened, it may throw an exception. The `catch` statement allows you to catch the error before it reaches the user. In some cases, your code may throw more than one kind of error. For example, when the preceding database is opened, it may not throw an exception of type `DBException`; rather, it may throw a regular `Exception`. To catch each possible exception, multiple exception statements can be combined.

```
try
{
  DatabaseObject.Open();
}
catch (DBException dbe)
{
  // log the error or report something to the user
}
catch (Exception e)
{
  // log the error or report something to the user
}
```

The `finally` statement can be used at the end of a `try-catch` block. Code inside a `finally` block is executed regardless of the exception thrown. Even if no exception is thrown, code in the `finally` block is executed.

```
try

{
  DatabaseObject.Open();
}
catch (DBException dbe)
{
  // log the error or report something to the user
}
```

```
catch (Exception e)
{
  // log the error or report something to the user
}
finally
{
  Console.WriteLine("executing finally statement");
}
```

Writing Loops in C#

C# supports several loop mechanisms, such as those seen in C++ and Visual Basic. The `for` loop is used to demonstrate the `break` statement. The `for` loop takes three expressions: the initializer, the expression to be evaluated, and the interator. The *initializer* initializes the loop variable and, optionally, declares it. When the expression in the loop evaluates to false, the loop exits. The *iterator* increments the loop counter. Usually in a `for` loop, a loop counter is used during the evaluation of the expression.

```
for (int i = 0; i < 10; i++)
{
  // do something interesting
}
```

In this `for` loop, the integer `i` is declared and initialized to zero. With each iteration of the loop, `i` is incremented by a value of 1. Once `i` is incremented to 10, the expression evaluates to false, and the loop exits.

A `for` loop can also be used to count backward.

```
for (int i = 10; i > 0; i--)
{
  // do something interesting
}
```

In the preceding loop, `i` is initialized to 10. Each iteration of the loop decrements `i` by one. Once `i` reaches 0, the loop exists.

A `do` loop and a `while` loop are similar. Both statements execute a block of code until a condition evaluates to false. The expression in a `do` loop is set at the bottom of the loop. Unlike a `while` loop, a `do` loop executes at least once regardless of how the expression evaluates.

```
do
{
  i++;
}
while (i < 10);
```

Even if i is initialized to 10, this loop executes one time. The condition in a while loop, on the other hand, is evaluated before the loop is executed. A while loop also places its condition at the top of the loop.

```
while (i < 10);
{
  i++;
}
```

Foreach loops can be used with collection classes or arrays. These loops iterate through each item in a collection or array until they reach the end of the items.

```
ClerkMonitor cm = new ClerkMonitor();
foreach (ClerkInfo ci in cm)
{
  Console.WriteLine(ci.Description);
}
```

In this loop, ClerkMonitor is a collection class that contains items of type ClerkInfo. Each iteration of the loop populates the variable ci with an instance of ClerkInfo. In this type of loop, the element type (in your case, ClerkInfo) must be declared inside the loop expression.

Method Parameters

Method parameters can be decorated with special statements that affect the behavior of parameters. These statements are used in a couple of places in this book, so you may want to pay particular attention to this section.

The ref statement allows you to pass in a parameter by reference. When the method executes, it sees the value the parameter has been set to in the code before the method has been called. If the method changes the value of the parameter, the new value is visible when the method returns.

In the code listed below, notice that the ChangeValue method decorates the j parameter with the ref keyword.

```
public class SomeClass
{
```

```
  public void ChangeValue(ref j);
}
```

The code listed below demonstrates the use of the ChangeValue method. Since j is a ref parameter, I must create my own integer instance in order to pass j to ChangeValue. If the j parameter was not a ref parameter, I could simply call sc.ChangeValue(1). After all, passing the value of 1 to ChangeValue would make the code more readable. I cannot do that with a ref parameter, however. If I were to pass a constant value such as the number 1 to ChangeValue, then the ChangeValue method would not be able to change the value of the constant (remember that constants cannot be changed once they are assigned a value). The C# compiler would not even compile the example below if I were to pass ChangeValue the constant 1.

```
int j = 1;
SomeClass sc = new SomeClass();
sc.ChangeValue(ref j);
Console.WriteLine(j.ToString());
```

If the ChangeValue method changes the value of j to 2, 2 is displayed when the method returns. Because j is set to 1 before the method is called, ChangeValue sees j as equal to 1 when the method is called. Methods that define ref parameters can be a little tricky to deal with. You must remember to use the ref statement both when you define the method and when you call the method. Ref parameters must also be initialized before they are passed to a method.

The out parameter works similarly to the ref parameter, but, with the out parameter, types passed in as parameters do not need to be initialized before they are passed. A method assigns the parameter a value before it returns control to the caller. out parameters work well in situations where the method must return multiple values.

```
ResourcePool rp;
SomeClass sc = new SomeClass();
sc.GetCount(out rp);
Console.WriteLine(rp.ToString());
```

In the preceding example, the rp variable isn't initialized. To call the method, declare the rp variable, and pass it in to the method call. Just as with the ref statement, the out statement must be used when calling a method.

Arrays

Dealing with arrays in C# can be a bit awkward, especially if you are coming from a C++ or Visual Basic background. In C#, arrays can be single dimensional, multidimensional, or jagged. Arrays can also be of any reference or value type (System.Object, int, double, bool, and strings, to name a few). All arrays, regardless of their types, inherit from System.Array. The Array class contains a number of methods and properties that help you work with arrays. This class allows you to perform binary searches, copy arrays, and sort arrays.

Look at how an integer array is declared.

```
int[] iAry = new int[10];
```

In C#, arrays are declared by using square brackets (as opposed to parentheses in Visual Basic). Instead of brackets' going behind the variable name, as in many languages, they go after the data type. The array is created by using the new keyword. Once the array is created, it is not possible to modify its dimensions. The dimensions of an array must be declared by using a literal value, such as 10 in the preceding example, or a constant variable. The C# compiler does not allow arrays to be declared with variable expressions. In other words, the following code example is illegal in C#.

```
int i = 10;
int[] iAry = new int[i]; // illegal!
```

Array elements are accessed by using square brackets. C# array elements start at position 0. This is akin to the C++ way of handling arrays. The following code uses square brackets to access the element in the first position of the array.

```
iAry[0] = 100;
```

Arrays can also be initialized when they are created.

```
int[] iAry = new int[10]  {1, 2, 3, 4, 5, 6, 7, 8, 9, 10};
```

To initialize an array, the initial values must be enclosed inside braces.

As I state previously, arrays can be multidimensional. Multidimensional arrays contain elements in two or more dimensions. A two-dimensional array can be declared as follows.

```
int[,] iAry = new int[3,2];
```

When I work with arrays with two or more dimensions, I like to think of them in terms of a table or matrix. The preceding two-dimensional array is laid out in memory very much like Figure C-1.

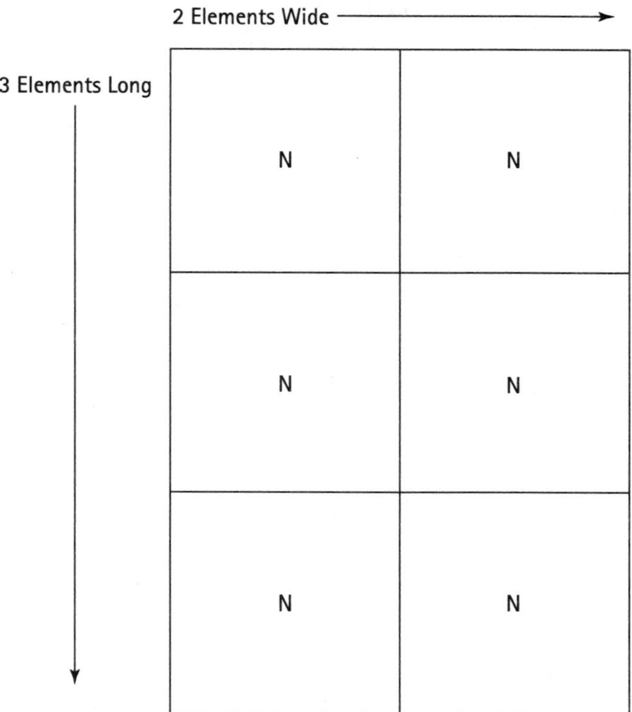

Figure C-1: Two-dimensional array

A comma is used to denote that there are two dimensions to this array. The array is 3-elements long and 2-elements wide. Adding commas and specifying the lengths of their elements can extend array dimensions. The following code creates an array that is 4-elements long, 3-elements wide, and 2-elements deep.

```
int[, ,] iAry = new int[4,3,2];
```

Multidimensional arrays can be initialized when they are declared. The two-dimensional array that precedes can be initialized as follows.

```
int[,] iAry = new int[3,2] {{12,3}, {4,23}, {99,0}};
```

If you continue with the table concept, the array, when it is initialized, looks something like Figure C-2.

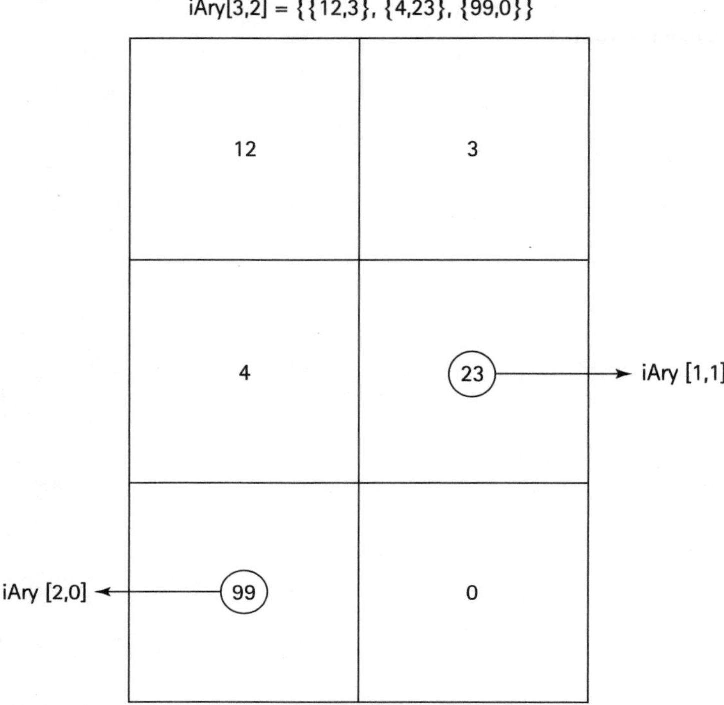

Figure C-2: Initializing a two-dimensional array

Basic Data Types

I refer to basic data types as integers, characters, strings, doubles and floats, and so on. C# has keywords that act as aliases for these kinds of types. Keywords in C# refer to structures from the `System` namespace. For instance, `int` is the keyword that refers to a `System.Int32` structure. Table C-1 lists the data type keywords in C# and their associated structures from the `System` namespace.

TABLE C-1 BASIC DATA TYPES IN C#

C# Keyword	System structure	Size (bits)	Value Range
`Sbyte`	`System.SByte`	8	-128 to 127
`Byte`	`System.Byte`	8	0 to 255
`Short`	`System.Int16`	16	-32768 to 32767
`Ushort`	`System.UInt16`	16	0 to 65535

C# Keyword	System structure	Size (bits)	Value Range
`Int`	`System.Int32`	32	-2147483648 to 2147483647
`Uint`	`System.UInt32`	32	0 to 4294967295
`Long`	`System.Int64`	64	-9223372036854775808 to 9223372036854775807
`Ulong`	`System.UInt64`	64	0 to 18446744073709551615
`Char`	`System.Char`	16	0 to 65535
`Float`	`System.Single`	7 digits	1.5×10^{-45} to 3.4×10^{38}
`double`	`System.Double`	15-16 digits	5.0×10^{-324} to 1.7×10^{308}
`bool`	`System.Boolean`	8	true or false
`decimal`	`System.Decimal`	128	1.0×10^{-28} to approximately 7.9×10^{28}

Enumerations are a special kind of data type. Enumerations contain a list of named constants. They can make code more readable, as they allow you to reference constants by using a name instead of the literal value. In C#, enumerations are declared by using the `enum` keyword. Enumerations can be declared as `byte`, `sbyte`, `short`, `ushort`, `int`, `uint`, `long`, and `ulong`. By default, enumerations are defined as `int`.

```
enum Animal
{
  Dog,
  Cat,
  Fish,
  Bird
}
```

A comma must separate each member in the enumeration. If values for the enumeration members are not explicitly defined, the first member defaults to 0. In the `Animal` example, the `Dog` member equates to 0; the `Cat` equates to 1, and so on. Members can be initialized to constant values if needed.

```
enum Animal
{
  Dog = 3,
  Cat,
  Fish ,
  Bird
}
```

Here, members are initialized starting at 3. `Cat` equals 4 and so on. In reality, each member can be initialized to any constant expression.

The two preceding examples do not define an underlying type for the enumeration. `Animal`, in this case, defaults to an `integer` enumeration. `Animal` can be defined as a `long`, as in the following example.

```
enum Animal : long
{
  Dog = 3,
  Cat,
  Fish ,
  Bird
}
```

Structures

A *structure* – also called a struct – is a data type that can contain other data types (`int`, `char`, `double`, and so on), constructors, methods, and fields. Structs are value types, which means a couple of things to a developer. First, memory for a value type is allocated from a thread's stack. Allocating memory from the thread's stack can provide a performance increase over allocating memory from an application's heap. Second, when dealing with structs, you are dealing directly with the struct itself, as opposed to a reference to the struct. This has implications when passing structs around in a program to different methods. When a struct is passed to a method, a copy of the struct is passed instead of a pointer or reference to the struct. You see in the next section that this differs from classes, as classes are passed by reference. Structs work well in situations where multiple values represent a single concept or entity. For instance, a struct works well if you need to represent map coordinates in an application. A struct representing map coordinates might contain integers representing longitude and latitude and a string representing location.

In the previous section, you see how each of the data-type keywords in C# aliases a structure from the `System` namespace. As a developer, you can define your own structs by using the `struct` keyword.

```
struct Location
{
  int longitude;
  int latitude;
  string location;
}
```

The preceding is a structure called `location` that contains a map coordinate and a description of the location. In an application, you can declare an instance of this struct and set the values of the fields.

```
Location Detroit;
Detroit.longitude = 1000;
Detroit.latitude = 99;
Detroit.location = "Joe Louis Arena";
```

In this example, I initialize the fields of the struct myself. There may be occasions, however, when you want the struct to initialize its fields instead. To do this, the struct must implement a constructor. *Constructors* are methods called when a struct is initialized. Constructors can contain parameters that can be used to initialize fields. A struct may implement multiple constructors.

If you want to initialize fields of the location struct, you can implement a constructor that takes the longitude, latitude, and location as parameters to the constructor.

```
struct Location
{
  int longitude;
  int latitude;
  string location;
  Location(int iLongitude, int iLatidude, string sLocation)
  {
    longitude = iLongitude;
    latitude = iLatitude;
    location = sLocation;
  }
}
```

To use this new constructor, the client code must be changed also. A client must use the `new` keyword when instantiating structs with parameterized constructors.

```
Location Detroit = new Location(1000, 99, "Joe Louis Arena");
```

Structs can also implement methods. For example, the `Location` struct might need a method to move from one location to another.

```
struct Location
{
  int longitude;
  int latitude;
  string location;
  Location(int iLongitude, int iLatidude, string sLocation)
  {
    longitude = iLongitude;
    latitude = iLatitude;
```

```
    location = sLocation;
  }
  void Move(int iLongitude, int iLatitude, string sLocation)
  {
    longitude = iLongitude;
    latitude = iLatitude;
    location = sLocation;
  }
}
```

When you are working with structs, you must remember these rules:

- Structs cannot declare parameterless constructors.
- Instance fields cannot be initialized in structs.
- Structs cannot support inheritance.

The C# compiler generates a parameterless constructor (also known as a default constructor) on your behalf. The default constructor is used to initialize the struct's fields to their default values. For integer types, this means they are initialized to 0; strings are initialized to an empty string (""). The compiler barks out an error if you try to implement your own default constructor.

Under most circumstances in C#, you can initialize a field to some value. This is not legal in structs. For instance, it is illegal to initialize the `longitude` field when you are declaring it in the struct.

```
struct Location
{
  int longitude = 1000; // illegal statement for a struct!!
  int latitude;
  string location;
}
```

The final rule to remember about structs is that they do not support inheritance. Inheritance allows you to derive functionality from another class by inheriting its properties, methods, and so on. If you need inheritance, you must use a class. You learn more about classes in the next section.

Classes

Classes are quite similar to structs. The main difference between classes and structs is that classes are reference types but structs are value types. When a class is passed to a method as a parameter, a reference to the class is passed instead of the actual bits that make up the class. A reference, in this sense, is the location in memory where the class resides. When a class is initialized, memory is allocated from the managed heap, as opposed to the threads stack. (Chapter 1 provides more information about .NET's managed heap.)

Like structs, classes can contain fields, methods, and constructors. The example that follows converts the `Location` struct from the previous section into a class.

```
class Location
{
  int longitude;
  int latitude;
  string location;
  Location(int iLongitude, int iLatidude, string sLocation)
  {
    longitude = iLongitude;
    latitude = iLatitude;
    location = sLocation;
  }
  void Move(int iLongitude, int iLatitude, string sLocation)
  {
    longitude = iLongitude;
    latitude = iLatitude;
    location = sLocation;
  }
}
```

The only difference between this class and the `Location` struct is the use of the `class` keyword. This C# keyword is used to declare a class.

As I stated previously, C# classes can support inheritance. Inheritance is commonly used when there is a parent-child relationship between classes. For instance, a class called `Dog` might have properties related to common characteristics of a mammal, such as fur and teeth. The `Dog` class might also have methods such as `Bark()` and `Sit()`. Another class such as `Labrador` might be able to use the functionality of the `Dog` class and extend upon it with methods such as `retrieve()`.

```
class Dog
{
  string Fur;
  int Teeth;
  Bark() { ... }
  Sit() { ... )
}

class Labrador : Dog
{
  Retrieve() { ... }
}
```

The Labrador class inherits the fields and methods of the Dog class by declaring the Dog class in its own definition (: Dog). When a client creates an instance of the Labrador class, it is able to access the Fur and Teeth properties and call the Bark() and Sit() methods. The client is also able to call the retrieve() method that the Labrador class implements. For example, the following client code is legal in C#.

```
Labrador lab = new Labrador();
lab.Bark();
```

Some languages allow a class to inherit from multiple base classes. A *base class* is any parent class a child class inherits. C# (or any .NET language, for that matter) does not support multiple inheritance.

Some classes in .NET act strictly as base classes. C# provides the abstract keyword to support this need. Abstract classes cannot be instantiated directly. The Dog class can be converted to an abstract class quite easily by adding the abstract keyword to the declaration of the class.

```
abstract class Dog
{
  string Fur;
  int Teeth;
  Bark() { ... }
  Sit() { ... )
}
```

Methods inside classes can also be declared abstract without making the entire class abstract. Classes that inherit from base classes with abstract methods must implement the abstract methods of the parent. In addition, the parent must not provide an implementation of a method it defines as abstract. As you can see in the Bark() method in the following example, methods are declared abstract by adding the abstract keyword to the declaration of the method.

```
class Dog
{
  string Fur;
  int Teeth;
  abstract Bark() { ... }
  Sit() { ... )
}
```

Sealed classes can be thought of as the opposite of abstract classes. Another class cannot inherit a sealed class. If, in this example, the Dog class is marked sealed instead of abstract, the Labrador class cannot inherit from the Dog class.

```
sealed class Dog
{
  string Fur;
  int Teeth;
  Bark() { ... }
  Sit() { ... )
}

class Labrador : Dog // this is an error!
{
  Retreive() { ... }
}
```

A field or method of a class can declare one of several modifiers that affect the accessibility of the member. Modifiers can be any of the following:

- `public`
- `protected`
- `private`
- `internal`
- `protected internal`

Public members can be accessed from any client or child class. Only child classes can access protected members. Only the class implementing the member can access private members. Only other types within the same project can access internal members. Only child classes within the same project can access protected internal members.

Some of these modifiers can be applied to the class itself. A class defined inside a namespace can be marked either `public` or `internal`. Classes that are members of other classes, however, can be marked with any of the access modifiers.

Properties

Properties are similar to fields in that they represent a type that is a member of a class or. struct. Properties wrap access to a field. They allow you to validate data a client is attempting to assign to a field. They can also be used to retrieve values upon a client's request. From the client's perspective, a property looks just like any other field. Just like fields, properties are declared with data types. The following class implements a property called `EngineSize`.

```
class Car
{
  private string m_EngineSize;
  public string EngineSize
  {
    get
    {
      return m_EngineSize;
    }
    set
    {
      m_EngineSize = value;
    }
  }
}
```

The EngineSize property is implemented with get and set methods. These methods are called accessors. The get accessor is called whenever the property appears on the left side of an equation or whenever the client needs to read the property value. The set accessor is used whenever the client assigns a value to the property. The client can use the property as if it were a field of the class.

```
Car car = new Car();
MessageBox.Show(car.EngineSize);
```

Inside of the set accessor, the variable on the right-hand side of the equation is called a value. This is a special keyword that represents the value the client is passing in. Regardless of the property's data type, the value keyword can always be used.

Properties can be made read-only or write-only depending on which accessor is implemented. For example, if you want to make the EngineSize property write-only, simply omit the get accessor.

```
class Car
{
  private string m_EngineSize;
  public string EngineSize
  {
    set
    {
      m_EngineSize = value;
    }
  }
}
```

If the client tries to read the value of the property, the compiler generates an error.

Indexers

Indexers are a rather neat feature of C#. They allow a class to be treated as if it were an array. The elements of the class can be iterated through as if they were elements of a normal array. Just like arrays, indexers are accessed by using square brackets and an index number. Indexers use accessors in the same way as properties do.

```
class CIndexer
{
  string[] names = new string[3] ("bob", "joe", "ralf");
  public string this [int index]
  {
    get
    {
      return names[index];
    }
    set
    {
      names[index] = value;
    }
}
```

This class implements an indexer that wraps an array of names. I try to keep things simple here, but usually you want to perform some logic to determine if the client has given you an index number that is out of range. In the declaration of the indexer, the `this` keyword is used. Classes use the `this` keyword to reference their own currently running instance. Next, inside the brackets, the index variable is defined. The class uses this variable to determine which element in the index the client wishes to access.

A client uses this indexer in the following manner. Notice how the client uses the class as if it were an array.

```
// client code
CIndexer indexer = new CIndexer();
for (int i = 0; i < 2; i++)
{
  Console.WriteLine(indexer[i]);
}
```

Unsafe Code

One of the most notable differences between C# and Visual Basic is that C# allows the use of pointers. Pointers run in an unsafe context. When the .NET runtime sees code that has been declared in an unsafe context, it does not verify that the code is type-safe. Although the memory to which pointers point is allocated from managed memory (see Chapter 1 for more information on managed memory and the Garbage Collector), the Garbage Collector does not see the pointer on the heap. Because the Garbage Collector does not know about pointers, special precautions must be taken to protect an application's pointers.

```
public unsafe static void Main()
{
  int I = 12;
  int* pI = &I;
  int J = *pI;
  Console.WriteLine(J.ToString());
}
```

The `Main()` method that precedes is declared by using the `unsafe` keyword. This keyword tells the C# compiler that the following block of code may contain pointers. Applications that use the `unsafe` keyword must be compiled with the `/unsafe` compiler option. This option can be specified when you use the command line compiler or the IDE.

The `pI` pointer is declared with using the `*` operator. The ampersand (`&`) operator returns the memory location of the `I` variable. In C#, the `*` and the `&` work the same way they do in C++. The `*` operator is used for pointers only. Do not confuse this with the multiplication operator in C#, although both use the same symbol. The `*` operator is used to return the value contained in the pointer's memory address. The `&` operator, on the other hand, returns the memory address of a type. In the declaration of the `pI` pointer, the memory location of `I` is stored in `pI`.

Although the code below compiles and runs, there is a potential problem. If the integer, `I`, were a field of a class, the application could run into problems if a Garbage Collection were to run just after the assignment of the pointer.

```
public unsafe static void Main()
{
  SomeClass sc = new SomeClass();
  int* pI = &sc.I; // this could cause problems!!
  int J = *pI;
  Console.WriteLine(J.ToString());
}
```

A Garbage Collection can run after the assignment of the pointer. If this occurs, the memory location of `sc` and its `I` field might change. This renders the pointer invalid, as the pointer is pointing to a memory location that is null or is occupied by another type. To avoid this problem, the `fixed` statement can be used to pin the `sc` instance in memory. By pinning a class in memory, you can prevent the Garbage Collector from changing the class's location.

```
public unsafe static void Main()
{
  SomeClass sc = new SomeClass();
  int J;

  fixed (int* pI = &sc.I)
  {
    J = *pI;
  }
  Console.WriteLine(J.ToString());
}
```

In a `fixed` statement, the declaration of a pointer and its assignment can be written inside parentheses. Any code that must be run using the pointer can be put in the code block that follows the fixed statement.

You can see from this appendix that C# is a fully featured language that contains many of the features (such as support for flow-control statements, loops, arrays, etc.) you have come to expect from a modern programming language. The purpose of this appendix was not to teach you the entire ins and outs of C# but rather to introduce you to the language and point out some of the language features that are used throughout this book. Now that you have read this appendix, perhaps the language features of C# and some of its quirks will not look so foreign to you as you make your way through the rest of the book.

Appendix D

Compensating Resource Managers

A COMPENSATING RESOURCE MANAGER (CRM) performs duties similar to a resource manager that I discussed in chapter 4. Resource managers are a crucial piece of a distributed transaction. They provide protected access to managed resources such as message queues and databases. CRMs provide you with a means to develop a pair of COM+ components that provide most of the services of a resource manager, without undergoing much of the effort required to develop a full-scale resource manager. Unlike a full-scale resource manager, a CRM does not provide isolation of data. (Isolation is one of the ACID rules from Chapter 4) Isolation hides changes to data from other clients while the data is being altered. CRMs provide the commit and rollback functionality of a full-scale resource manager.

The most common use of a CRM is to provide protected access to the file system. Applications must often access the file system to write data and to move or delete files. CRMs also provide a good way to manage XML text documents. As XML becomes more widely adopted, it is likely that XML documents will contain business data that must be managed within a transaction. Because there is no resource manager for the Windows file system, CRMs help fill this void by allowing you to protect access to files within a COM+ transaction. CRMs also allow you to stay within the familiar transactional-development model of COM+.

The classes you need to write a CRM in C# are in the `System.EnterpriseServices.CompensatingResourceManager` namespace. In this section, you learn to write a CRM by using classes from this namespace. Also, you learn about the CRM architecture and requirements CRM components and applications must meet. If you have not read Chapter 4 before reading this appendix, I highly recommend that you do so. Chapter 4 gives you the background you need to understand the concepts and terminology in this appendix.

Introducing the Compensating Resource Manager

A CRM consists of three components:

- Worker
- Compensator
- Clerk

The *worker* component is the part of the CRM visible to clients. Worker components implement business or data logic of the CRM. For all intents and purposes, worker components are regular COM+ components that are CRM aware.

The worker component is a transactional component whose transactional attribute – ideally – is set to `Required`. `Required` ensures that the worker runs in the client's transaction. Also, `Required` ensures that the component runs within a transaction if the client does not have one. If the worker does not run in a transaction, this pretty much defeats the whole purpose of a CRM. CRMs are intended to be used in situations in which the client is another component running in a transaction. If the client aborts its transaction, the work of the CRM can be rolled back.

The worker component must write entries to a log file. Later, the compensator uses these entries to either rollback the work of the worker or to make it permanent. Log entries should be made before the worker performs its work. This concept is known as *write ahead*. To understand why write ahead is so important, consider the following scenario. A worker component executes five lines of code, each modifying data in some way. On the sixth line, the worker writes an entry to the log file. One day, while the worker is running, someone trips over the server's power cord and unplugs the server just as the third line of code is being executed. The power failure causes the entire system to shutdown (I know an Uninterruptible Power Supply prevents this). At this point, data is in an inconsistent state. Because the worker has not written anything to the log, you have no way to determine what data has been updated and what data has not. The worker can prevent this scenario by writing records to the log before it performs its work. This is not a guarantee that a catastrophic failure will not cause problems, but it does help you guard against these types of problems. Write ahead introduces another problem, however. If a worker uses write ahead and something like a power failure occurs immediately after, log records may appear for things that have not happened. The compensator must have enough savvy to know how to handle these situations. Later in this appendix, you learn a technique for handling this condition.

The *compensator* component either commits the work of the worker or undoes its work, depending on the outcome of the transaction. If the worker's transaction commits, the COM+ runtime invokes the compensator to commit the transaction. The compensator is notified (via a method call) of every log the worker has written. At this time, the compensator may look at each log record and use that information to make the worker's actions permanent.

In the event the transaction is aborted, the compensator must undo any work the worker component has performed. The compensator is notified of every log record the worker writes. This gives the compensator an opportunity to undo any work the worker has performed.

A compensator might be notified multiple times of a transaction's outcome (commit or abort). This may happen if failures occur during the final phase of the transaction. For this reason, a compensator's work must result in the same outcome each time the compensator is called. If a compensator is written in this fashion, it is said to be *idempotent*. For example, if a compensator opens an XML file and adds some elements, this is not considered idempotent. If the compensator is called multiple times, multiple elements may be added to the XML file. If, on the other hand, the compensator opens an XML file and changes an attribute on an element, this might be considered idempotent. Changing the value of an XML element multiple times does not result in different outcomes, assuming the attributes value is set to the same value each time. In reality, idempotency is a hard thing to accomplish without a little help. In most cases, it is sufficient to implement enough logic to make the compensator's action idempotent. If, for instance, you have to add an element to an XML file, you can implement logic to determine if the element exists. If the element does not exist, you can add it. By checking for the existence of the element, you are, in effect, making the action idempotent. This rule should make you aware of the fact that the compensator can be called multiple times during final phases of a transaction.

Be clear that the client never uses the compensator component. Instead, the COM+ runtime instantiates and consumes the compensator at the appropriate times. As a CRM developer, you develop both the worker and compensator components.

The *clerk* component has two responsibilities: it registers the compensator with the *Distributed Transaction Coordinator (DTC)* and writes records to the log file. The compensator must be registered with the DTC so that the DTC knows which component to invoke once the worker's transaction has ended. The worker object uses the clerk to perform this action. In the .NET Framework, the worker registers the compensator component when the clerk class's constructor is called. Other options, such as what phases (transaction abort, transaction success, and so on) the compensator should be notified of, are also defined at this time. You go into these options in more detail in the next section.

The main job of the clerk is to write records to the log file. Log records are written to a memory buffer before they go to disk. This improves performance, as it minimizes disk access. As log records are written, they go to memory. Once the buffer is full, they are written to disk. This does present a problem, however. If the worker's log entries are not stored on disk but rather held in a volatile memory buffer, log records can be lost if an application problem exists that causes the application to crash. To prevent this, the clerk has a method that forces records held in memory to be written to disk. It is highly recommended that worker components use this method before they begin their work. Later, you learn how this is done.

Figure D-1 shows how all of these components fit together within the scope of a transaction and within the logical scope of the CRM. In Figure D-1, you can see that the worker component runs within the transaction of the client. You see also that the worker, compensator, and the clerk work together to form the CRM.

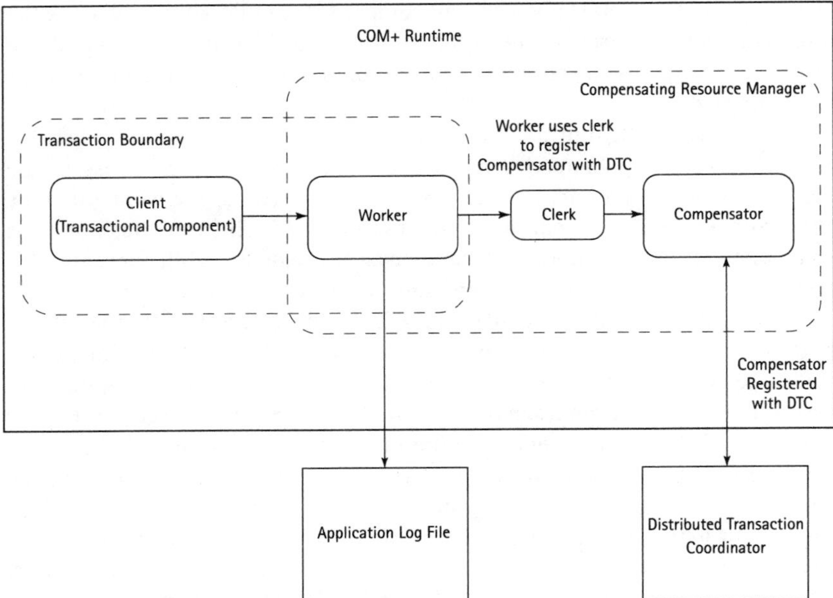

Figure D-1: Components of a CRM application

COM+ creates the log file when an application containing CRM components starts. The log file is located in the `%systemroot%\system32\dtclog` directory. This is the same directory that stores the log file for the Distributed Transaction Coordinator. COM+ creates a log file for each server application that contains a CRM. The log file is named by using the application ID of the log file with a `.crmlog` extension. Remember that the application ID is a GUID used to identify an application uniquely inside COM+. A CRM log file in this directory might look something like `{57206245-EAA4-4324-92CD-0DBAB17605D5}.crmlog` (including the curly braces).

Unfortunately for us developers, the CRM log file is a binary file that cannot be easily viewed with Notepad or another text editor. As you know, each COM+ server application must run under a configured identity. By default, this is the Interactive user account. Server packages can also be configured to run under a user account other than Interactive user. If an application is configured to run under an account other than Interactive user, the log file for that application is secured so that only that user can access the file. However, if the application is configured to run as the Interactive user, the log file inherits permissions from its parent directory (`dtclog`). Incidentally, the `dtclog` folder inherits permissions from the `system32` folder by default. So why bother to secure the CRM log files? The log files can contain sensitive information, such as account numbers or whatever else you decide to put in the log. You should be aware that if the identity of the application changes, an administrator has to change the security settings on the log file. COM+ does not change this for you automatically.

COM+ provides support for CRMs by creating and ultimately managing the CRM log file and by invoking the compensator when the transaction completes. To gain this support, a COM+ server application package must have the Enable Compensating Resource Managers attribute checked. Figure D-2 shows where this attribute is located on the application's Advanced settings tab.

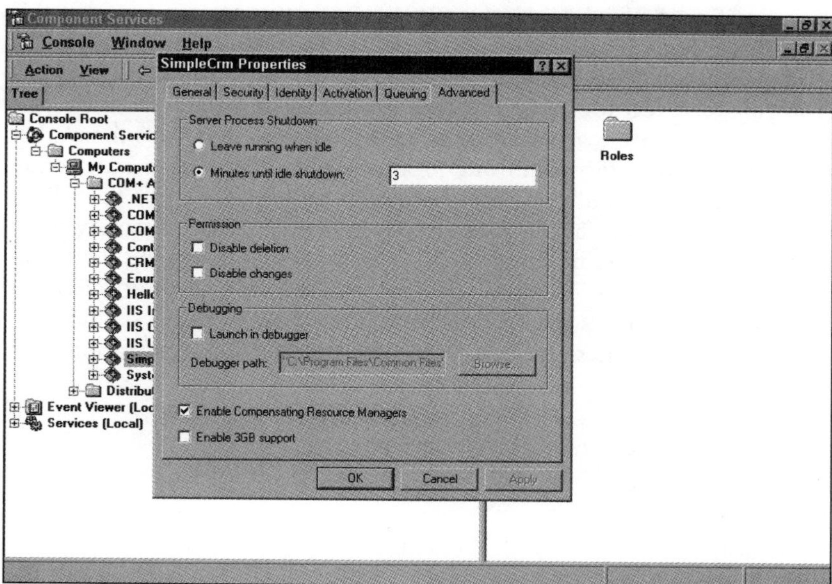

Figure D-2: Enabling CRM support

Without this setting, COM+ does not provide any of the services I have mentioned. In addition, the clerk component cannot be instantiated unless this attribute is enabled.

COM+ supports a recovery phase for CRMs. The recovery phase occurs if an application stops due to either an operating-system crash or some unrecoverable error inside the application itself. When the application starts again, COM+ reads the application's log file to determine if a transaction is pending completion. If a pending transaction exists, COM+ contacts the DTC service to determine the outcome of the transaction. The application does not start on its own. It starts when a component in the application is invoked. This may not be the optimal time to perform a recovery on a CRM. I suggest looking into the COM Administration API documentation for ways to start a CRM application when the system boots or during nonbusy times of operation. This way, you can avoid a potentially costly recovery while clients are trying to access your components.

Developing Compensating Resource Managers with C#

As I mention in the beginning of this appendix, CRMs are developed using classes from the `System.EnterpriseServices.CompensatingResourceManager` namespace. Unless specifically noted, all classes mentioned in this section are from this namespace.

Before you get into the nitty-gritty of this namespace, write a simple CRM application so you can get a feel for how the classes in this namespace interact. In this example, a console application acts as the client. The console client calls the worker component to move a directory from one location to another. If the transaction succeeds, the directory is moved from its temporary location in `c:\temp` to its final destination. If the transaction fails, it is moved from the temporary directory to its original location. The compensator component is responsible for moving the directory from the temporary location to the source or destination directory. For the compensator to know what source and destination directories it should use, the worker logs both directories to the log file. The code for this application is in listing D-1.

Listing D-1: CRM sample application: moving directories

```
using System;
using System.IO;
using System.Reflection;
using System.EnterpriseServices;
using System.EnterpriseServices.CompensatingResourceManager;

[assembly: AssemblyKeyFile("C:\\crypto\\key.snk")]
[assembly: ApplicationActivation(ActivationOption.Server)]
[assembly: ApplicationCrmEnabled]

namespace XCopy
{

  [Transaction(TransactionOption.Required)]
  public class CWorker : ServicedComponent
  {
    private Clerk clerk;
    public override void Activate()
    {
      clerk = new Clerk(typeof(XCopy.CCompensator),
                        "Compensator for XCOPY",
                        CompensatorOptions.AllPhases);
    }
```

```
  public void MoveDirectory(string sSourcePath,
                            string sDestinationPath)
  {
    clerk.WriteLogRecord(sSourcePath + ";" + sDestinationPath);
    clerk.ForceLog();

    int iPos;
    string sTempPath;

    iPos = sSourcePath.LastIndexOf("\\") + 1;
    sTempPath = sSourcePath.Substring(iPos,
                            sSourcePath.Length - iPos);

    Directory.Move(sSourcePath, "c:\\temp\\" + sTempPath);
  }
}

public class CCompensator : Compensator
{
  public override bool CommitRecord(LogRecord rec)
  {
    string sSourcePath;
    string sDestPath;
    string sTemp;
    int iPos;
    GetPaths((string)rec.Record, out sSourcePath, out sDestPath);
    iPos = sSourcePath.IndexOf("\\");
    sTemp = sSourcePath.Substring(iPos,
                         sSourcePath.Length - iPos);
    Directory.Move("C:\\temp\\" + sTemp, sDestPath);

    return false;
  }

  public override bool AbortRecord(LogRecord rec)
  {
    string sSourcePath;
    string sDestPath;
    string sTemp;
    int iPos;

    GetPaths((string)rec.Record, out sSourcePath, out sDestPath);
    iPos = sSourcePath.IndexOf("\\");
    sTemp = sSourcePath.Substring(iPos,
```

Continued

Listing D-1 *(Continued)*

```
                              sSourcePath.Length - iPos);
      Directory.Move("C:\\temp\\" + sTemp, sSourcePath);

      return false;
    }

    private void GetPaths(string sPath,
                          out string sSourcePath,
                          out string sDestination)
    {
      int iPos;
      iPos = sPath.IndexOf(";");
      sSourcePath = sPath.Substring(0, iPos);
      iPos++;
      sDestination = sPath.Substring(iPos, sPath.Length - iPos);
    }
  }

  public class CClient
  {
    static void Main(string[] args)
    {
      CWorker worker = new CWorker();
      worker.MoveDirectory("c:\\dir1", "c:\\dir2");
    }
  }
}
```

Take a look at this code from the top down. First, declare the namespaces you want to use. Because this application performs work on the file system, you must declare the `System.IO` namespace. This namespace contains the `Directory` class you use to move the directories around the file system. The final `using` statement declares the `CompensatingResourceManager` namespace. This should be the only other namespace that is new to you. All of the other namespaces should look familiar, as you have seen them in almost every other `ServicedComponent` class in this book.

In the assembly-attribute section, define the COM+ application to run as a server package, as this is one of the requirements for a CRM. Also, notice a new attribute called `ApplicationCrmEnabled`. This attribute enables CRM support for the application. It also causes the Enable Compensating Resource Managers check box from Figure D-2 to be checked when the application is registered in COM+.

The first class defined in the `XCopy` namespace is the worker component: `CWorker`. This component inherits from the `ServicedComponent` class, just as any other COM+ component does. This class requires a transaction.

Every time the `CWorker` class is activated, it creates a new instance of the `Clerk` class. (Remember that activation and instantiation are two different things in COM+. COM+ activates a component when the COM+ runtime calls the `Activate` method that the component overrides from the `ServicedComponent` class. COM+ instantiates a component when the client of the component calls the C# keyword `new`.) The `Clerk` class constructor registers the compensator component within the COM+ runtime. `Clerk` defines two constructors, which differ by their first parameter. The preceding example involves the constructor that takes a `System.Type` class as the first parameter. The `typeof()` keyword appears in other chapters of this book. Just to refresh your memory, the `typeof()` keyword is a C# keyword that returns the `System.Type` class for a given type. In this example, you pass in the name of the `Compensator` class.

The `System.Type` class is the starting point for applications that use reflection. *Reflection* is a technique that allows a developer to determine the various characteristics of a type. With reflection, a developer can determine what attributes a class is decorated with, how many constructors a class supports, and each method and property the type supports, among other things. In the case of the `Clerk` class, the type the `typeof()` keyword returns allows the .NET runtime to determine what methods the class supports.

The second parameter in the `Clerk` constructor is a description field that can be used for monitoring the CRM. The last parameter is an enumeration that tells the .NET runtime and COM+ what phases of the transaction you want to be notified of. In your case, you want to be notified of all the phases of the transaction, so pass `CompensatorOptions.AllPhases`. There may be occasions on which you want to be notified only of the commit or abort phases of the transaction. By passing a different value for this enumeration, you can be notified of only those phases.

The `MoveDirectory` method of the `CWorker` class performs the business-related work for this CRM. Before the worker component does any real work, it must first record what it is going to do in the CRM log file. Logging its actions before it does any work, the `worker` component is practicing the write-ahead technique I mention previously. In my example, I write a single record to the log file. This record contains the source and destination directories. The instance of the `Clerk` class is used to write the log entry. Notice that I combine the source and destination directories into one log entry. I do not want to write two entries to the log (one for the source directory and another for the destination directory) because this results in two notifications of the compensator component when the transaction commits. If this is the case, the compensator becomes confused, as it gets only the source or destination directories upon each notification. The `WriteLogRecord` method does not force the record to be written to the log. Instead, it writes its data to the memory buffer I mention previously. To write the record to the log permanently, I must call the `ForceLog` method.

Once I write the log entry and force it to the log file, I am free to go about with the work of the worker component. I move the source directory to a temporary location in `c:\temp`. I do not want to move the directory to the destination, as I do not know if the transaction will commit or abort. Based on the outcome of the transaction, I let the compensator decide if the directory should be moved to the destination or back to the source directory.

Next, the compensator is defined in the source code. The compensator component inherits from the `Compensator` class. This class derives from the `ServicedComponent` class. When the application is registered in COM+, both the worker and compensator show up as serviced components.

The `Compensator` class provides many virtual methods used for all phases of the transaction. To keep things simple for this first example, I implement only the `CommitRecord` and `AbortRecord` methods. COM+ calls these methods when the transaction commits or aborts, respectively.

If the transaction commits, I read the log record to determine the destination directory. I have to do a little string manipulation here to parse out the paths for each directory. Once I get the destination directory, I move the directory from its temporary location to the destination directory. If the transaction aborts, I move the directory back to the source directory.

The client for the worker component is a simple console application. It creates a new instance of the worker component and calls the `MoveDirectory` method, passing in the source and destination directories. In a real-world application, the client is most likely another transactional component, but a console application works fine for our purposes.

If everything goes right within the `MoveDirectory` method, the transaction commits. Once the `MoveDirectory` method returns, the transaction ends and COM+ invokes the compensator component, calling the `CommitRecord` method.

Of course, things do not always happen as we expect. For example, the source directory may not exist. In this case, an exception is thrown, which dooms the transaction. This can cause problems down the line for the compensator in its `AbortRecord` method. If the source directory does not exist, the worker is not able to move the directory to the temporary location. If the transaction aborts, the compensator tries to move a directory in the temporary location that does not exist. To correct this situation, add a little logic to the compensator and worker to make sure they do not try to access directories that do not exist. The code in Listing D-2 shows a more robust `MoveDirectory` method. Similar logic can be placed in the compensator's `CommitRecord` and `AbortRecord` methods.

Listing D-2: Robust MoveDirectory method

```
public void MoveDirectory(string sSourcePath,
                          string sDestinationPath)
{
  clerk.WriteLogRecord(sSourcePath + ";" + sDestinationPath);
  clerk.ForceLog();
```

```
  int iPos;
  string sTempPath;

  iPos = sSourcePath.LastIndexOf("\\") + 1;
  sTempPath = sSourcePath.Substring(iPos,
                       sSourcePath.Length -  iPos);

  if (Directory.Exists(sSourcePath))
  {
    Directory.Move(sSourcePath, "c:\\temp\\" + sTempPath);
  }
}
```

Now the directory is moved only if the source directory exists on the file system. This prevents the transaction from aborting, as you are not trying to move a directory that does not exist.

Granted, most applications require more sophisticated logic than this. For example, you may want the transaction to abort if the client does not have proper access rights to move the directory. The code in Listing D-3 moves the directory only if the user has the correct privileges. If the client does not have the rights to move the directory, the transaction is aborted.

Listing D-3: Revised MoveDirectory checking for access rights

```
public void MoveDirectory(string sSourcePath,
                          string sDestinationPath)
{
  clerk.WriteLogRecord(sSourcePath + ";" + sDestinationPath);
  clerk.ForceLog();

  int iPos;
  string sTempPath;

  iPos = sSourcePath.LastIndexOf("\\") + 1;
  sTempPath = sSourcePath.Substring(iPos,
                       sSourcePath.Length - iPos);

  if (Directory.Exists(sSourcePath))
  {
    try {
      Directory.Move(sSourcePath, "c:\\temp\\" + sTempPath);
    }
    catch (SecurityException se)
    {
```

Continued

Listing D-3 *(Continued)*

```
        clerk.ForceTransactionToAbort();
      }
    }
}
```

In this version of `MoveDirectory`, I catch the `System.Security.SecurityException` exception. This exception is raised if the client does not have rights to move the directory. For this example, you can assume that the server application that hosts the CRM is running as the Interactive-user account. The Interactive-user account allows the application to run under the security context of the direct caller. A more sophisticated implementation of this practice is to check the call chain by using COM+ role-based security and to verify that each user in the call chain has rights to move the directory. However, simply catching the error suffices for this example.

The `ForceTransactionToAbort` method is the important thing to focus on here. As the name suggests, this method forces the transaction to abort. This allows you to implement logic that determines if the transaction should be aborted, rather than just relying on an error to be thrown or throwing one yourself.

The `CommitRecord` and `AbortRecord` methods are not the only methods COM+ calls when the transaction completes. A compensator can also be notified during the first phase of the physical transaction (see Chapter 4). During this phase, the following three methods are called (in the following order) on the compensator.

1. `BeginPrepare`
2. `PrepareRecord`
3. `EndPrepare`

All three of these methods are virtual. They are called only if you decide you need them in your application. It is not strictly necessary for you implement these methods. These methods are not called during the recovery phase of a CRM transaction. The intent of these methods is to allow the compensator to prepare its resources with the expectation that the transaction is going to commit. If the transaction is not going to commit, there is little point in preparing resources. Because of this reasoning, these methods are not called if the transaction has aborted.

After the methods of the prepare phase are called, the commit methods are called in the following order.

1. `BeginCommit`
2. `CommitRecord`
3. `EndCommit`

BeginCommit passes a boolean flag to the compensator. This flag indicates whether or not the compensator is being called during the recovery phase. If the value of the parameter is true, the compensator is being called during the recovery phase. You have seen the CommitRecord method. This is the method the compensator should use to commit the work of the worker component. The EndCommit method notifies the compensator that it has received all log notifications.

A compensator is notified of an aborted transaction in a manner similar to the way in which it is notified when the transaction commits (minus the prepare phase, of course). The methods that follow are called in order during an aborted transaction.

1. BeginAbort
2. AbortRecord
3. EndAbort

Just as with the BeginCommit method, the BeginAbort method is called with a flag indicating whether the compensator is being called from normal operation or from the recovery of the application.

The final technique I want to show you is the monitor support built into the classes of the CompensatingResourceManager namespace. The ClerkMonitor class is a collection class that contains a list of ClerkInfo classes. The ClerkInfo class gives you access to properties relating to all of the compensators currently running within an application. The ClerkInfo class supports the following list of properties.

- ActivityID of the compensator
- Instance of the Clerk used to register the compensator
- Compensator class instance
- Description specified when the compensator is registered
- InstanceID
- Transaction Unit of Work

In the code that follows, I have added another class to the XCopy namespace.

```
public class CMonitor : ServicedComponent
{
  public void ListCompensators()
  {
    ClerkMonitor cm = new ClerkMonitor();
    cm.Populate();
```

```
    ClerkInfo ci = cm[0];
    Console.WriteLine(ci.Description);
  }
}
```

Once I create the `ClerkMonitor`, I must call the `Populate` method to fill the collection with the known compensators and related CRM information. The `Description` field that is printed out to the screen is the same `Description` field used when the worker component registers the compensator. Because this application has one worker and one compensator component only, I need to access only the first index of this collection. If more workers and compensators exist, I can loop through the collection with a `foreach` loop.

Index

Symbols & Numbers

A

G

H

I

J

K

L

N

S

T

U

V

Hungry Minds, Inc. End-User License Agreement

4. **Restrictions on Use of Individual Programs.** You must follow the individual requirements and restrictions detailed for each individual program in Appendix A of this Book. These limitations are also contained in the individual license agreements recorded on the Software Media. These limitations may include a requirement that after using the program for a specified period of time, the user must pay a registration fee or discontinue use. By opening the Software packet(s), you will be agreeing to abide by the licenses and restrictions for these individual programs that are detailed in Appendix A and on the Software Media. None of the material on this Software Media or listed in this Book may ever be redistributed, in original or modified form, for commercial purposes.

5. **Limited Warranty.**

   (a) HMI warrants that the Software and Software Media are free from defects in materials and workmanship under normal use for a period of sixty (60) days from the date of purchase of this Book. If HMI receives notification within the warranty period of defects in materials or workmanship, HMI will replace the defective Software Media.

   (b) HMI AND THE AUTHOR OF THE BOOK DISCLAIM ALL OTHER WARRANTIES, EXPRESS OR IMPLIED, INCLUDING WITHOUT LIMITATION IMPLIED WARRANTIES OF MERCHANTABILITY AND FITNESS FOR A PARTICULAR PURPOSE, WITH RESPECT TO THE SOFTWARE, THE PROGRAMS, THE SOURCE CODE CONTAINED THEREIN, AND/OR THE TECHNIQUES DESCRIBED IN THIS BOOK. HMI DOES NOT WARRANT THAT THE FUNCTIONS CONTAINED IN THE SOFTWARE WILL MEET YOUR REQUIREMENTS OR THAT THE OPERATION OF THE SOFTWARE WILL BE ERROR FREE.

   (c) This limited warranty gives you specific legal rights, and you may have other rights that vary from jurisdiction to jurisdiction.

6. **Remedies.**

   (a) HMI's entire liability and your exclusive remedy for defects in materials and workmanship shall be limited to replacement of the Software Media, which may be returned to HMI with a copy of your receipt at the following address: Software Media Fulfillment Department, Attn.: *C# COM+ Programming*, Hungry Minds, Inc., 10475 Crosspoint Blvd., Indianapolis, IN 46256, or call 1-800-762-2974. Please allow four to six weeks for delivery. This Limited Warranty is void if failure of the Software Media has resulted from accident, abuse, or misapplication. Any replacement Software Media will be warranted for the remainder of the original warranty period or thirty (30) days, whichever is longer.

(b) In no event shall HMI or the author be liable for any damages whatsoever (including without limitation damages for loss of business profits, business interruption, loss of business information, or any other pecuniary loss) arising from the use of or inability to use the Book or the Software, even if HMI has been advised of the possibility of such damages.

(c) Because some jurisdictions do not allow the exclusion or limitation of liability for consequential or incidental damages, the above limitation or exclusion may not apply to you.

7. **U.S. Government Restricted Rights.** Use, duplication, or disclosure of the Software for or on behalf of the United States of America, its agencies and/or instrumentalities (the "U.S. Government") is subject to restrictions as stated in paragraph (c)(1)(ii) of the Rights in Technical Data and Computer Software clause of DFARS 252.227-7013, or subparagraphs (c) (1) and (2) of the Commercial Computer Software - Restricted Rights clause at FAR 52.227-19, and in similar clauses in the NASA FAR supplement, as applicable.

8. **General.** This Agreement constitutes the entire understanding of the parties and revokes and supersedes all prior agreements, oral or written, between them and may not be modified or amended except in a writing signed by both parties hereto that specifically refers to this Agreement. This Agreement shall take precedence over any other documents that may be in conflict herewith. If any one or more provisions contained in this Agreement are held by any court or tribunal to be invalid, illegal, or otherwise unenforceable, each and every other provision shall remain in full force and effect.